# THE OFFICIAL

# Duke Nukem® 3D

## Strategies & Secrets™

by Jonathan Mendoza

SAN FRANCISCO     PARIS     DÜSSELDORF     SOEST

| | |
|---|---|
| Associate Publisher | GARY MASTERS |
| Acquisitions Manager | KRISTINE PLACHY |
| Project Editor | MAUREEN ADAMS |
| Production Coordinator | LABRECQUE PUBLISHING SERVICES |
| Developmental and Copy Editor | TERRENCE O'DONNELL |
| Book Design and Production | WILLIAM SALIT |
| Proofreader | TORY McLEARN |
| Cover Designer | ARCHER DESIGN |

3D Realms Entertainment is a division of Apogee Software, Ltd.
*DOOM* and *Heretic* are registered trademarks of id Software, Inc.
Dark Forces™ © 1994 Lucas Film, Ltd.

SYBEX is a registered trademark of SYBEX Inc.

TRADEMARKS: SYBEX has attempted throughout this book to distinguish proprietary trademarks from descriptive terms by following the capitalization style used by the manufacturer.

Every effort has been made to supply complete and accurate information. However, SYBEX assumes no responsibility for its use, nor for any infringement of intellectual property rights of third parties which would result from such use.

Library of Congress Card Number: 96-68697

ISBN: 0-7821-1794-5

Manufactured in the United States of America

10 9 8 7 6 5 4 3 2 1

# DEDICATION

To Special Guest Villain, an Austin, Texas pop band whose musical stylings kept my toes tapping and my fingers plucking (the QWERTY keyboard) in the wee hours.

# ACKNOWLEDGEMENTS

I take my wig off (since I don't wear a hat) to the Duke Nukem 3D development team. These guys deserve—and are almost assured—a special place in the annals of the computer game industry. They have found a suitable vehicle to channel their incredible energy, intelligence, and imagination. I am particularly grateful to George Broussard, Scott Miller, and Greg Malone for taking precious time from an inhuman development schedule to reply to my e-mail, answer my dumb questions and share his wit, insights, and good humor. The next person on my list is Terry O'Donnell, who, in the role of developmental and copy editor, helped me shape this book into the mess it is in today. Other persons worthy of recognition for their sometimes questionable but always unwavering support, include my dear colleagues Raleigh, Carol, Jovita, and Vickey. Thank you, too, Diana, because you've always been there for me. Finally, I owe a great deal to Gary Masters, associate publisher at Sybex, for believing I could write and giving me the opportunity to do it. Gary, the carpal tunnel is only a minor inconsequence. But most of all, I want to thank you, the intelligent reader and game enthusiast, for wanting to know more and pushing the PC game industry to keep outdoing itself.

*Jonathan Mendoza*
e-mail address: jonathan@sunscape.com
CompuServe address: 73771,1637

# TABLE OF CONTENTS

# CHAPTER 5
# Lunar Apocalypse $\qquad$ 114

# INTRODUCTION

The future never seemed so stark, real, and utterly compelling. *Duke Nukem 3D* blazes uncharted trails in the 3D action game genre, immersing you into an ominous and futuristic universe that is as imaginative and alluring as it is deadly. More than a technical and artistic achievement, *Duke Nukem 3D* is virtual red-hot candy for the senses.

## DUKE'S NEVER-ENDING SAGA

As Duke Nukem, you return to Los Angeles in a stolen alien vessel, expecting a hero's welcome. After all, you defeated the Rigelatins and blew up their ship in *Duke Nukem II*. Before that, you saved humanity from the clutches of Dr. Proton and his assassin automatons in the original *Duke Nukem*. But, instead, you're nearly blown out of the sky. L.A. is under siege. A wave of alien races landed while you were gone, and they've taken over. Their intentions aren't clear, but one thing is for sure—all over the city there are hundreds of helpless human females encased in cocoons who don't look particularly happy. Welcome back to Earth, Nukem. You're here just in time to save humanity (again) and find out what the aliens want with our chicks.

## THE LOAD-DOWN ON THE SOFTWARE

The full version of *Duke Nukem 3D* consists of three unforgetable episodes:

- L.A. Meltdown
- Lunar Apocalypse
- Shrapnel City

Each episode, in turn, contains a number of levels. L.A. Meltdown, which is included with this book/CD-ROM package, is widely available as shareware. It has five levels and one secret mission (for a total of six levels). Lunar Apocalypse and Shrapnel City each have eleven levels (two of which are secret). Altogether, then, the full version offers twenty-eight exciting, virtual 3D environments to explore and conquer.

## WHO IS DUKE NUKEM AND WHY SHOULD ANYONE CARE?

Intrepid, fearless, buff, blond, and good looking, these qualities might be used to describe many West Coast surf riders. But there's a lot more to Duke Nukem, a twenty-first century Californian, than his legendary way with the waves and perfect, comic book jawline. Duke Nukem might well be humanity's last hope from complete and irreversible annihilation at the hands (or extremities, anyway) of alien invaders with dark, sinister machinations.

> ✎ **NOTE**
> This book is your guide to all twenty-eight *Duke Nukem 3D* levels. It will be your trusted and faithful companion as you set out on yet another excellent adventure in the continuing Duke Nukem saga. It also brings you close up with the real people who made this game happen and lets you in on their insights and muse-chasing.

Duke Nukem's fame dates back to his now historic defeat of Dr. Proton. In the original and very endearing *Duke Nukem*, a "scrolling screen" action game, Duke is pitted against Dr. Proton and his legions of evil robots. Armed with a powerful laser gun, Duke overcomes perilous traps and multitudes of metallic assailants. Eventually, Duke brings Dr. Proton's reign of terror to a screeching halt.

In his second adventure, while giving a TV interview (and shamelessly plugging his autobiography, *Why I Am So Great*), Duke is snatched by a UFO in *Duke Nukem II*. Millions watch in disbelief as Duke disappears in a luminous blue beam, right in front of the studio cameras. The UFO's occupants, the dreaded Rigelatins, want to drain Duke's brain thought patterns and port them onto their X5G Think-o-matic War Computer. Simply stated, their objective is to squeeze Duke's mind dry for the knowledge they need to bring Earth buckling to her knees. But our resourceful Duke refuses to go down that way. Using a small, hidden explosive in his molar, Duke breaks free, destroys the Rigelatins' ship, and heads back to Earth in a stolen alien vessel.

### Nukem's Current Enigma

This brings us to the present game, *Duke Nukem 3D*; a sophisticated, virtual-reality experience and Duke's most challenging adventure to date. Here's what transpires:

After piercing mother Earth's atmospheric veil, Duke directs the tiny, one-man vessel to his hometown, Los Angeles. But no sooner does he reach L.A. airspace, when a sudden blast renders the capsule into falling junk. Barely able to eject, and precisely at the right moment, Duke miraculously saves himself by landing on the roof of a downtown skyscraper.

L.A. is under siege by a colorful assortment of hostile alien races that have apparently stormed the town and taken it over. Reptilian assault troopers and captains, mutated alien operatives known as pig cops, and monstrous octopus-like octabrains have a tight grip on the city. But for all their physical diversity, the aliens share equally in one regard—their contempt for humanity leaves no room for a shred of mercy. Why are the aliens here? As Duke Nukem, you plan to find out. Meanwhile, you must explore your surroundings, get heavier weaponry, and kick some serious alien butt.

By the time he reaches the second episode, Lunar Apocalypse, Duke begins to glean the aliens' Machiavellic agenda. They intend to crack the Earth apart like a giant walnut and reap her bountiful mineral resources. The aliens' plan is most deplorable and cruel, albeit, cleverly ingenious. By aiming their weaponry at California's San Andreas Fault, they expect nothing less than to render planet Earth into a pile of rocks for their subsequent interstellar mining operation. In other words, they plan to pound our home planet with the equivalent of a cosmic wrecking ball. Meanwhile, there's also something very strange happening to human females. Large numbers of them are encased in slimy, pod-like cocoons. Is there a twisted bio-genetic experiment going on? As Duke Nukem puts it, are the aliens "messing with our chicks?"

Will the aliens' fiendish plan succeed? Is humanity's fate irrevocably bleak? Will Earth be ravished, her richness decimated by the rush of sinister miners from outer space? And will the fate of Earth's female population be entombed in their cocoons? Or will new, undreamt-of life spawn from such a most unholy union?

There's only one human alive that can answer these questions. His name is Duke Nukem—your assumed identity in this simulation, no matter which gender you happen to be. Humanity awaits your reply. What's it going to be, Duke Nukem?

## HAVE YOU GOT THE RIGHT HARDWARE?

Besides nerves of steel, finely tuned reflexes, and above-average intelligence, to play *Duke Nukem 3D* you need the following:

- 486/66 CPU or better (a Pentium is recommended)
- 8MB of RAM minimum
- VGA graphics card
- Sound card (Gravis UltraSound, Sound Blaster, WaveBlaster, etc.)

You can also play *Duke Nukem 3D* in higher resolutions—up to 800 x 600—if you have a VESA compliant video card. Most of these cards have adequate drivers. But if you experience video problems, try using UNIVBE, a driver widely available online. Depending on your playing style and preference, you might consider using a Gravis

Gamepad or joystick—though most players do quite well with the keyboard and mouse combination alone.

# WHY DUKE NUKEM 3D IS SO GREAT

Here are a few of the reasons why *Duke Nukem 3D* soared all the way to number one on the Internet's top 100 Games List, just days after its shareware release.

## It's the 3D Engine, Man

Considering the level of the competition and the magnitude of the stakes, upping the ante in the electronic, 3D action game realm is not inconsequential. But 3D Realms Entertainment, Apogee's brainchild (solely spawned to create advanced 3D games), has done just that with its Build engine, the powerhouse behind *Duke Nukem 3D*. As a 3D-rendering workhorse and development tool, the Build engine gives its creators myriad new ways to construct convincing, interactive, and creative virtual architectures. That's why in *Duke Nukem 3D*, you can experience:

- **Floors above floors**  Although games like *DOOM*, *Heretic*, and *Dark Forces* let you climb or descend, their playing field doesn't allow the existence of one floor above another. In *Duke Nukem 3D*, you have complete freedom to roam. You can visit and explore areas directly above or below you.

- **Underwater movement**  To solve certain puzzles, you will have to cross dangerous underground sewage systems or traverse the length of long, sinewy bodies of water. You will be surprised to find how realistic your movement and displacement become when you're submerged.

- **Chase view**  Press a function key and see yourself from a third-person perspective, as though you were placing a *virtual camera* behind Duke Nukem.

- **Slanted floors and surfaces**  No longer restricted to flat areas, Duke Nukem can climb along steep, angular, and highly irregular terrain.

- **The ability to look up and down**  Your viewing vantage point is not restricted to a flat plane. You can actually look up and look down. In fact, while hovering with a jetpack, you can get a bird's-eye view of your environment.

## Duke Is Only As Good As His Tools

Besides the merits of *Duke Nukem 3D*'s Build engine, there are other nifty innovations that make *Duke Nukem 3D* the megahit it is destined to become. The full version of the game offers the following features:

- **Support for up to eight players in an IPX network, which is common in most office settings:** Depending on your point of view, installing *Duke Nukem 3D* on the office network could be seen as a productivity drain or as a cathartic and ultimately beneficial release of energy. *Duke Nukem 3D* is a featured attraction of Dwango and TEN, online platforms for multi-player games. (The shareware version supports only four players.)

- **A dazzling assortment of weaponry and equipment:** Your arsenal runs the gamut from semiautomatic pistols, shotguns, pipe bombs, and a rocket propelled grenade, to more exotic weapons such as a crystal-powered shrinker, a freezethrower, wall-mounted laser trip bombs, and a doubled-barrelled devastator. (The last four weapons are available only in the game's full version.) Among the useful nonweapon items you can score are scuba gear for diving, jetpacks for hovering over the scenery, night vision goggles for optimum vision in dark conditions, protective boots for running or crossing over toxic canals and pools, and even testosterone-laden steroid pills for sudden power surges.

- **Build, a map tool editor:** This tool can let you create additional *Duke Nukem 3D* levels in real time and in 3D. Modifying existing levels is also a breeze with this tool. Even if you have never so much as decorated a room before, you might discover there's a hidden architect inside you waiting to be let out.

- **Edit Art, a dedicated bitmap editor:** With this program, you can place new graphic elements into your maps, whether these are new aliens, weapons, or textures. In sharing its development tools with you, the enthusiast, 3D Realms' philosophy is manifest and encapsulated by Greg Malone, *Duke Nukem 3D*'s producer, who sums it up this way: "Give the power to the users."

## BETWEEN THE COVERS

This book, written in close collaboration with 3D Realms and Apogee designers, coders, dreamers, and artists at large, is your official handy reference to the coolest, most inventive 3D action game this side of *DOOM* and *Descent*, the inimitable *Duke Nukem 3D*.

### Not Another Silly Strategy Book

*Duke Nukem 3D Strategies & Secrets* is not your average hint and strategy guide. This substantive tome is chockful of timely and useful information. Between its covers you are likely to find the knowledge to become a skilled and serious, if not an outright formidable, contender. But beyond any skills you might acquire, there's another reason why having this book will make you feel good.

Throughout these pages, you will read amusing anecdotes and inside stories from the talented members of 3D Realms' *Duke Nukem 3D* team. Find out what agonies and triumphs paved the way for *Duke Nukem 3D* to reach fruition.

To accommodate new as well as experienced players, this book is composed of three parts:

- Part I   The Basics of *Duke Nukem 3D*
- Part II   Duking It Out
- Part III   Duke Nukem's Cognoscenti

PART I  THE BASICS OF *DUKE NUKEM 3D* This section of the book is required reading for every new *Duke Nukem 3D* player. If nothing else, it can help you avoid an early demise by giving you the basic tools and information to start your foray in Duke's fantastic universe.

For those who just cannot wait to get into the action and prefer learning on the fly, the very first chapter takes you on a brief, but instructional, tour of Hollywood Holocaust, the very first level in L.A. Meltdown. If you're more of a studious type, you might skip the tour and focus instead on Chapters 2 and 3. These Chapters get you acquainted with your powerful arsenal and equipment, introduce the unsavory company you will keep, and show you some essential fighting and strategy skills (for both solo and multiplayer modes). You also get a briefing on using the game's menus and controls. Finally, you will learn how to interpret and understand the set of maps that introduce each level in Part II, and you will be given some tips to help you reign victorious in your own episodes.

**PART II DUKING IT OUT** This is where the flying shrapnel from the pipe bomb meets tough alien flesh. If you are already familiar with the material in Part I, then you are ready to go bust heads, and so you must. Here is where you get to roll up your sleeves, grit your teeth, and get ready for an all-out assault to thwart the aliens' dark conspiracy. This section provides complete descriptions of each level, detailed maps, proven strategies, and other helpful information. Find out the best routes, execute the most effective techniques, and score all the power-ups, weapons, and equipment you possibly can amass. If you want to know every secret in every level, this is the place to go for answers.

**PART III *DUKE NUKEM'S COGNOSCENTI*** This section of the book is a bag-ful of goodies to supplement your *Duke Nukem 3D* enjoyment. First and foremost, there is an interview with the creative talent at 3D Realms and Apogee. Peek inside the heads of some of the most notable forces in the PC game industry, and see how ideas and concepts churn in there. You also get in on the creative and technical labor of love that gave birth to the heroic *Duke Nukem 3D*.

Another chapter runs you through the fundamentals of using the Map Editor and Edit Art to guide you as you create your own virtual structures and render some bitmaps.

## WHAT THE CD-ROM IS PACKING

Besides L.A. Meltdown (the shareware episode of *Duke Nukem 3D*), the enclosed CD-ROM supplements the information in this book with:

- Blazing walk-through demos of all the game's levels, except for the secret levels

- Detailed, full-color graphics of each level's texture or surface map and black and white renderings of each level's line map, all in PCX format

- Shareware versions of many other popular offerings by Apogee and 3D Realms as well as previews of coming attractions

The shareware game versions are stored in a directory named **Apogee**. The surface maps are stored in a directory named **Tx-maps**, and the line maps are stored in a directory named **Lin-maps**.

> **WARNING**
> The CD-ROM's walk-throughs can only be viewed if you have the full version of *Duke Nukem 3D*. Check the SYBEX forum in CompuServe (GO SYBEX) or the Sybex Web site (www.sybex.com) for availability of walk-through files for the shareware levels. You will get unpredictable results if you attempt to run the demos with the shareware version of the game.

## Viewing Walk-through Demos

The CD-ROM included with this book contains a collection of demo files for all but the secret levels in *Duke Nukem 3D's* three episodes. In the *Blazing through . . .* sections in Part II, *Duking it Out*, you will see boxed references labeled *Disc Demo*, which contain the particular demo file name you can copy to your *Duke Nukem 3D* directory. Each file presents a demonstration *walk-through* of play in a particular level. They allow you to take a break from your keyboard, sit back, and see one way to *blaze through* and solve a particular level.

## Copying Demo Files

Do the following to copy a desired demo file from the CD-ROM into your *Duke Nukem 3D* directory or folder.

1. If the CD-ROM included with this book is not already loaded, insert it into your CD-ROM drive and access the Blaze folder. Remember to start your computer in MS-DOS mode.

2. Copy the .dmo file for the walk-through you wish to view to your *Duke Nukem 3D* directory. The files are named according to episode number and level number; for example, Hollywood Holocaust's demo file is named E1-L1.dmo, Hotel Hell's demo file is named E3-L8.dmo, and so on.

3. With the *Duke Nukem 3D* directory active, copy the walk-through file so that it writes over the file named Demo1.dmo. For example, enter the following command to copy the walk-through for Lunar Apocalypse's Warp Factor level:

   **copy E2-L3.dmo demo1.dmo**

You will be prompted whether to write over the existing demo1.dmo file. Press Y to respond affirmatively.

4.  Start the game and the demo, by entering the following:

    **duke3d /x blaze.con**

The game will start as usual, and you will see the walk-through you chose appear on screen. Because the main menu automatically appears over the demo, press the Esc key so you can view the demo unobstructed on a full screen.

# READY, AIM . . .

In short, this book delivers the goods, the information, and the insight to prepare you for what is sure to be a thrilling and most memorable action-game joyride. Welcome to the not-so-distant universe of *Duke Nukem 3D*.

**NOTE** Before you can view any of the walk-throughs included on the CD-ROM, you must first copy the file Blaze.con into your *Duke Nukem 3D* directory. You need only do this once. Start your computer in DOS mode. If you are running Windows 95, press Alt+F4 and select **Restart the computer in MS-DOS mode**. Load the CD-ROM (included with this book) into your CD-ROM drive and access the Blaze directory. Then simply copy Blaze.con to the directory where you installed the game. The default name is Duke3D.

**WARNING** If you want to retain the original Demo1.dmo file, either copy it to another directory or copy it to another file name within the game directory.

# PART
# I

# THE BASICS OF
# DUKE NUKEM 3D

Getting down to the basics, that's what this section of the book is all about. Think of it as your basic training to get you into shape for the ensuing mayhem. If you are a new player, the information in Part I is particularly germane to your survival. If you are a veteran of past *Duke Nukem* campaigns, then this part of the book will allow you to work out the kinks and get your feet wet with this new 3D version. Here is what you will find in Part I:

❉ Chapter 1, *Spare Me the Details, I'm Ready to Pummel Alien Flesh*, provides a crash tour of getting started in Hollywood Holocaust, the first level in the L.A. Meltdown episode.

❉ Chapter 2, *Duke's Enemies, Weapons, and Power-Ups*, details the inventory of weapons and power-ups at your disposal and the roster of adversaries you will encounter.

❉ Chapter 3, *Mapping Out Strategy and Winning*, provides you with recommended game plans for tackling each level in every episode, including the secret levels!

# 1

# Spare Me the Details, I'm Ready to Pummel Alien Flesh

Itchy fingers? Say no more. If you have already installed the game and consider yourself a person of action who doesn't need much in the way of explanations, you're in the right place. This lean and mean chapter dispenses with formal briefings and introductions, places you smack in the middle of the action, and guides you through some interesting alien encounters as you learn to interact with your new virtual environment.

## YOUR MISSION

Simply stated, your mission in Hollywood Holocaust (as it is in every level) is threefold:

✧ Build your arsenal with weapons, ammunition, power-ups, and special cardkeys that grant you access to locked areas.

✧ Destroy the enemy.

✧ Find the exit and move on to the next level.

To accomplish your mission, you must rely on quick reflexes, keen powers of observation, and a penchant for holding on to dear life.

### GETTING YOUR BEARINGS

After escaping from the tentacles of an alien brain-drain device and destroying the craft where you were held captive, you head back to Earth and your native Los Angeles.

But the small alien vessel you escaped in is shot down from the sky. Miraculously, you're able to eject at the last instant and wind up atop a downtown building. Apparently while you were gone, another wave of hostile aliens landed and took over the city. Their plans are uncertain, but there's death and destruction everywhere. And the dozens of human females encased in cocoons attest to a bizarre and fiendish alien biogenetic experiment.

# A CRASH TOUR OF HOLLYWOOD HOLOCAUST

Get ready to mix it up on the streets of Hollywood! This crash tour gives you some basic tools so you can embark upon your own exploration with a measure of confidence. The crash tour shows you how to do the following:

- Start the game.
- Get acquainted with basic movements and shooting.
- Gather weapons, ammo, and power-ups.
- Blow away a few aliens.

> **SEE** For a more thorough introduction to *Duke Nukem 3D*'s menus, controls, and environment, see Chapter 2, *Duke's Enemies, Weapons, and Power-Ups* and Chapter 3, *Mapping Out Strategy and Winning*.

## STARTING THE GAME

You can only start *Duke Nukem 3D* from the DOS prompt. So, be sure your computer is running either in DOS or a Windows 95 DOS window. Then make the game directory active. (For example, enter the command **cd\duke3d** to change the current directory to "duke3d.") Then follow these steps to start *Duke Nukem 3D*:

1. With the game directory active, at the DOS prompt type **duke3d** and press Enter. In a few seconds, the program loads and the main menu appears (see Figure 1.1).

> **SEE** If you haven't installed *Duke Nukem 3D* on your system yet, see Appendix A, *Installation and Setup*.

> TIP
>
> Although you can run *Duke Nukem 3D* in a DOS window (in Windows 95), 3D Realms, the makers of *Duke Nukem 3D*, recommends that you run the game with your computer operating under DOS. If your computer's CPU is any version earlier than a Pentium 90, you will get smoother game play and avoid competing with Windows 95 for system resources.

2. Use the arrow keys to move the spinning selection cursors next to the **New Game** option and press Enter. Now you must choose an episode to play, as shown in Figure 1.2.

3. Choose **L.A. Meltdown**. Next you get to choose the skill level at which you want to play, as shown in Figure 1.3.

4. Choose **Let's Rock**.

After a few seconds, you find yourself as Duke Nukem on the rooftop of a downtown building, watching your ruined vessel plummeting to the ground and leaving a trail of

**FIGURE 1.1:** The *Duke Nukem 3D* main menu lets you start a new game, set game options, or load a saved game.

FIGURE 1.2: Select an episode to play on this screen. Shareware users can only choose L.A. Meltdown; the full version of the game lets you choose any episode.

FIGURE 1.3: Select a skill level on this screen. What will it be today?

smoke in its wake. You also see your hands loading a hand pistol with a clip—now you're ready to rock!

## IT'S TIME FOR ACTION

Take advantage of the relative calm on the rooftop to get acquainted with Duke's basic moves and controls. Because most people find the mouse/keyboard combination ideal, the discussions of play techniques will assume that you too are using this same setup.

### Looking Around and Picking Stuff Up

The first thing you should notice is that you are viewing everything through Duke's eyes. You have, for all practical purposes, become Nukem himself. Press ↑ to walk forward a few steps. Notice how your hand and your entire perspective weave slightly, just as if you're really walking.

> **TIP**
> Press F1 twice anytime for a list of movement options and other keystroke controls.

Walk backwards by pressing ↓. You will probably bump against a small wooden crate. Turn on your axis by pressing either ← or →. You can also execute a swift 180-degree turn by pressing the Backspace key. Go ahead, try it.

Standing in front of the crate, press A and ↑ simultaneously to jump up onto it. Press Pg Dn to look for a pistol clip behind the crate. Move forward to drop behind the crate and pick up the clip. To pick up any item on the floor, you simply walk over it. To pick up items on higher surfaces, like tables or compartments, you simply get as close to them as you can.

Now sidestep around the crate by pressing Alt and either ← or → at the same time. Use the direction keys to walk around the roof's central structure. Look up into the L.A. skyline by pressing Pg Up. Be sure you stand at a safe distance from those C-9 canisters over in the corner. It's time to blow them up and hit the streets.

> **TIP**
> The 180-degree spin move (press the Backspace key) is extremely useful when you are being chased or attacked from the rear.

### Blowing Stuff Up

Any time you have a weapon in your hands, you are aiming in the general direction in which you are moving. To obtain a higher accuracy rate, you have a crosshair at your reach any time you need it. Press the I key to activate (display) a small and unobtrusive crosshair. Press the I key a second time when you want to turn the crosshair off.

Aim at the C-9 canisters, and shoot at them by pressing either Ctrl key. To use the mouse to shoot, click the left mouse button. If you changed the defaults with the Setup program, then use the mouse button you assigned to this function. Brace yourself for the explosions. Notice that the metal fan near the canisters is also blown to bits, leaving a gaping opening.

## Running and Aiming

Run to the gaping hole where the metal fan used to be. To inject speed into your movements, press the Shift key in combination with the desired direction key. After a while, it becomes natural to run or execute your movements with extra speed in this manner. But in certain situations, it is best to move slowly and deliberately with sudden bursts of speed.

Drop into the metallic air duct, and fall down to the street level. You will probably suffer a few bruises from the fall. If your status bar's display is turned on, a quick look at it might show a slight decrease in health. You won't have a whole lot of time to rub your sore spots, though, before an assault trooper notices you from his spot on top of a large crate across the street.

Press Shift and ↑ to run toward the shameless invader, aiming your weapon slightly upward to catch him before he can reach ground level or use his jetpack to escape. To aim upward, press the Home key. In situations where you need to aim downward, press the End key. Pressing these keys is like pointing

**WARNING** Avoid standing too close to the C-9 canisters while you are shooting them. They're highly flammable. You can be seriously harmed if you're too close when a canister goes off. By the same token, C-9 canisters and other volatile materials you will routinely see on every level can prove highly useful in battle. Use their explosive power to your advantage when you see your enemies standing near them.

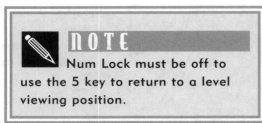

**NOTE**

Num Lock must be off to use the 5 key to return to a level viewing position.

your head and your sight in the desired direction and keeping it there. To return to a normal viewing position, press the 5 key on the numeric keypad.

With the immediate danger gone, take a look around and assess the situation. You are at what appears to be the famous Hollywood "Walk of Fame," but the name seems hardly fitting when your fifteen minutes could be suddenly cut short. Your only friend right now is the gun in your hand. If you are to have a fighting chance, you must secure some heavier firepower.

## Jumping and Uncovering Secrets

Looking around, you can't help but notice the "Innocent" billboard at the end of the street. Somehow you sense there's something not so innocent about the sign. So you decide to get up there and investigate for yourself. But how can you get up there? The large wooden crate gives you an idea.

Take a short running start toward the large crate (press Shift and ↑ together). As you pick up speed, punch the A key at the proper moment to let the inertia carry your jump forward as you land on the top of the crate. Once on top, take a second hop onto the slanted surface of the nearby building. It's a bit slippery, but you can hold on. Aiming higher, turn toward the ledge where the "Innocent" sign sits, and hop up a third time. If you fall off on your first attempt, don't give up and try again.

When you finally land on the ledge, listen for the small hydraulic platform that lifts a rocket propelled grenade (RPG) launcher right below the sign. Walk over and grab it immediately. You now have a weapon of awesome destructive power hoisted on your shoulder. Before you hurt yourself with it, put it away by pressing the 2 key on the keyboard to change back to the pistol. (You can also use the keypad when Num Lock is enabled.)

## Operating a Monitor and Finding Another Secret

With the pistol in hand, jump back onto the building's slanted surface. Move parallel with the building along the slant to the second or third window and jump inside right through either one-way window. Notice the box of grenades on the platform in the middle of the room. As you walk over to get them, don't be caught with your guard down by the trooper who comes shooting at you from the dark corner of the L-shaped room. Dispose of the trooper and grab the grenades. Notice that as you grab them a message at the top of the screen informs you that you picked up something useful.

While you're in the apartment, take a second to scope out the security monitoring system. Walk over to the monitor on the wall at the northwest end of the room and activate it with the spacebar. Press the spacebar again and notice how the scene on the monitor changes. You are in effect gaining access to multiple cameras installed throughout the level and can see what's going on in other areas of the Hollywood Holocaust level.

> **TIP**
>
> To push or pull a door open, activate a switch, turn on a monitor, or open a compartment, all you have to do is get near the device and press the spacebar.

Pull back from the monitor using ↓. Now go back to the south end of the room, and notice the movie poster on the wall. Could it be hiding something? Press the spacebar. Sure enough, it lifts and reveals a bottle of steroid pills.

The steroids could come in handy later, so stow them away. In other words, just walk up to them to pick them up. Again, notice the message near the top of the screen informing you of your good find.

## Boosting Your Health and Learning the Sidestep

Jump out of the room through one of the windows. Land on the slanted surface, and follow it toward the south end of the street. Near the end of the street, you will see a glowing object on the inclined ledge—an atomic health unit. Take this precious power-up. It gives you a whopping 50 percent boost to your health indicator. Always keep a watchful eye on your health status; don't let it fall below 50 percent for very long, if you can help it.

> **TIP**
>
> If you want to turn off the messaging feature, press F8. See Chapter 2, *Duke's Enemies, Weapons, and Power-ups*, for a detailed discussion on changing game options.

By this time, you will have attracted the attention of some additional troopers. Run toward the small alley directly across the street. Take cover behind the wall and poke your head out, sidestepping enough to take pot shots at the troopers while avoiding their shots at you. To sidestep, simply press the Alt key in combination with either the ← or →keys. Sidestep moves are extremely important as they allow you to step out of the way of incoming projectiles. Of course,

> **TIP**
>
> You may notice medkits lying about here and there as you make your way through the levels. These are identified by their red-cross symbols. They come in two sizes and can also boost your health, although not as much as do healing atoms.

you can also try sidestepping very quickly by pressing the Shift key along with either of these combinations.

When the troopers are no longer a factor, run back toward the movie theater's box office. Switch to the RPG launcher by pressing the 5 key on top of the keyboard.

At a prudent distance, aim directly at the box office. Ideally, you want to annihilate the alien hiding there and also blow a big hole in the wall. With this objective accomplished, pull out your gun again and venture forth into the theater, where more enemies, weapons, and power-ups abound.

## TAKE IT FROM HERE

Your crash tour ends here, Duke. From this point on, you get to direct and star in your own action adventure pictures. Maybe an Oscar is a pipe dream. Settle for surviving and reaching the next level. And of course, save humanity along the way.

If the crash tour gave you enough to whet your thirst for more, feel free to go directly to the blood and guts—meat and potatoes, if you prefer—part of the book: Part II, *Duking It Out*. However, if you care to be somewhat more enlightened about the company you will keep, the weapons at your disposal, and other goodies, go ahead and read Chapter 2.

> **NOTE**
>
> If the numeric keypad's Num Lock is turned on, you can also use it to change weapons.

# CHAPTER 2

# Duke's Enemies, Weapons, and Power-Ups

Before plunging head-first into a mission that could determine the fate of life on Earth as we know it, why not get acquainted with Duke's adversaries and the weapons and equipment that can be used to defeat them? Newbies and veterans alike will benefit from the factual information in this chapter. If perchance you went aboard the crash tour of Hollywood Holocaust in Chapter 1, then you already have been exposed to a few members of the invading alien races. You also might

have learned something about the game's options, weapons, and the way you maneuver your player. On the other hand, you might have skipped the tour altogether and chosen to start with this chapter instead. Whatever the case, this chapter provides the solid foundation you need to enter Duke's universe knowing what to expect and how to handle your-self. In particular, this chapter delves into the following:

- Operating the game
- Evaluating Duke's alien foes
- Presenting Duke's arsenal
- Controlling Duke's moves
- Reading Duke's status bar
- Checking out the online maps

# OPERATING THE GAME

Operating *Duke Nukem 3D* is simple and straightforward. This section explains the simple mechanics for:

- Starting a new game
- Saving a game
- Loading a saved game
- Quitting a game

## STARTING A NEW GAME

Here's how to start the action. (Be warned that you might not only be starting a new game but also a brand new addiction.)

**SEE** If you haven't installed *Duke Nukem 3D* on your system yet, see Appendix A, *Installation and Setup*.

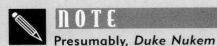

**NOTE** Presumably, *Duke Nukem 3D* is already loaded and running on your system. If it isn't, in DOS, access the game's directory (cd\duke3d). Then, type **duke3d** and press Enter. The game loads in a few seconds.

1. If the main menu isn't showing, press Esc.

2. At the main menu, use the arrow keys to move the rotating radioactive signs (the screen cursors) to the NEW GAME command, as shown in Figure 2.1, and press Enter.

3. At the Select An Episode screen, move the cursors to the episode of your choice and press Enter. (See Figure 2.2.)

4. At the Select Skill screen, move the cursors to the skill level you feel you can handle and press Enter. (See Figure 2.3.)

Get a move on, Duke, it's bust heads or lose.

## SAVING A GAME (F2)

It is always a good idea to save a game in progress at regular intervals. That way, if you come to a premature demise, you can always pick up the game from where you left off. Otherwise you must start from the level's beginning.

FIGURE 2.1: It all starts with that first game.

**FIGURE 2.2**: The Duke saga continues with your choice of three different episodes.

**FIGURE 2.3**: Just how much pain can you possibly enjoy? You get to decide on this screen.

> **TIP**
>
> Another incentive to saving your games has to do with your weapon, ammo, and power-up cache. If you are killed and haven't saved your current game, you will have to start over at the level's beginning and forfeit your entire arsenal.

To save a game in progress, do the following:

1. Press the F2 key. The game pauses and the Save Game screen appears, as shown in Figure 2.4.

2. Move the cursor to the slot where you want to save the game, type a name in the space, and press Enter.

You can save a game under any name, phrase, or description you want, but it can be no longer than 19 characters. Also, you can type over names for games that have been saved previously. When you save over a game, however, be aware that the first game is lost from memory.

The frame on the left side of the screen captures the current scene and then returns you to the game. Then you can continue kicking butt or protecting your own.

## LOADING A SAVED GAME (F3)

After you have saved one or more games, you can load any of them anytime and continue playing. This is how you do it:

> **TIP**
>
> Use Quick Save (F6) after you have already saved a game. As you make further progress into a level, you can update your saved game without having to type a name each time. Simply press the F6 key and then select Y (for Yes) to answer the *Save over last game?* prompt.

1. If you are in the middle of a game, press the F3 key. (Otherwise, press Esc to display the main menu and then choose Load Game.)

2. At the Load Game screen (see Figure 2.5), move the cursor to the name for the game you wish to load.

Notice that the frame on the left side of the screen shows the scene where the level will start.

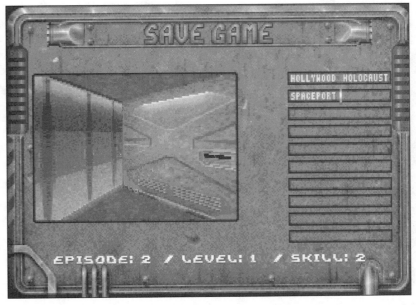

**FIGURE 2.4:** Not to sound alarmist, but you had better save your game before you die and lose your entire arsenal.

3. Press Enter.

The game picks up where it left off, and you are back in business.

## QUITTING A GAME

To quit a game in action:

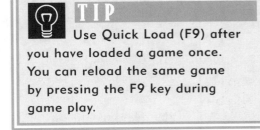

**TIP** Use Quick Load (F9) after you have loaded a game once. You can reload the same game by pressing the F9 key during game play.

1. Press the Esc key to display the main menu.
2. Move the cursors to the Quit command and press Enter.
3. When you are prompted whether to quit to DOS, type **Y** and press Enter.

Now you can go back to normal life.

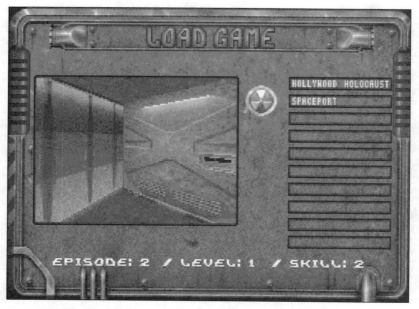

**FIGURE 2.5:** Choose the game you want to relive all over again.

# ADJUSTING THE GAME ENVIRONMENT

If you want to settle in for a productive and satisfying session of *Duke Nukem 3D*, you might as well tweak the game's environment options to set them up just the way you like them. Adjustable options for game play include the following:

- Picture adjustments
- Sound adjustments
- Mouse sensitivity
- Parental control (Adult Mode)

The remainder of this section shows you how to set things just right for you.

## PICTURE ADJUSTMENTS

The picture adjustments over which you can exercise control include the following:

- Resolution (the level of detail)
- Shadows (whether your enemies cast them)
- Screen tilting
- Screen size
- Brightness

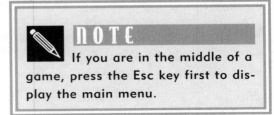

NOTE
If you are in the middle of a game, press the Esc key first to display the main menu.

You adjust all of these options from the same Options screen. To make your adjustments, do the following:

1. At the main menu, move the cursors to the Options command and press Enter. The Options screen is displayed, as shown in Figure 2.6.

2. Move the cursor to the option you wish to adjust, and make the desired adjustments as described in Table 2.1.

3. When you are finished setting your adjustments, press the Esc key to go back to the main menu.

If you were in the midst of a game, you will return to the game with the new adjustments in place.

## SOUND ADJUSTMENTS

The sound adjustments at your command include the following:

- Music
- Sound effects
- Ambient noise

**TABLE 2.1: DUKE NUKEM 3D GAME OPTIONS**

| OPTION | DESCRIPTION | ADJUSTMENT | SHORTCUT |
|---|---|---|---|
| Detail | This option controls the level of resolution you will see on your screen. You have two choices: High and Low. With most systems, High is the only choice. Even machines as basic as 50 Mhz 486s can still take advantage of the High detail level. | Press Enter to toggle between the High and Low levels. | Press F5 to toggle between the High and Low levels during game play. |
| Shadows | This option controls whether your enemies will cast shadows or not. Characters that cast shadows require a little more computational power. | Press Enter to toggle between shadows and no shadows. | |
| Screen Tilting | When turned on (the default state), this option enhances the 3D effect by causing Duke to jerk his head (and thus, your view) whenever he is hit or dies. | Press Enter to toggle between screen tilting and no screen tilting. | |
| Screen Size | This option controls the size of the game play area on your screen. A larger game play area requires more cycles per second of computational power. Therefore, the larger the screen, the slower the game will run. Of course, with Pentium 90s or higher, the speed difference is barely noticeable. | Press ← or → to decrease or increase the screen size respectively. | Press the − or + keys during game play. |
| Brightness | This option controls how dark or light the picture appears. | Press ← or → to decrease or increase the level of brightness respectively. | Press F11 to cycle through the eight levels of brightness during game play. When you reach the desired level, press the Esc key. |

FIGURE 2.6: Tweak the game options to your heart's content.

Like their picture counterparts, the sound adjustments can also all be made from the same screen. Here is how to set your own sound adjustments:

1. At the main menu, move the cursors to the Options command and press Enter.

2. At the Options screen, move the cursors to the Sound option and press Enter. The Sounds screen appears, as shown in Figure 2.7.

3. Use the arrow keys to highlight the sound option you want to control and make your adjustments, as indicated in Table 2.2.

4. When you have adjusted the sound levels to your desire, press the Esc key to get back to the main menu.

FIGURE 2.7: Tweak all the knobs you want to make sound adjustments.

## TABLE 2.2: DUKE NUKEM 3D SOUND OPTIONS

| OPTION | DESCRIPTION | ADJUSTMENT |
|---|---|---|
| Sound | This option controls whether you hear anything at all. | Press Enter to toggle between sound on and sound off. |
| Music | This option controls whether you hear any music at all. (The music, sound effects, and ambient sound can be controlled independently.) | Press Enter to toggle between music on and music off. |
| Sound Volume | This option controls how loud the sound effects will sound. Sound effects include explosions, alien growls, and the normal sounds that happen naturally as you interact with the environment. | Press ← or → to decrease or increase the sound volume respectively. |
| Music Volume | This option controls how loud the music will sound. | Press ← or → to decrease or increase the music volume respectively. |

| OPTION | DESCRIPTION | ADJUSTMENT |
|---|---|---|
| Duke Talk | This option controls whether you hear Duke speak during game play. A man of few words, Duke is known to use a few colorful expressions from time to time. | Press Enter to toggle between talking and silent modes. |
| Ambiance | This option controls whether ambient sounds are present or absent. Ambient sounds are not necessarily produced by your interaction with the environment. They are simply the natural sounds of the environment you are visiting. | Press Enter to toggle between ambient sounds on and ambient sounds off. |
| Flip Stereo | This option controls the sound signals going to the right and left channels. You can switch the direction of the signals so the left channel becomes the right channel and vice versa. | Press Enter to switch the stereo channel signals. |

## MOUSE SENSITIVITY

For most players, the mouse is a most useful interface device that allows you to move swiftly and deliberately. In the aiming mode, the mouse gives you a great degree of control in choosing and isolating your targets. Set the sensitivity of your mouse to your liking and improve your all around scores. To set mouse sensitivity do the following:

1.  At the main menu, move the cursors to the Options command and press Enter.

2.  At the Options screen, move the cursors to the Mouse Sensitivity option and press ← or → to decrease or increase the sensitivity, respectively.

## PARENTAL CONTROLS

If you want to keep the more mature material from the prying eyes of youngsters and other, shall we say, prudish types, you can exercise the game's built-in parental controls.

The procedure involves turning off Adult Mode and setting up a password. Without the password, the player is barred from viewing human flesh. However, you will still see plenty of blood, guts, and gore. To turn off Adult Mode:

1. At the main menu, move the cursors to the Options command and press Enter.

2. At the Options screen, move the cursors to the Parental Lock option and press Enter. The Adult Mode screen appears, as shown in Figure 2.8.

3. Press Enter to turn off the adult content of the game. The program will prompt you for a password, so you can turn the adult material back on when you wish.

4. Type a password of up to 12 characters and press Enter.

From this point on, if you wish to view the adult content while playing the game, you will have to access the Adult Mode screen, turn on adult content, and type the correct password.

**FIGURE 2.8:** Keep prying eyes locked out. Exercise your parental controls.

# EVALUATING DUKE'S ALIEN FOES

However unsettling, it's time to talk about the unsavory company you will keep when you play *Duke Nukem 3D*. The hostile and predatorial cast of alien characters paying you a visit is quite motley. Obviously a fiendish predatory alliance of unprecedented proportions, the alien invaders are not here merely to study, explore, and dissect cattle. They've assembled with the common goal of subjugating our world. Their agenda also includes bio-genetic experimentation with unwilling human females. If you are to fight and reach any level of success, you should definitely find out all you can about these uninvited guests. It's up to you to crash their party in a big way and find out the best way to bounce them back to the void where they belong.

## ASSAULT TROOPERS (TROOPERS)

These reptilian-looking bipeds sport green vests, laser pistols, and jetpacks. The first wave to invade the Earth, the assault troopers form the grunt front lines of the alien alliance. Because they are highly mobile and capable of hovering, assault troopers are never easy to deal with. Although they can be killed with a few rounds from your handgun, assault troopers are seldom discouraged from their pursuit. As their designated prey, you should never let your guard down when a trooper lurks around. Each time a trooper's blast hits you directly, you will experience as much as a 15 percent drain on your health.

## ASSAULT CAPTAINS (CAPTAINS)

These guys, who sport the higher ranking red vests, make up the next higher echelon in the alien hierarchy. Like their minion troopers, the captains also sport laser pistols and jetpacks. But in addition, they wear phased-induced teleporter devices on their wrists. A captain can dematerialize at will only to reappear when you least expect it, usually behind your back and firing at you point blank. Don't let this happen to you, for each time you suffer a hit, you experience a commensurate health drain of up to 20 percent. Ouch! One way to avoid being caught from behind is to back up against a wall when a captain has gone invisible. He will have no choice but to reappear in front of you. Then your odds are a bit more even.

## PROTOZOID SLIMERS (SLIMERS)

Equipped with a very simple nervous system, these evolutionary throwbacks resemble a giant mutated amoeba. After sensing your presence, protozoid slimers emerge from their egg pods for the sole purpose of sucking your brain through your nose. What drives them to do this is a complete mystery, but it appears to be hard-coded in their genes. Slimers also like to crawl up your pant legs and work their way up to your nose. These creatures are also quite elusive, as they are able to crawl along walls and ceilings. They can also stretch their gelatinous bodies and bounce from ceiling to floor. The best way to dispose of slimers is by stomping on them or shooting them with your handgun. The ripper chaingun is also a good weapon to possess when you are surrounded by a colony of slimers.

## PIG COPS

At one point, these guys' motto was "to protect and to serve." But after undergoing advanced mutation, the L.A. police force has become a mindless army of slaves serving the aliens' beckoning. The dreaded pig cops are indeed faithful servants and ruthless killers. Toting shotguns and exhibiting absolutely no fear, pig cops are determined, unyielding opponents. Often announced by their growling snort, pig cops are good shots. It isn't rare to see a pig cop drop to the ground to take careful aim before firing.

Your chances of overcoming an encounter with a pig cop get better if you are armed with a shotgun. But even so, and as if they weren't tough enough, many pig cops wear protective body armor. This can be a mixed blessing. Sometimes you can kill a pig cop and claim his weapon or body armor. If they are available, you will see these items fall next to a pig cop's bloated carcass. Get shot by a pig cop and expect at least a 20 percent drain in your health. If you aren't wearing a body armor, the damage reaches in the magnitude of 25 percent or even higher.

## RECON PATROL VEHICLES (RPVS)

Highly maneuverable and fast, RPVs are single-user, anti-gravity transports that allow pig cops to take to the air. Every RPV is equipped with powerful side-mounted laser cannons. A well-trained pig cop can give chase and swoop upon you in his RPV. In addition, RPVs can hover indefinitely, allowing pig cops to get a fix on you and keep you in the line of fire. Get hit by the RPV's laser cannon and experience a major health loss of as much as 30 percent. Besides the laser cannon, each RPV is also equipped with an automatic ejection seat. This means that even when you pluck one from the air, the pig cop will emerge from the wreckage and come chasing after you.

## ENFORCERS

Armed with blazing ripper chainguns, enforcers are charged with dispatching the remaining human opposition. Their powerful hind legs enable these reptilian-looking creatures to leap great heights. Their toughness is partly due to the fact that many enforcers wear protective armor. Enforcers tend to run in packs, so when you see one, you can usually expect to see a few more. The shotgun is a good weapon to use against enforcers, when you are facing them at mid ranges. Usually one or as many as three shotgun blasts are enough to put enforcers out of existance. Sometimes a dying enforcer will drop his ammo load, which you can use for your ripper chaingun, or his armor plate, which you can also use for your own protection.

## OCTABRAINS

Resembling a giant octopus with three ferocious eyes, an octabrain's massive brain matter and trifocal vision make him a mysterious and most heinous enemy. These unsightly creatures prefer to lurk in dark and moist places and are also known to take to the air as easily as they dominate the depths of bodies of water. Octabrains have a penchant for pouncing suddenly into view. Then, by focusing their immense mental energy into a focused emanation, an octabrain can nearly paralyze you from a single shock, shaving your health by as much as 50 percent. At close quarters, an octabrain relies on razor sharp, serrated teeth to saw you in half.

## BATTLELORD

Each episode has one or more *bosses*, and the Battlelord is the first boss you will encounter in the level known as The Abyss. A true mastodon, the Battlelord is the dead-

liest of all the aliens you will encounter in the L.A. Meltdown episode. The Battlelord's sheer size is enough to scare you silly. Once you feel the impact of his over-under ripper chain-gun, which also doubles as a mortar launcher, you'll be praying for and seeking shelter. A sustained attack can decrease your health at the rate of 5 to 10 percent per second. In the midst of a lead flurry, the Battlelord can switch modes and launch spherical explosives at your feet.

You'd better run. You'd better hide. You'd better devise a strategy before confronting the Battlelord. If you can stay alive long enough to drive home about 30 to 35 rounds with your RPG launcher, you might enjoy the spectacle of watching the massive Battlelord crumble to the ground. This giant menace does not believe in going gently into the night.

## BATTLELORD SENTRY

A smaller version of the original Battlelord, the battlelord is not quite as ferocious as his taller cousin and is easier to kill, but he still packs a respectable amount of fire power and should never be underestimated.

## ASSAULT COMMANDER (COMMANDER)

A massive hovering torso on a free floating anti-gravity deck, the assault commander is a most formidable opponent for three main reasons. For one, in spite of his stately port, he can levitate and dash through the air quite gracefully. Also, he can render you to shreds in a matter of seconds. His anti-gravity deck is equipped with sharp blades, and it doubles up as a food processor of sorts. One of the commander's favorite methods of killing involves dropping over his victim with the blades at full spin. Finally, the commander is extremely dangerous even at long ranges. His posterior end, for lack of a more anatomically correct term, is capable of launching deadly projectiles. Get hit by one and loose as much as 50 to 75 percent of your health.

The best way to defend yourself and prevail over the assault commander is to keep him at bay, dodge his incoming projectiles, and hit him with one or two RPG rounds. If you are in close quarters, you can use the shrinker to bring him down to size and then simply stomp him flat. If you don't have the RPG, the freezethrower can also be extremely effective. Blast the commander until he turns blue, then break him into shards with a simple bullet from your handgun or even by kicking him with your mighty foot.

## SENTRY DRONE (DRONE)

This enemy is a mindless automaton with a simple program running through its silicon-based brain: Seek Duke Nukem and destroy him. Sporting anti-gravity units, sentry drones are highly maneuverable and elusive. They can hover and dart through the air at fast speeds. Once they trace you, drones will simply dive at you at full speed, delivering an explosive charge capable of reducing your health by up to 35 percent. Drones are a lot easier to deal with when they are at a distance, where you can pepper them with the ripper chaingun until they explode. If you hear the whinning pitch of a sentry's anti-gravity unit engaging, you had better seek shelter behind a thick door, wall, pillar, or whatever. A diving drone will often crash against obstacle in its zeal to execute its program.

## MOON ASSAULT LEADER

Sporting dual mounted rockets on his shoulders and a fast-speed chaingun in his underside, the Moon Assault Leader is one ferocious alien beast. The heavy harness around his reptilian body holds his weapons and also protects him from injury. Sharp eyesight, lightning quick reflexes, and a self-contained arsenal are among the top predatorial characteristics gracing this grotesque creature. Whenever you are forced to contend with the Moon Assault Leader, you will do well to start out with as much health and armor as you can possibly amass. Then you might not have much of a choice but to play a deadly cat-and-mouse game, with you relegated to the role of the rodent. A combined assault of all your heavy weaponry can eventually incapacitate the Moon Assault Leader.

### CYCLOID EMPEROR (EMPEROR)

A true abomination if there ever were one, the Cycloid Emperor is a deadly walking nightmare. This one-eyed giant is dangerous for many reasons. First, there's his lethal breath, which is capable of emanating energy blasts in rapid succession. You can be over-whelmed and outmatched in a matter of seconds, if you sustain a full breath assault. Then there's the Emperor's built-in devastators. Just as powerful as your own devastator, the Emperor can fire charges directly from the built -in ports in his mechanical, claw-like upper extremities.

# PRESENTING ARMS

Ask anyone who's ever saved the world and they'll tell you the same thing: The right hardware and firepower make all the difference. Although you will face what seem like insurmountable odds, when used diligently, your weaponry will see you through the worst. Naturally, knowledge and mastery of your weapons affect your success rate directly. And equally important is knowing the conditions when a specific weapon is most effective.

Every time you start a new *Duke Nukem 3D* game, you enter holding only a hand-gun. The first order of business is to find more weaponry and ammo so you can defend yourself and prolong your own survival. This section details each weapon you can find as you make your way through each level. Bear in mind that some levels may not contain all of the weapons at your disposal in *Duke Nukem 3D*.

### THE MIGHTY FOOT

Ironically, your first arm is your foot. Even when completely unarmed, you can still kick like a mule. It is possible to stomp a pig cop to death, for instance, but it sure isn't pretty. Just hope that you are not often forced into such disagreeable situations. The mighty foot also comes in handy when you simply want to bash through an air duct grill, break a window, or deliver a coup-de-grace to an agonizing opponent. Until the next best weapon comes along, isn't it comforting to know your foot can always carry you through?

## THE HANDGUN

The smooth, metallic grip of the semi-automatic handgun is certainly more reassuring than relying solely on your mighty foot. The least powerful of all your weapons, the handgun is a godsend when no other weapon is in sight. The handgun lets you fire 12 rounds in succession before you have to reload it. That's when you leave yourself open for a second or two.

Whenever you find a handgun, it comes fully loaded and you have enough clips to fire 48 rounds. The clips you run into are good for 12 rounds each. The maximum number of bullets you can carry is 200. You can usually finish off assault troopers and assault captains with 3 to 5 shots. A pig cop requires at least 5 and maybe more. Taking on an octabrain with a handgun would be rather chancy, but you can do it if you can keep a safe distance and shield yourself from its mental energy blasts.

## THE SHOTGUN

Getting hold of a shotgun lets you assert yourself with a little more authority. Your first move in any level is to find a shotgun if you don't already have one. A proverbial work-horse, the shotgun lets you make short work of most bipedal aliens (with the exception of the massive Battlelord and the other vociferous bosses from Lunar Apocalypse and Shrapnel City). Pig cops carry shotguns. Occasionally, you might be able to wrestle a pig cop's weapon. With a shotgun, you must pump to reload every time after firing. This takes about a second, leaving you open for an instant.

Any shotgun you find comes with 10 shells, unless you retrieve one from a pig cop you've just killed, and then the number of shells depends on how many shells the pig cop fired. Shotgun ammo also comes in boxes of 10 shells. The most shells you can carry at any time is 50. If your aim is exceedingly good, you can off most troopers and captains and even pig cops with a single blast. But because of its spread, the shotgun is most effective at medium or close distances. You can knock out an octabrain with three solid shots. Recon Patrol Vehicles also make suitable targets for the shotgun. You can plunk one from the sky with about 2 to 4 good shots.

## THE RIPPER CHAINGUN

The ripper chaingun is an excellent weapon for sweeping down hostile crowds. Accuracy, though good to have, is not mandatory for this weapon's effectiveness. The major drawback to the ripper chaingun is, of course, its voracious consumption of ammunition. Find a ripper chaingun and use it most effectively in crowded situations. Each ripper chaingun you find comes with 50 rounds, as do its ammo cases. You can carry up to 200 rounds at once.

Secure a ripper chaingun and shred through most troopers and captains with short, concentrated one- or two-second bursts. Pig cops might require a few more rounds. The ripper chaingun is particularly effective against octabrains. With it, you can stand your ground and square off. The sustained impact of its bullets on an octabrain's pulpy flesh will keep it from mustering one of its lethal mental energy blasts.

## THE ROCKET PROPELLED GRENADE (RPG) LAUNCHER

You can almost afford to be cocky when you score the RPG launcher. In terms of sheer explosive power, no other weapon equals the impact of an RPG projectile. Not only can you blow opponents to bits from long distances, but you can also blow holes right through some building walls and even dig tunnels into solid rock. But for all its sheer power, the RPG launcher is rather slow in sending off its load. Avoid drawing the launcher unless you are ready to use it.

Every RPG launcher you find comes with 5 rounds, as does each case of ammo. A single projectile is capable of rendering a crowd of aliens into gruesome confetti. The octabrain is also highly succesiptible to this weapon. When you face off any of the bosses, pray you have a well stocked RPG launcher. The most ammo you can carry for this weapon tops off at 50 rounds.

> **☠ WARNING**
> If you accidentally discharge an RPG launcher near a wall, the blast could cause you serious damage or even kill you.

## PIPE BOMBS

Crude, but extremely effective, pipe bombs are a guerrilla-type of weapon that you can fling and detonate remotely. Nearly matching the explosive power of the RPG launcher, pipe bombs are strategic weapons. The fact that you can detonate them from a distance lets you set up traps for your adversaries. Here is a likely scenario: You drop a bomb, make your enemy chase you, turn a bend, and then push the detonator at the right moment. After a powerful *KA-BOOM*, you might hear an unpleasant splat as alien innards spray the walls.

> **☠ WARNING**
>
> If you detonate a pipe bomb while you are standing nearby, you can kill yourself accidentally—and that is never fun—or seriously maim yourself. The most pipe bombs you can amass and carry at any one time is 50.

Pipe bombs are also ideal when you can drop them into enclosed areas where enemies happen to be congregated. The main disadvantage of using pipe bombs is that after deploying one, you are basically unarmed until you detonate it or draw another weapon, which well could be another pipe bomb. In fact, there are situations where you will want to carpet an area with pipe bombs and detonate them all at once. Explosions of this type are quite extraordinary.

## WALL-MOUNTED LASER TRIP BOMB (LTB)

Another highly strategic weapon, the laser trip bomb is only available in the full version of *Duke Nukem 3D*. This clever wall-mounted device is ideal for restricting your

enemies' range of movement. Deploy a trip bomb on a wall, and it automatically projects a sensitive laser beam onto the opposing wall or surface. Any disturbance, however slight, to the beam triggers the trip's bomb's plastic explosives.

You can create explosive walls by lining up trip bombs at different heights. Once deployed, a trip bomb's sensing beam stays active until it is violated and the explosives are discharged. Perhaps something to consider when deploying trip bombs is that, not only are you restricting your enemy's movements, but you are restricting your own as well. So use them judiciously. At any one time, the most trip bombs you can carry is 20.

## THE SHRINKER

Powered by glowing green shrinker crystals, this weapon has the effect of shrinking your opponents to the size of bugs you can flatten with your foot. This weapon is only available in the full version of *Duke Nukem 3D*. Be aware, though, that the shrinker's effects last only temporarily. So immediately after using it, you should rush your shrunk opponent and squash him like a grape.

## THE DEVASTATOR

A double-barreled weapon of awesome destructive power, the devastator launches explosive charges with concentrated impact. After pulling the trigger, watch the barrels' pumping action as they dish out a flurry of charges. This weapon makes short work of most enemies, including assault commanders and enforcers. Like the RPG, exercise caution when using this weapon in close quarters. The explosive charges can harm you as well as the enemy.

## THE FREEZETHROWER

Falling under the exotic category, a freezethrower could easily turn into a workhorse, provided you find enough ammo to keep it going. When you connect with the freezethrower, your victim's molecular structure is radically changed to ice. Of course the tougher the opponent, the more charges it takes to turn him into ice. Once the opponent is in the catatonic ice state, you can simply kick him or shoot him to break the ice without uttering a word, so to speak. Beware that the effect of the freezethrower lasts only a few seconds, and your opponents will thaw out and act like nothing happened.

# DUKE'S POWER-UPS

In rounding out and complementing a well-stocked arsenal (useful equipment like jet-packs and beneficial devices like atomic health units), the game's power-ups constitute another key element to victory. Not necessarily destructive, power-ups are items and equipment that bestow you with special abilities. For instance, a jetpack is a power-up that lets you hover over the landscape. Other power-ups can give you tremendous health boosts, let you see in the dark, or allow you to traverse underwater terrain or safely negotiate canals of flowing toxic sludge. The details for each power-up follow; and remember, always use the right tool for the job.

## MEDKITS

Medkits come in two sizes: small and large. In addition, portable medkits are also available. The small and large medkits increase your health by 10 and 30 percent, respectively. Whenever you grab either of these two medkits, your health is increased immediately (but never to go over 100 percent).

The portable medkit carries a full 100 percent of health, which you can use to restore your health level up to 100 percent. Unlike the two smaller medkits, this item is activated and used only when you press the M key. However, each time you use it, a corresponding percentage is deducted from it to replenish your health level up to 100 percent. For example, if your health is currently at 70 percent and you press M to activate a portable medkit, your health will go up to 100 percent. The portable medkit, on the other hand, will go down to 70 percent, which is available the next time you decide to use it.

## ATOMIC HEALTH UNITS

Atomic health units look like large, glowing, blue atoms and they are truly lucky finds. A single atomic health unit will cause your health to soar by 50 percent, even above and beyond 100 percent. The upper limit to the health you can amass with atomic health units tops off at 200 percent. In a very real sense, atomic health units give you a new lease on life and help you even the often ridiculous odds against surviving.

## ARMOR

An armor can make the difference between mortal or merely flesh wounds. When you slide into an armor, you are suddenly better able to absorb punishment before it takes its toll on your health. Although often found in secret places, some-  times you can strip armors from the bodies of dead pig cops. Just like you shouldn't engage in chancy activities without proper protection, you should always strive to wear an armor when facing your oppo- nents. A fresh armor gives you 100 percent of protection. Armors do, however, tend to wear out with every impact you sustain. When your armor percent- age goes below 50 percent, you should definitely exercise more care, and pay more attention to your defensive techniques.

## KEYCARDS

Keycards come in the primary colors red, yellow, and blue. Although used for noth- ing more than opening special doors or latches, keycards are often hidden or found in remote or seemingly inaccessible places. More often than not, your strategy for solv-  ing a level includes determining what cards you need and in what order you must have them. Without the proper card or card combi- nations, many level areas will remain a mystery and completely beyond limits. To use a keycard, you simply walk up to the door in question and press the spacebar.

## STEROIDS

Like keycards, steroids are often well out of view. When you happen upon these unassuming little brown flasks, you might not be too impressed. But  the pills inside pack a hell of a kick in more ways than one. After you acti- vate this item (you select it with the [ key and then press Enter), you will learn to appreciate the sudden rush of energy and speed. Your kick will become at least twice as powerful and your movements will be greatly accelerated. A flask of steroids is good for about 30 seconds. So use them judiciously, and try not to abuse them. You might consider limiting their usage to fighting situations in close quarters with multiple enemies. Also, if you wish to traverse long distances in a hurry without stopping to admire the scenery or engaging many enemies, learn to rely on the power of the steroid.

## HOLODUKE

Is it real or is it holoduke? This holographic likeness of yourself is of great value as a strategic device. Like steroids and keycards, holodukes are often found in unexpected or hard-to-reach places. When you deploy the holoduke (by pressing the H key), an image of yourself is left at the spot where you stand. The holoduke has a limited life span of about 35 seconds. You can disengage it by pressing the H key a second time. After deploying it, you can hide and wait for your enemies to go after the fake Duke and leave themselves open for your retaliation from the rear. You can also plant a pipe bomb at the feet of the holoduke and detonate it when your unsuspecting adversaries get near it. Perhaps a bit sly, but this war is to the death, and you didn't start it in the first place.

## JETPACK

This is perhaps the single most useful power-up anybody can ask for. With one of these babies safely strapped to your back, you can take to the air. The steel gray jetpack gives you a most significant strategic advantage. No longer earthbound, your options suddenly multiply. Once you find a jetpack, you can activate it by pressing the J key. Then you can ascend or descend with the A and Z keys, respectively. To turn the jetpack off, you simply press J a second time.

A new jetpack is fueled up to 100 percent, but goes down to 0 percent in about 45 seconds of continued usage. With a jetpack you can reach high places and uncover secrets that would otherwise remain a mystery. A jetpack also allows you to plot direct, short routes to certain destinations. In many cases, a jetpack can allow you to blaze through a level by letting you circumvent all manner of obstacles in the earthly terrain.

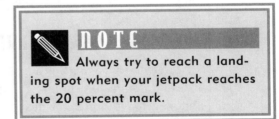

**NOTE**
Always try to reach a landing spot when your jetpack reaches the 20 percent mark.

## NIGHT VISION GOGGLES (NVG)

With a pair of these, you gain the ability to see in the dark. While your view won't be as good as in daylight, you will certainly gain a clear advantage over opponents and aliens lurking in the darkness. After scoring the NVG, you can turn them on by pressing the N key. The 100 percent mark goes down to 0 percent in about 35 seconds. Save the NVG by pressing the N key a second time.

## SCUBA GEAR

There is simply no way you can get through some levels without going underwater— 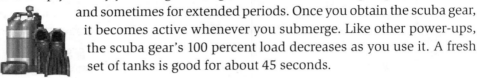 and sometimes for extended periods. Once you obtain the scuba gear, it becomes active whenever you submerge. Like other power-ups, the scuba gear's 100 percent load decreases as you use it. A fresh set of tanks is good for about 45 seconds.

## PROTECTIVE BOOTS

Although not exactly fashionable footwear, a pair of protective boots is a lot more than mere goulashes. They can keep you from coming into direct contact with the toxic liquids and chemicals that circulate through many levels like the poisoned veins of a hopeless junky. Like the scuba gear, your protective boots are smart. They know when to turn on and off.

# CONTROLLING DUKE'S MOVES

Knowing your enemies and being intimately acquainted with your weapons is only half the battle. The other half of your success hinges on your technique and execution. This section summarizes the keyboard controls for moving your Duke around. As you become a more experienced player, your moves will become second nature.

## WALKING, TURNING, AND RUNNING

Walking in *Duke Nukem 3D* is a no-brainer; it's almost like chewing gum. Just press the arrow key for the direction you want to go. To run, you simply press and hold down the Shift key in addition to the desired arrow key. If you like, you can leave Run mode on by pressing the Caps Lock key. Press the Caps Lock key a second time to disengage the Run mode.

Besides the arrow keys, you can also execute common turning maneuvers with other keys. For example, to execute a quick 180 degree turn, press the Backspace key. To take a quick glance to your left or right, without changing your direction, press the Insert and Delete keys, respectively. After you release either of these keys, your view returns to the forward position.

## LOOKING AND AIMING UP AND DOWN

To look up or down momentarily, press PgUp or PgDn, respectively. After releasing either of these keys, your view returns to the normal, level position.

Unlike looking up or down, aiming up or down changes your view until you change it back. To aim up press the Home key until you reach the desired aiming position. Do the same thing with the End key to aim down. To go back to a level view, press 5 on the numeric keypad.

## MOVING AND AIMING WITH THE MOUSE

The more you learn to rely on the mouse/keyboard combination, the better a player you will become. The mouse duplicates many of the keyboard controls and it offers a single source to exercise multiple techniques. Three-button models are preferred over two-button models because they add an extra button for control.

The *Duke Nukem 3D* Setup program lets you assign functions to each mouse button, or you can use the default assignments as shown in Table 2.3.

**NOTE** To aid you in aiming, you can turn on a crosshair any time you like. Just press the I key. An unobtrusive crosshair will appear to indicate where your weapon is aiming currently. Press the I key a second time to turn off the crosshair.

**NOTE** With the Setup program, which is explained in Appendix A, *Installation and Setup*, you can also assign actions to double-clicks. For example, you can assign the middle button for jumping when it is double-clicked. The only double-click default is Open (as in open doors), and it is assigned to the secondary mouse button.

### TABLE 2.3: THE DEFAULT MOUSE BUTTON FUNCTIONS

| MOUSE BUTTON | SINGLE CLICK |
| --- | --- |
| Primary | Fire |
| Middle | Move forward |
| Secondary | Strafe |

In certain situations, particularly when you are stationary, you can turn on Aim mode for the mouse by pressing the U key. This simple action turns the mouse into a most responsive aiming tool. While in Aim mode, you can perform all the aiming techniques described in Table 2.4.

| TABLE 2.4: MOUSE FUNCTIONS IN AIM MODE. | |
| --- | --- |
| AIMING DIRECTION | MOUSE ACTION |
| Up | Pull mouse back. |
| Down | Push mouse forward. |
| Left | Push mouse to the left. |
| Right | Push mouse to the right. |

You can also combine motions so you can aim upward as you turn to your left or aim downward as you look to the right. To turn off Aim mode, press the U key a second time during game play.

## JUMPING AND DUCKING

Just like in previous incarnations of *Duke Nukem* and *Duke Nukem II*, *Duke Nukem 3D* provides you with extensive use of jumping and ducking maneuvers. Sometimes the only way to reach a platform, an air duct, or another elevated surface, is to jump as high as you can. By the same token, other areas will remain undiscovered unless you get down to crawl on your hands and knees. Both of these operations are very simple. You jump by pressing the A key. You can also take running jumps by pressing Shift and ↑ together and then punching the A key at the right moment (after you pick up some momentum to carry you forward). To duck, you simply press the Z key.

## SHOOTING AND CHANGING WEAPONS

You can fire the weapon you are currently holding by pressing either of the Ctrl keys. When you don't have any weapons, or if your mighty foot is the currently active weapon, you will see your right leg raise and snap a powerful kick, when you press the Ctrl key.

To change weapons, all you have to do is press the number key associated with the weapon you want. Each weapon is always associated with the same number as shown in Table 2.5.

| TABLE 2.5: WEAPONS AND CORRESPONDING NUMBER KEYS | |
|---|---|
| **WEAPON** | **NUMBER KEY** |
| Mighty foot | 1 |
| Handgun | 2 |
| Shotgun | 3 |
| Ripper chaingun | 4 |
| RPG launcher | 5 |
| Pipe bombs | 6 |
| Shrinker | 7 |
| Devastator | 8 |
| Laser trip bombs | 9 |
| Freezethrower | 0 |

# READING DUKE'S STATUS BAR

The status bar appears at the bottom of the screen during game play, and it is your feedback mechanism to find out how well or poorly you are doing. The status bar lets you monitor your health and the current percentage of your armor, as well as various other aspects of your arsenal. As you can see in Figure 2.9, the status bar's ergonomic design lets you appraise your conditions at a glance.

The status bar allows you to keep tabs on the following indicators:

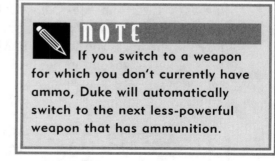

**NOTE**

If you switch to a weapon for which you don't currently have ammo, Duke will automatically switch to the next less-powerful weapon that has ammunition.

1.  The Health indicator displays your current health status. Under optimum conditions, and with enough atomic health units, your health can soar to 200 percent.

2.  The Armor indicator displays the percentage of armor you have left. It can reach up to 100 percent with a fresh armor.

3. The Weapons indicator shows you the weapons you have available through their number designations (2 for the handgun, 3 for the shotgun, 4 for the chaingun cannon, and so on). This indicator also shows the number of rounds you have versus the maximum number of rounds you can carry.

4. The smaller Ammo indicator to the right shows you the number of rounds available for the weapon that is currently in your hands.

5. The Inventory indicator shows the power-up that is currently selected. You can change power-ups with either the [ or ] key. To activate a selected power-up, you simply press Enter.

6. The Keys indicator shows you the installation keycards you have in your possession, if any.

You can increase the screen size but still retain a minimized status bar, as shown in Figure 2.10.

# CHECKING OUT THE ONLINE MAPS

As you begin to navigate in ever more complex *Duke Nukem 3D* installations, you will find the online maps to be quite handy. The online maps are available in two modes: first, as overhead line maps that you can superimpose over the actual area where you are moving; second, as textured maps that completely block the view of your immediate surroundings. The line map only shows the dividing lines between the installation's various rooms and areas. The textured map shows additional installation details, such as the surface qualities of rocky terrain, liquid expanses, and concrete or metallic areas.

**FIGURE 2.9:** Keep abreast of your vitals with the status bar.

To view the online line map, simply press the Tab key once. To view the textured map, press the Tab key a second time. To get back to the normal view, press the Tab key a third time. Once you are displaying an online map, you can size it to your needs by pressing the - or + keys on the keyboard.

While you are viewing the textured map, you can choose to continue moving, and the map will show your movement and progress. However, if you are moving while viewing the textured map, you will not be able to view your enemies and counter their onslaughts. If you wish to explore the map on screen and be able to scroll around and blow up different sections without moving physically in the level, you can turn off the Follow mode. Just press the F key while watching the map on screen. Use the arrow keys and - and + to scroll and zoom in and out of map sections. Press the F key a second time to turn Follow mode back on.

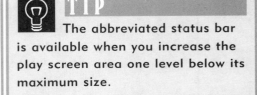

> **TIP**
> The abbreviated status bar is available when you increase the play screen area one level below its maximum size.

FIGURE 2.10: The minimized status bar keeps you appraised of your most vital indicators, health, and weapons.

CHAPTER

3

# Mapping Out Strategy and Winning

Just how does one become a *winner*? There's always the self-help book route or the lottery. And then there's true discipline and a fiery passion for what you do. Duke falls in with the latter group, and his motivations are not solely for personal gain. (Although, he was pushing his autobiography, *Why I Am So Great,* when he was snatched by the Rigelatins at the start of *Duke Nukem II*—but that's another story.) This time Duke is looking further than the self. He is contemplating the delicate and perilous balance by which humanity's fate can be decided—one way or another. The two sections in this chapter cover:

- Fighting solo
- Using the level maps

> **SEE**
> For more details on playing DukeMatch or Co-Op modes, see Appendix B, *Multiplayer Tips and Online Resources*.

Fighting Solo describes a few skills and techniques that any serious player should master. Using the Level Maps shows you how easily and intuitively it is to read the level maps you will see for each level in Part II of this book.

# FIGHTING SOLO

Most players will experience solo fighting before playing in DukeMatch or Co-Op modes, and there is a good reason for this. You will want to hone your skills before duking it out with the big boys. To be not just a good, but a superior solo player, you must master:

- Moving with agility
- Fighting with grace
- Exploring with intelligence

## MOVING WITH AGILITY

Your chances for overcoming your opponents are directly related to how well you can move in your virtual environment. Naturally, being fleet of foot and light on your toes will allow you to be able to elude your attackers and retaliate with impunity. After learning the basics of getting from point A to point B, you should inject speed into your movements by pressing Shift in conjunction with the other keys.

### Sidestepping and Strafing

Sidestepping and strafing will allow you to dole out punishment and then take shelter quickly behind a wall or other inanimate object. Sidestepping is also very important when you come around corners or sudden turns. When you sidestep around a corner, you will be in a better position to fire your weapon accurately. The last thing you want to happen is to be blind sided by an incoming projectile. Recall that you use the Alt key and either ← or → to execute sidestepping.

### Strategic Movement

Good gaming strategy dictates that you learn to take advantage of your full range of motion. You can look up and down with the PgUp and PgDn keys, and you can look to either side with the Insert and Delete keys, no matter where you are in any level. Use the A and Z keys to jump and duck, respectively. There will be many opportunities to

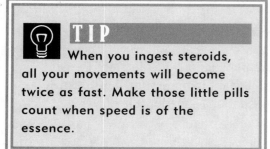

**TIP**

When you ingest steroids, all your movements will become twice as fast. Make those little pills count when speed is of the essence.

duck behind a counter only to jump up and surprise your enemies.

Be aware that you are not the only one who can duck. Pig cops will routinely drop to the ground and aim up at you. When this happens, you too should drop to the ground and beat the pig cop to the trigger.

As for jumping, in certain situations, especially if you don't have a jetpack, you will have to hop onto crates, elevated surfaces, and even on wall indentations to reach high places. Put all of your movements together, and soon they will become second nature.

The 180-degree turn is also a very useful technique to master. For example, you can use it as an offensive strategy against an opponent who is chasing you. As you are running away, hit the Backspace key to execute a smooth 180-degree turn, and you will be suddenly staring at your pursuer down the barrel of your weapon.

## FIGHTING WITH GRACE

Fighting gracefully is never easy. It takes skill and hours of practice. But it can be done. Just what is involved in fighting with grace? It turns out that the most graceful and effective fighters are those who are intimately acquainted with their arsenal, know their opponents as they know themselves, and can master the rudiments and elements of their environment.

### Get the Heavy Weapons

Whenever you start a new game, your first concern should be to find a respectable weapon. This doesn't mean the pistol is inconsequential. In fact, the pistol is an extremely useful weapon when shooting at mid-range or long-range targets. But the pistol will seem ineffective when you are confronting enemies in close range—especially enemies that can fire rapidly, like enforcers and the Battlelord.

You will fare much better against these kinds of enemies when you are able to score a shotgun. Make the shotgun your workhorse. Of course, be aware that after firing a shot, you must take a second to reload. Seek shelter when you are loading your shotgun. Once you obtain a devastator, a shrinker, or the exotic freezethrower, you can become quite formidable. But just the same, don't become overly dependent on these weapons because they are not very common and their ammo does not come quite so readily.

## Know Your Enemy

Every opponent you face has strengths and weaknesses. Learn to minimize the former and exploit the latter. Assault troopers, for instance, aren't exactly very bright or quick. Their hovering ability gives them a clear advantage, but if your aim is good and you are quick on the trigger, they're as good as sitting ducks.

Assault captains have a device that lets them teleport at will. When in their presence (or absence), back into a corner or against a wall so they're forced to appear within your field of vision.

Enforcers are a different beast altogether. Their rapid-fire ripper chainguns are nothing you want to step in front of for very long. Their heavy armors also make them quite hardy. Couple that with their leaping ability, and you can see why you don't want to engage enforcers in the open. Whenever you find yourself in their unpleasant company, look for objects that you can use as shields (walls, panels, crates, rocks, or anything else). Then strafe and deliver your response. The shotgun is the weapon de rigueur when it comes to enforcers.

Octabrains are very dangerous indeed. With their hovering ability and debilitating mental energy blasts, they can inflict great harm even from a distance. However, you are faster and more supple of movement. By far the quickest way to dispose of them is to use the RPG launcher or the devastator, but you can also save the exotic weapons for more critical moments. If you are good at strafing, you can take on an octabrain at mid-range with nothing more than your shotgun. Sidestep out of the way of their mental energy blasts, deliver three solid shotgun blasts, and the octabrain will collapse like a deflated hot-air balloon.

The ripper chaingun is another choice weapon for dealing with many a cantankerous octabrain. Keep the octabrain squarely in your sights, and squeeze the ripper chaingun's trigger until the beast is riddled with hot lead. A sustained ripper chaingun attack will keep the octabrain from working up its thunderous mental blasts. The freezethrower is also quite effective against octabrains. Once an octabrain becomes an ice statue, switch to the handgun and shatter the beast out of existence with a single coup de grâce.

If you are suddenly overcome by several octabrains in close quarters, then look to the shrinker to save the day. You will probably sustain some injuries, but if you were to rely on other weapons at close range, you might be damaged even worse. Use the shrinker to reduce your opponents to size and then stomp them with your mighty foot. When using the shrinker, you want to rush your opponent as you unload a charge. As though it had a mind of its own, your mighty foot knows what to do and will instinctively stomp the little devils into nasty stains on the floor.

The bosses for each episode, however, are not overcome so simply. To overcome the stronger and meaner alien beasts, you must rely on your heavier weaponry. Also, if you can help it at all, you should avoid engaging the big boys, the episode bosses, when your health falls below 80 percent. The Battlelord, for instance, is nearly unbeatable. About the best way to deal with this fierce alien predator is to maneuver him into a position where he cannot reach you, but you can still unload your arsenal on him. Make the Battlelord chase you into a smaller opening that you can get through but that he cannot. Most door thresholds are too small for the Battlelord to pass through. Get him stuck near a door threshold, and have your way with him. Of course, you will have to rely heavily on a combination of the RPG launcher, the devastator, and even the freezethrower to bring the Battlelord down once and for all.

Bringing down the Moon Assault Leader, seen only once at the conclusion of Lunar Apocalypse, will require you to be even more ingenious and resourceful. Because he is kept in check behind a sealed chamber, you will want to set him up before facing him. He is stronger and faster than the Battlelord. He also fires high-potency twin rockets from his shoulder-mounted turrets. Your fate will be much more favorable if you can ingest steroids right before the inevitable encounter because you will be dodging rockets and running away from this massive, heinous beast.

Before releasing the Moon Assault Leader from his cage, set up every laser trip bomb you have just outside the door. Your jetpack can aid you with this task. Then drop a bunch of pipe bombs before opening the door. Inflict as much punishment as you can early on, before he even has a chance to aim or fire. Then, run for your life, and try to hit him with the RPG launcher and the devastator as you run in circles around him. You can also be sneaky and activate the holoduke at the opposite end of the open chamber to fool the Moon Assault Leader. If he bites the bait, you can punish him from the back. If necessary, seek shelter behind the door and lock him out as you catch your breath and collect your thoughts.

Your best bet against the Cycloid Emperor—whom you only have to face at the conclusion of Shrapnel City inside a football stadium—is to maneuver him, much like the Battlelord, into a defenseless position. You can do this by drawing him near the bleachers. If you don't have all the weaponry you need, you will have to dash around to collect more ammo and other power-ups. Deploy the holoduke to keep him occupied as you go around collecting what you need. It also helps to boost your speed with steroids or prolong your life with the aid of the plentiful atomic health units on the field. The key is to keep him near the bleachers as much as you can, of course.

## Master the Rudiments of the Environment

The other aspect of the formula for fighting with grace involves a natural feel for the assortment of terrain you will be traversing. Every level and every episode in *Duke Nukem 3D* offers a wide variety of architectures—from the urban decay of L.A. Meltdown and the space-age constructions of Lunar Apocalypse to the ruinous surroundings of Shrapnel City. The more familiar you are with the particular trappings of the terrain, the better you can deal with the alien menace. Throughout many levels, you will run into passive explosive devices, such as fire extinguishers or C-9 canisters. When a group of aliens is unlucky enough to be standing next to such devices, shoot the canisters and then take cover from the flying alien viscera.

Oftentimes, even a simple elevator can help you overcome serious adversity. Whenever you board an elevator, you don't know what could be waiting for you at the end of the ride. If it's something unpleasant, and often it is, you want to stay in the elevator and reach for a pipe bomb. As soon as the elevator door opens, throw the pipe bomb outside and close the door immediately. As the elevator takes you back to your starting point, feel free to detonate the bomb. A variation on this technique is to open an elevator and drop a pipe bomb or two. Then activate the elevator to make it go up or down (whichever way it happens to go). When the elevator reaches its destination, detonate the pipe bombs to clear the way for you before you actually get on and ride it.

Your biggest allies, by far, are the walls, rocks, and other surfaces that surround you. There are times when you should face nasty situations head on, but the line between bravery and insanity gets ever so fine so very quickly, particularly when your ego is as big as Duke's. Just remember that there's more at stake here than your own pride. Use walls, rocks, and other surfaces as shields. Use the time to plot a path or a course of action. Sometimes retreating is not totally dishonorable. Regroup and come back with a vengeance.

## EXPLORING WITH INTELLIGENCE

Given the diversity and the types of ground you will be covering, you must make the most of every sense and take in as much information about your whereabouts as possible. Learn to identify switches, and look for areas that might be obvious and not so obvious hiding places. There are many compartments and secret doors throughout almost every level. Often, a locked gate or a force field is linked to a switch in a remote part of the installation. Begin to see and anticipate what the mechanical and electronic devices do in each level. Frequently, monitors are placed next to important switches. Look at the monitor before and after pressing a switch to find out if you were successful in removing a barrier.

When you spot visible cracks on walls, rocks, and other surfaces, it usually means that you can blow a hole through them with a pipe bomb or the RPG launcher. The devastator is also capable of punching holes through certain surfaces. You can count on finding useful items in holes or tunnels you happen to unearth when you blow up these surfaces.

Use the security monitoring systems for your cause. Prying eyes watch you at almost every step. Most levels are wired with a network of cameras and monitors. Whenever you see a monitor, it is always a good idea to walk up to it and press the spacebar. You will gain access to cameras spread throughout the level. Look for power-ups and weapons as well as for possible enemies. Try to look for signs that might identify where the particular chamber you are looking at is found. Ask yourself: Is it a big or small chamber? Are there any keycards visible? What aliens might lurk there?

Be sure to activate your overhead map when necessary. (Just press Tab once.) Switch to the textured map by pressing Tab a second time. Identify the areas where you have already been, and try to determine where you should go next. If a certain area is barred by a security latch requiring a keycard, notice what color the keycard should be. And then attempt to find it.

# USING THE LEVEL MAPS

Every level description in *Part II*, *Duking it Out*, has two maps to help guide you along the way. The first map is a textured representation of the level's layout or floor plan, showing you the main areas of interest as well as a prominent route to follow. The marked route closely follows the recommended route that is described in detail in each *Blazing through...* section. The second map is a wire frame, or line map, of the level's layout that also shows significant weapon, ammo, power-up, and keycard locations. When you put together the information from each level's set of maps, you should have a very good idea of what you must do to get where you need to go.

## THE ROUTE MAPS

The textured route maps provide you with essentially three types of information for each level: its different types of terrain, a recommended route from its starting point to its exit, and the locations of key switches that open up or unlock certain areas. As you can see in Figure 3.1, the map's textures reflect the types of terrain you will be traveling as you make your way through the level. For instance, rocky terrain, smooth

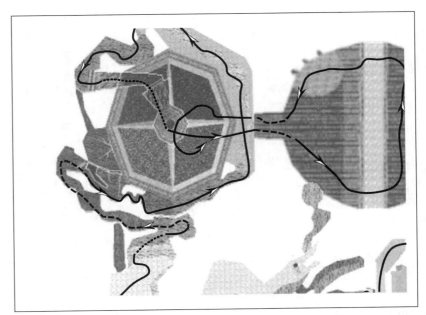

**FIGURE 3.1:** Use the textured maps to identify prominent level features and to find out the route to follow.

surfaces, air ducts, and even toxic canals and water pools can be readily made out on the textured maps.

The recommended route to follow appears as a *solid line* when you are traveling along a more or less level surface. A *dashed line* along the path indicates areas you must climb, whether it's along a slope, a stairway, or by riding an elevator or a platform. A *dotted line* along the path, by contrast, indicates areas you must descend, as when you are going downstairs or jumping from a high place to a lower area.

To make the map as easy to read as possible, significant locations and items are identified liberally with descriptive labels. In particular, the locations of the locked latches that can only be opened with the keycards are each identified by the keycard's color initial—B for blue, R for red, or Y for yellow—within a triangle. This tells you which keycard you will need to open a latch for a door or gate to gain access to areas otherwise out of reach.

## THE LINE MAPS

The second map in each level's set represents a wire frame, or line drawing, of the level's overall layout. The main purpose of this map is to point out the general locations of the more significant weapons, ammunition, and power-ups that you can get a hold of as you battle your way to the level's exit. Each item is identified with a label, as you can see in Figure 3.2. These maps also reveal the locations of the often crucial keycards that are necessary to access areas vital to your successful completion of the level.

For one level, the Tier Drop level in Shrapnel city, the map showing weapon and power-up locations is represented with a set of texture or surface maps instead of a line drawing. This level's particular configuration could not be represented meaningfully as a line map and, therefore, consists of four textured or surface maps to show the locations of collectable items.

**NOTE**
If you would like to view the PCX files that contain the map graphics, open a graphics viewer capable of displaying PCX format files and access the map files stored on the CD-ROM. The texture or surface maps are in a directory named Tx-maps; the line maps are in a directory named Lin-maps.

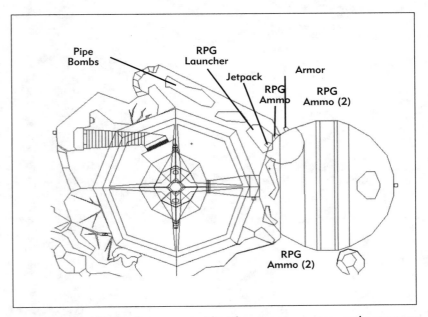

FIGURE 3.2: Use the line maps to identify weapons, ammo, and power-ups.

# PART

# II

# DUKING IT OUT

It doesn't take the prognostication of a psychic to determine that you know and appreciate a good action game, especially if that game engages your mind and dazzles your eye. Perhaps that's why you choose to play *Duke Nukem 3D*. Perhaps there are other—maybe deeper—reasons. Whatever your reasons, this part of the book lays out the information you need to venture into all three of the *Duke Nukem 3D* episodes:

- ✳ Chapter 4  L.A. Meltdown
- ✳ Chapter 5  Lunar Apocalypse
- ✳ Chapter 6  Shrapnel City

Whether you want to blaze through each level—getting from its ominous starting point to its welcomed exit—without distraction, or to take in all of the attractions that the level has to offer, this section is filled with the strategy and hints that will make each episode as exciting as it promises to be.

# L.A. Meltdown

L.A. Meltdown is the introductory episode in Duke Nukem's latest and most demanding adventure. At the conclusion of *Duke Nukem II*, our hero had beaten the Rigelatins and deflated their dreams to enslave humanity. Against all odds, Duke had managed to destroy the invaders' interstellar ship and get away in a stolen vessel. Expecting a hero's welcome, Duke is instead nearly blown out of the sky as he enters L.A. airspace.

Apparently, during the time Duke was kidnapped, another wave of malevolent aliens arrived, storming the town and terrorizing the citizenry. Once again, it's up to Duke to save the day (or at least his own skin) and maybe learn more about the aliens' questionable motives, which clearly involve scores of young human females, who are turning up all over town in strange cocoons. They are still alive, but understandably, they are not very cheery.

There are six levels in L.A. Meltdown. (One of these is a secret level, accessible only if you can find the special secret exit within one of the other levels.) With levels built in and around Los Angeles, L.A. Meltdown places you in a wide assortment of backdrops and terrain. Early on, you'll find yourself in the midst of urban and moral decay as you traverse Hollywood Holocaust and penetrate deep inside The Red Light District. Later on, just minutes away, you'll be doing time in the prison island of Death

Row. Your reward for escaping Death Row? How about a tour of the Toxic Dump's drum processing plant and its perilous canyons and underwater passages. And then there's the Launching Facility, complete with a rocket to the moon. Near the end of the episode, you'll be in the desert, hiking along tenuous mountainside trails, overlooking deep canyons, or crawling in long, dark, and moist caverns as you seek to uncover the buried secret of The Abyss.

# HOLLYWOOD HOLOCAUST

The word in the streets is that the streets aren't safe for anyone anymore. Sure, things weren't exactly peachy before the aliens' arrival. After all, this is L.A. in the mid twenty-first century. But since the aliens landed and began encasing human females in sticky cocoons and murdering anyone who stood in their way, the situation has degenerated considerably.

A wise woman once said, "Before you can walk, you must crawl." Hollywood Holocaust gives you every opportunity to crawl until you find your footing and introduces you to Duke Nukem's interactive, futuristic, and perilous 3D environment. Use this level to get acquainted with many of the architectural constructs you will find later. Also, if you can find one or both RPG launchers, the jetpack, and the pipe bombs, you'll be eternally grateful in the next level.

## MAPS AND ROUTE

In spite of being the first *Duke Nukem 3D* level, Hollywood Holocaust's design is deceivingly simple, as shown in Figure 4.1. But as you are about to experience, solving this level is anything but simple. However, if you prevail, you can collect a sizable cache of goodies to fortify yourself for The Red Light District, as you can see in Figure 4.2.

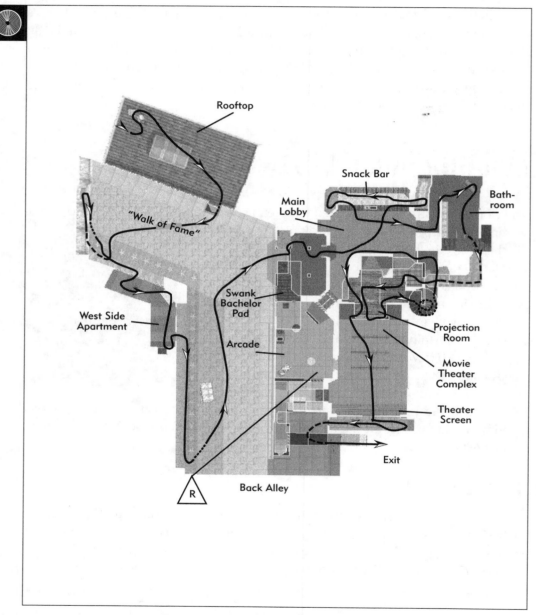

**FIGURE 4.1:** Welcome to Hollywood Holocaust with its promise of infamy and misfortune.

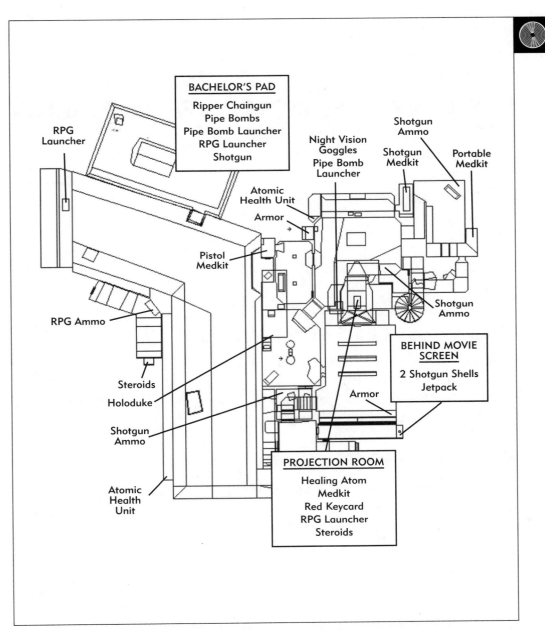

**FIGURE 4.2:** Don't be too dazzled in tinsel-town, just collect as many of these items as you can to build up your arsenal.

## THE GOODS

Table 4.1 shows a rundown of the items you might be able to collect in Hollywood Holocaust. A jetpack can help you get to a nice cache of weapons in this level.

| TABLE 4.1: THE GOODS IN HOLLYWOOD HOLOCAUST | | |
|---|---|---|
| **WEAPONS** | **AMMO** | **POWER-UPS** |
| 2 shotguns | 7 cases | 1 portable medkit |
| 1 ripper chaingun | 1 case | 3 atomic health units |
| 3 RPG launchers | 5 cases | 2 armors |
| | | 2 steroid flasks |
| | | 2 jetpacks |
| | | 1 NVG |
| | | 1 holoduke |

## BLAZING THROUGH HOLLYWOOD HOLOCAUST

Here's how you can complete this level as soon as superhumanly possible and experience a definite adrenaline rush. (Do not attempt the following if you are on any medication.) Start *Duke Nukem 3D*; select New Game, the L.A. Meltdown episode, and the Let's Rock skill level; and get ready to rumble.

### On Top of the Skyscraper

❖ **Grab some ammo and hit the street.** Take the ammo behind the crate. Shoot the C-9 canisters from a safe distance, and drop down the metal chute to reach the street level.

### On the Street

1. **Get the RPG launcher.** First, jump on top of the large crate near the northwest side. From the crate, jump onto the slanted surface of the building. From the slanted surface, jump onto the small ledge on the perpendicular wall (with the "Innocent" sign). Walk on the ledge toward the sign, and an RPG launcher emerges from a secret compartment below.

2. **Raid the secret apartment.** Jump back onto the slanted ledge, and walk over to the second window. Jump through the window, and you will be inside an apartment. Take the RPG ammo and the steroids from behind the "Biker Bimbos" poster.

3. **Take the atomic health unit.** Exit the apartment through its southern-most window, and follow the slanted ledge of the building southward toward the atomic health.

4. **Blast into the movie theater.** Jump back to the street and run north toward the street corner to get in position across from the movie the-ater's box office. Switch to your RPG launcher, and launch a rocket into the theater's box office. Then run inside through the demolished box office wall.

Watch out for trooper snipers in the apartment at the southeast end of the street. Also, the movie theater's foyer and lobby are congregating grounds for troopers and captains. Expect to see a pig cop or two there also.

## Inside the Theater

1. **Score a shotgun and another atomic health unit.** Swing the lobby's doors open and raid the snack bar. Take the shotgun from the small adjacent locker room on the east side of the snack bar. Then run out to the snack bar's west side, and take the atomic health unit from behind the secret door, which should now be open.

2. **Stop by the bathroom.** Enter the bathroom, climb over the stalls, and tear through the air duct grill. Crawl in and follow the bend 90 degrees to the right.

3. **Make your way to the projection room.** Drop into a small, dark metallic chamber and dispose of the troopers guarding their cocooned victim. Then, feel for the secret door along the west side of the room that leads to the projection room.

4. **Storm the projection room and start a movie.** Shoot your way inside and grab the red keycard. Find and push the switch to the right of the projection window to start the evening's feature attraction.

5. **Shoot the screen.** As the curtains open and the action begins, shoot another RPG into the middle of the screen. You will blow a hole big enough to crawl through and for a very good reason, as you will soon see.

6. **Score a jetpack and some shells.** Descend into the movie room via the spiral staircase, and crawl behind the screen. Take the jetpack and the shotgun shells. Then exit through the window at the west end.

7. **Get out of Hollywood Holocaust.** Activate the jetpack and levitate onto the red-glowing corridor. Get to the exit switch and punch it.

## ADDED ATTRACTIONS IN HOLLYWOOD HOLOCAUST

You haven't seen much in Hollywood Holocaust if you haven't experienced:

- Fun and games at the theater's arcade
- A swank bachelor's apartment

### Fun and Games at the Arcade

Besides the obvious reason for entering the arcade—and you can guess what that is—there is one other compelling factor: the holoduke. This likeness of yourself can be deployed to fool your opponents into thinking it's really you. Also, if you weren't able to secure the jetpack, your only way out of Hollywood Holocaust is to go through the arcade.

Inside the theater's lobby, approach the southwest corridor toward the neon "Arcade" sign. Activate the metal elevator and surprise any enemy that could be riding in it. Usually a shell in the face does the job. Climb inside and ride the elevator to the top level. Again, be ready to unload a few rounds on the awaiting pig cop (or pig cops, depending on the skill level you chose). Before venturing forth, notice the C-9 canisters in the southeast corner of the room. Hit any of them with a bullet, and take shield as best you can. Flying guts are likely to redecorate the walls.

When the commotion dies down, enter the arcade. Walk up to the *Duke Nukem II* video-game machine and press the spacebar. A secret compartment raises to show the slightly translucent holoduke (see Figure 4.3). Take it quickly because the compartment remains open but a second or two. Then march toward the security door, and use the red keycard to open it. Have your shotgun handy. You will meet a trio of pig cops in succession.

As you climb the ramp of the small metallic room, the wall behind the wooden crate blows up, and you might find yourself nose-to-snout with a most unfriendly pig cop. You might want to duck behind the crate and stand up only to shoot your weapon. With the pig cop out of the way, proceed into the narrow dark corridor. Shoot directly at the red, beady eyes shining in the far corner. It's another pig cop. If you hit the fire extinguisher behind him, you will make short work of him.

> **TIP**
> Avoid a nose-to-snout confrontation with a most unfriendly pig cop as you leave the arcade. Duck behind the crate and stand up only to unload the shotgun.

Now all you have to do is open one more latch, walk onto the metal bridge, and face off any other pig cops, assault troopers, or assault captains that are still alive. Then you can choose to check out the swank apartment next, or simply run straight for the level's exit.

**FIGURE 4.3:** Move quickly if you want to grab the holoduke before the compartment closes.

## The Swank Apartment over the Movie Theater

There is a cushy third-floor apartment above and to the right of the movie theater's marquee. While you don't have to visit this cool bachelor pad to solve this level, there are some compelling reasons to consider dropping in. For one thing, there is some impressive booty in there: one ripper chaingun, an RPG launcher, a case of ammo for it, and some pipe bombs. Besides that, you can kick back on the soft couch, enjoy a dry martini, and even take in a titillating clip on the television. You can access the apartment in one of two ways:

- With the jetpack
- Through deft footwork and precise jumping

**USING THE JETPACK** The simplest way to reach the secret apartment involves using the jetpack. This means that you must first get it if you don't already have it. (The jetpack is hidden behind the movie screen. You have to blow a hole in it to reach the other side.) Once you have it, simply get near the tall palm tree to the right of the theater and activate it. Ascend to the third story, by the marquee, and go in right through the window. Enjoy the amenities.

**USING DEFT FOOTWORK AND PRECISE JUMPING** To reach the apartment in this manner, you have no choice but to visit the arcade first. (See *Fun and Games at the Arcade* above.) If you haven't been able to get the jetpack, this is, in fact, the only way to reach the cozy cove. But you must also possess the red keycard to be able to unlock a special latch in the arcade. The red keycard is inside the projection room. After taking care of business in the arcade, and exiting via the door with the red key latch, be prepared to trade shotgun blasts with a few pig cops.

As you emerge onto the bridge leading directly to the level's exit, drop carefully onto the narrow ledge that skirts the building and ends right by the theater's marquee. Hug the wall and follow it as it turns 90 degrees to the west and then makes another 90 degree turn to the north. Stop in front of the palm tree. Then aim your sights up, and jump so that you land right on top of the tree. Turn to face the building, and jump straight through the window. (Figure 4.4 shows you these locations.) Once inside, relax for a few seconds, check out the goods, and don't forget to collect the weapons.

FIGURE 4.4: This is the way to the swank apartment.

## COVERT DETAILS

Table 4.2 lists a complete rundown of the secrets in Hollywood Holocaust.

| TABLE 4.2: THE SECRETS IN HOLLYWOOD HOLOCAUST | | |
|---|---|---|
| **AREA IN LEVEL** | **SECRET ITEM** | **HOW TO GET IT** |
| The Walk of Fame | RPG launcher | A secret compartment below the "Innocent" graffiti emerges as you approach it. |
| | steroids | These are behind the poster in the second-story, west side apartment. |
| | shotgun ripper chaingun RPG launcher pipe bombs | A swank bachelor's apartment above and to the right of the theater's marquee is where you will find this weapons bonanza. |
| The movie theater | pipe bombs | These are in a secret compartment above the trash can by the elevator to the arcade. |

*(Continued on next page)*

*(Continued from previous page)*

| AREA IN LEVEL | SECRET ITEM | HOW TO GET IT |
|---|---|---|
| | armor | This item is in a hidden elevated chamber on the west side of the main lobby. Open the chamber by activating the cash register behind the snack bar. Then stand on a receding (unseen) pillar below and slightly to the right of the chamber and press the spacebar to activate it. |
| | RPG launcher | Behind a secret wall on the west side of the projection room is where you will find it. This wall raises when you jump on top of the projector to grab an atomic health unit. |
| | a secret wall that opens | The secret wall is at the southwest corner of the projection room. The adjoining room is a dark metallic chamber with a female in a cocoon. The chamber is also accessible through an air duct on the east side that connects it to the theater's bathroom. |
| | jetpack shotgun shells | These are behind the movie screen. |

# THE RED LIGHT DISTRICT

As with all major cities in the world, L.A., too, has its seedy side. And you are about to witness it in some graphic detail. Complete with an adult bookstore and peep-shows, The Red Light District offers many attractions for the seeker of fleshly delights. But beware of everyone you meet, for many pack a trick or two up their skirt. (By the way, you might want to get some cash before entering the district. Tipping is heavily encouraged.) This level introduces a new addition to your enemies' arsenal, the recon patrol vehicle (RPV).

With its many side attractions and surplus of temptations, it would be easy to lose one's head in The Red Light District. Definitely more physically demanding than Hollywood Holocaust, this level will surely test your stamina. Your chances to make it through The Red Light District are high as long as you move swiftly in the open spaces and very carefully when there isn't as much leg room. To solve this level, you must acquire all the keycards in a specific order: blue, yellow, and red. To get the yellow keycard, you must first demolish the condemned building on which it sits. A final word or two—if you don't have a jetpack when you reach the area behind the curtain in the gentleman's club, you will have to draw open the curtains and endure a good ol' fashion barroom brawl.

## MAPS AND ROUTE

The Red Light District offers many distractions indeed. But don't get too distracted because your enemies will die trying to prevent you from getting to the floor show. On the route map shown in Figure 4.5, notice the locations of the special latches that require the blue, yellow, and red keycards to unlock them. The keycards' locations are shown on the map in Figure 4.6. The blue keycard gives you access to a detonation switch, and the yellow and red keycards provide you access to the bar and floor show areas.

## THE GOODS

Table 4.3 shows a rundown of the items you might score in The Red Light District.

### TABLE 4.3: THE GOODS IN THE RED LIGHT DISTRICT

| WEAPONS | AMMO | POWER-UPS |
|---|---|---|
| 2 shotguns | 3 cases | 1 portable medkit |
| 2 ripper chainguns | 1 case | 4 atomic health units |
| 1 RPG launcher | 5 cases | 2 armors |
| 3 pipe bombs | | 1 steroid flask<br>1 jetpack<br>3 NVGs<br>2 holodukes |

## BLAZING THROUGH THE RED LIGHT DISTRICT

Ready for some fast action? You've come to right place. Can you handle the hard and fast lane ahead? Do your best to keep up. Of course, nothing prevents you from exercising your freedom of choice. Feel free to wander, explore, and take a few risks.

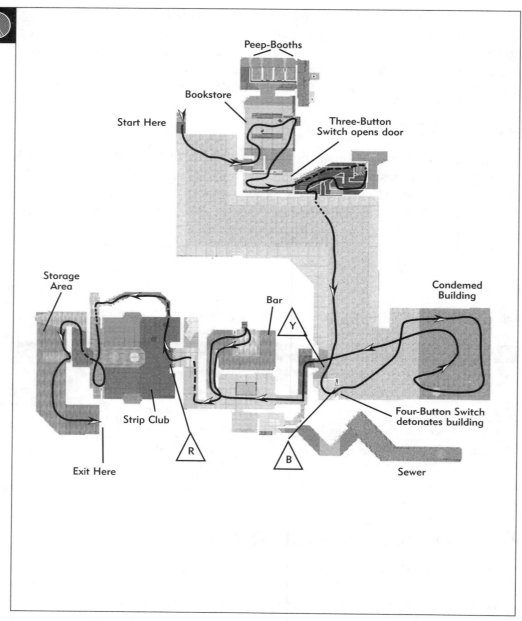

**FIGURE 4.5:** What will be your pleasure (or demise) in The Red Light District?

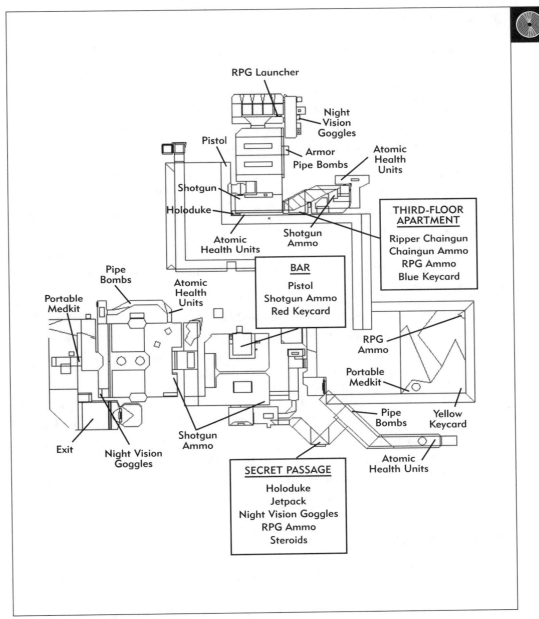

**FIGURE 4.6:** It's places like these your mom warned you about, but there's lots of weapons and power-ups to gather.

## In the Bookstore

1.  **Head for the bookstore.** The second you come out of the elevator, run straight for the bookstore's entrance to your left. Do not waste time engaging the pig cop on the hovering recon patrol vehicle (RPV). It's almost always a loosing battle. Also, beware that standing on the other side of the steel door is another pig cop. Pour lead into his countenance the second you see the red of his eyes.

2.  **Search for good material.** After looking over the good material, open the secret door behind the magazine rack, and take the armor and pipe bombs. Also raid the area behind the counter for a shotgun (by the monitor) and the atomic health on top of the magazine racks. While you're reaching for the atomic health, push against the corner where the magazine racks converge and uncover the holoduke behind the secret compartment.

3.  **Access the upstairs alcove.** Activate the two outside switches on the east wall to unlock the red door, and proceed into the dark, sloping corridor. Guarding off the troopers creeping in the dark, run to the elevator at the end of the hall, and ride it to the alcove upstairs.

4.  **Get more goods and go.** Take the RPG ammo on top of the mattress and look behind the small compartment in the wall for the blue keycard. Chop down the troopers in the adjacent room, and take the ripper chaingun rounds. From the window in this room, take pot shots at the RPVs and the troopers outside and across the street. When you've softened them up a bit, jump out the window and onto the wide avenue below.

## On the Main Avenue

1.  **Access the 3D Realms Demolition quarters.** Run toward the south end and enter the small partition along the building labeled "3D Realms Demolition." Shoot your way in, right through the awaiting pig cop.

2.  **Uncover the combination switches.** Activate the blue keycard reader to reveal two circular switches on each of its sides.

3. **Use the right combination.** Activate the two inside switches to uncover a detonator switch. Push it and watch the condemned building across the street crumble to the ground.

4. **Collect the yellow keycard, ammo, and a portable medkit.** Run out into the rubble and collect more RPG ammo, the yellow keycard, and a portable medkit.

5. **Enter 3D Realms Demolition's headquarters.** Use your newly acquired yellow keycard to open the latch that unlocks the metal door to 3D Realms Demolition's headquarters.

## Inside the 3D Realms Demolition Building

1. **Check out the bar.** Go up the ramp, past the pool table, and take a right into the bar.

2. **Duck for the red keycard.** Open the secret door behind the bar, and crawl inside to grab the red keycard.

3. **Head for the floor show and into the duct.** With the red keycard in hand, enter the floor show area. Find the air duct near the northeast corner, blow it open, and jump inside by climbing a nearby table (see Figure 4.7). Drop into the narrow corridor below to reach the area behind a large red curtain.

4. **Elevate to freedom?** Activate the jetpack to reach the platform above. Go around to the south into a warehouse-like space with an angular ceiling and a few wooden crates. Battle a few obstinate pig cops around the crates. Then run around the bend to locate the exit switch. Now get ready to do a little bit of time as you await your turn on death row.

> **TIP**
> The bookstore is another known hangout for alien troopers, pig cops, and captains. Use doors and video shelves for protection. Often, you can surprise your opponents by jumping on top of the shelves and shooting down at them.

> **TIP**
> Don't be too hasty to run over to the rubble in search of the yellow keycard. It could be your undoing. Wait until the explosive charges go off completely before rushing out.

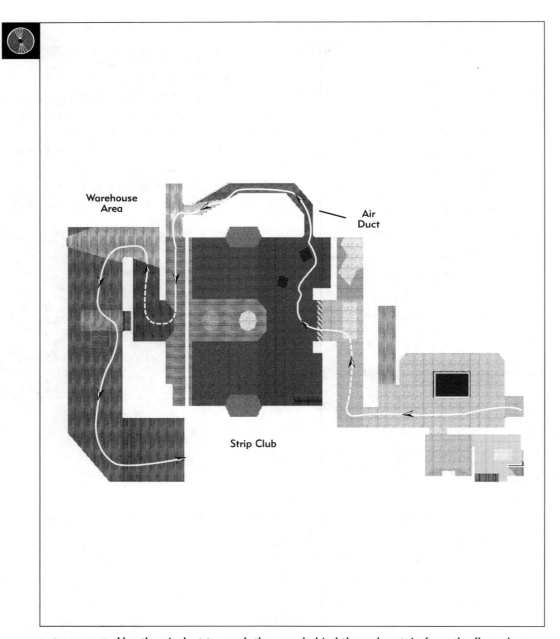

**FIGURE 4.7:** Use the air duct to reach the area behind the red curtain from the floor show.

## ADDED ATTRACTIONS IN THE RED LIGHT DISTRICT

For all the cheap thrills one might experience in The Red Light District, it goes without saying that there's a heavy price to pay. This section highlights some of the tough encounters you might have. It also describes areas you might want to visit if you just can't get enough. Get ready to:

- ✥ Take in a peep show or two.
- ✥ Square off in the bar and take the red keycard.
- ✥ Cause a serious commotion in the floor show.

**DISC DEMO**
Check out The Red Light District demo on the CD-ROM. You can find it in the folder labeled "Blaze" in a file named E1L2.BLZ. At this point you will find yourself crawling through this duct and about to run into some nasty pig cops at the other end—better not be low on ammo!

### Catching a Sneak Peek at the Peep Show

If you never as much as walked into an adult bookstore before because you felt self-conscious or embarrassed, don't worry. Besides stocking a wide variety of magazines and videos, the bookstore also has a discreet row of peep stalls in the back, where you might enjoy a few private screenings. Not only that, but you will be able to lay your hands on a choice piece of hardware, a loaded RPG launcher.

After taking the armor and pipe bombs behind the secret magazine rack, head toward the north end of the bookstore. Turn quickly to the right side as you cross the threshold and dispense with the awaiting pig cop. Then turn your attention to the west side of the hallway. As you come around the corner, pounce on the pig cop. Turning eastward now, clear the way of assault troopers and captains lingering about. Then run to the end of the hallway, and open the door to the stall at the very end. Open the small screen and grab the RPG. If you are not easily offended by erotic sights, visit the other stalls. But beware of the occupants inside. Pig cops are known to like movies too. The best technique for emptying the stalls is to open the door, stand aside, and catch the enemy as he pokes his head out to look.

## Squaring Off at the Bar

The second you enter the bar inside the 3D Realms Demolition building, it might seem like everyone knows your name and wants you dead. Yet, you have no choice but to go in search of the red keycard. When you reach the top of the ramp, avoid stepping inside the bar right away. Instead, stand just outside, pepper the aliens with your shotgun, and then take refuge behind the wall.

After thinning out the gnarly bar crowd, throw a pipe bomb down the ramp and then rush in behind the counter. As you enter this area, you will cross a trigger that causes a few pigcops to materialize. In a few seconds, the gang of bad pig cops, hot after your trail, will make its way up the ramp. Crouch under the bottle rack and open the secret compartment. Crawl inside to grab the keycard. In the process, push the thumb-activated detonator. That should take care of at least one pig cop and damage the rest. Switch to the shotgun and hold your ground inside the little crawl space (see Figure 4.8). From this cubbyhole, shower with bullets anything that moves outside.

> **TIP**
> If you need a respite to gather your wits, you can close the small door to the tiny compartment. Just press the spacebar again.

Once the noise dies down, crawl out and be sure to check out the TV monitor. Remember the now infamous slow-speed chase of a particular white bronco?

## A Final Show Down in the Bloody Floor Show

The floor show in The Red Light District is nothing short of extraordinary. The instant you step in through the heavy metal door, you will see three separate stages appear. The main stage emerges from the floor and dominates the center of the room. Two side stages descend from the ceiling. As with many other danger areas, it's always best to proceed cautiously. Rather than running in and risking an ambush, open the door and pick off as many troopers and pig cops as you can from the outside.

**FIGURE 4.8:** Crawl into the small compartment below the bar for protection and to grab the red keycard.

Once it's safer to venture in, find the air duct in the northeast corner of the room, blow it open, and jump inside. Follow the duct to the end. You will run into another grill. Tear through it, and then drop a pipe bomb into the narrow space below and detonate it. Repeat the procedure if necessary. You want to blow up the vicious pig cops in the confined space before you jump down from the duct. When you do jump down, switch to the RPG launcher and aim up at the pig cop on top of the large platform. If you have the jetpack, you'll be able to avoid a nasty scene. Simply activate it, reach the top of the platform, and proceed around the corner into a darkened warehouse. After a final turn, you'll be facing what appears to be the exit switch.

> **TIP**
>
> Anytime you can confront your opponents indirectly, such as from behind walls or to one side of an entrance to a room, you stand a better chance of dodging enemy fire. Strafing across, you can also unload your own offensive.

**WARNING**

Be warned against getting too physical with the dancers. Tipping is encouraged and accepted, but if you dare to shoot a dancer—accidentally or not—you will pay dire consequences. Every time a dancer dies, a captain and a trooper materialize on the scene.

However, if you don't have the jetpack, you'll have to draw the curtains open. The only problem with that is that the floor show area will be repopulated with scores of pig cops. With that in mind, approach the switch at the south end of the corridor and activate it. As the curtains begin to draw open, engage the RPG launcher and slaughter as many pig cops as you can. You can also run to the north side of the corridor (it's best to avoid the main floor, for as long as you can) and throw pipe bombs into the moshing pig cops.

Eventually, climb the main stage, face the west side, and take a flying jump onto the elevated platform. Then simply follow the path to the exit. But don't be terribly disappointed when you find yourself captive at the end of this level.

## COVERT DETAILS

The secrets of The Red Light District are exposed for all to see in Table 4.4.

### TABLE 4.4: THE SECRETS IN THE RED LIGHT DISTRICT

| AREA IN LEVEL | SECRET ITEM | HOW TO GET IT |
| --- | --- | --- |
| The bookstore | holoduke | This item can be found in the secret compartment behind the counter and above the magazine racks, at the southwest corner. |
| | armor and pipe bombs | These items are behind the middle bookshelf on the east side. |
| The demolished building | atomic health | This healthy find is in the sewer, underneath the manhole cover. |
| The strip bar | ripper chaingun | This handy weapon is behind the north side stage. |
| | pipe bombs | You will find these in the air duct at the northeast corner. |
| | NVG | These are on top of a metallic box at the southwest end of the main floor and behind the massive curtain. |
| The crate area | portable medkit | This item is behind the secret compartment along the east wall, right by the wooden crates. |

# DEATH ROW

You open your eyes in Death Row only to be momentarily blinded by a sudden and painful electrical jolt. Collecting your wits and taking stock of your surroundings, you notice you're the center piece in an execution room. The rigid chair you're on is anything but inviting. (The last thing you recall is when the aliens took you prisoner at the conclusion of your Red Light District tour of duty.) Before enduring another blast, you jump off the chair and realize you are completely unarmed. It appears as though your seconds in Death Row are numbered. Indeed, you are trapped in a correctional facility where good behavior means absolutely nothing.

The only way out of Death Row is via an aquatic escape. You must endure a rough ride to the area known as Cell Block 2. There is said to be a tunnel there that might lead either to an awaiting submarine or a horrific death in the clutches of fierce octabrains and their alien allies. Your path through Death Row will send you on a search for all three keycards (in the order blue, yellow, and red). If you can survive the first few seconds in Death Row, you might yet have a fighting chance.

## MAPS AND ROUTE

Look over Figures 4.9 and 4.10 to help you plot your imminent jailbreak. You're at liberty to choose your own path, but the recommended route leads straight to a chance for freedom.

## THE GOODS

Don't waste your time while doing time. You can actually amass a good deal of loot, even while you are behind bars. Check out Table 4.5 for a complete list.

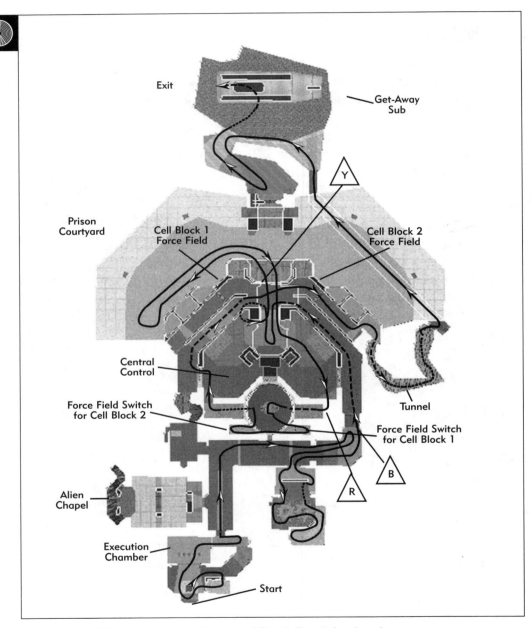

Exit

Get-Away
Sub

Prison
Courtyard

Cell Block 1
Force Field

Cell Block 2
Force Field

Y

Central
Control

Force Field Switch
for Cell Block 2

Force Field Switch
for Cell Block 1

Tunnel

B

Alien
Chapel

R

Execution
Chamber

Start

**FIGURE 4.9:** They say that breaking out of Death Row is hard to do.

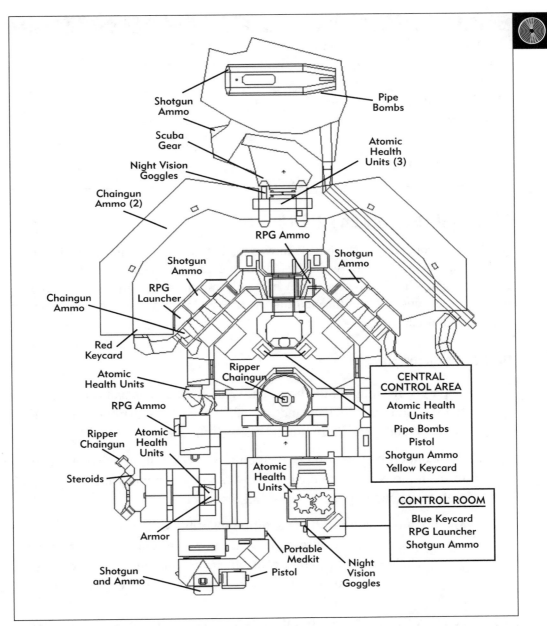

Shotgun Ammo

Pipe Bombs

Scuba Gear

Atomic Health Units (3)

Night Vision Goggles

Chaingun Ammo (2)

RPG Ammo

Shotgun Ammo

Shotgun Ammo

RPG Launcher

Chaingun Ammo

Red Keycard

Ripper Chaingun

**CENTRAL CONTROL AREA**

Atomic Health Units

Atomic Health Units

Pipe Bombs

RPG Ammo

Pistol

Ripper Chaingun

Atomic Health Units

Shotgun Ammo

Yellow Keycard

Steroids

Atomic Health Units

**CONTROL ROOM**

Blue Keycard

RPG Launcher

Shotgun Ammo

Armor

Portable Medkit

Shotgun and Ammo

Pistol

Night Vision Goggles

**FIGURE 4.10:** Because you must start this level with nothing in your arsenal, better look for the first weapon you can find.

| TABLE 4.5: THE GOODS IN DEATH ROW | | |
|---|---|---|
| **WEAPONS** | **AMMO** | **POWER-UPS** |
| 1 shotgun | 1 case | 2 portable medkits |
| 2 ripper chainguns | 4 cases | 7 atomic health units |
| 2 RPG launchers | 2 cases | 2 armors |
| 3 pipe bombs | 1 case | 2 steroid flasks |
| | | 1 scuba gear |
| | | 2 NVGs |
| | | 1 holoduke |
| | | 1 pair of boots |

# BLAZING THROUGH DEATH ROW

All claustrophobia aside, Duke Nukem was made to roam with unbridled abandon. Dark, squalid corridors and walls, steel bars, a completely restrictive life style, and Duke simply don't mix. However, you can greatly minimize your time in the big house. Follow these steps to blaze through the Death Row level. As always, you're free to roam, but don't get caught.

## In the Execution Area

1. **Get a pistol.** Jump off the hot chair. Walk around the small control room to the east, open the door, and rush for the small compartment to get a handgun and a clip. Turn around and pelt the pig cop.

2. **Get a shotgun.** Throw the switch on the left side of the window. Jump through the window as the chair lowers to the ground. Duck inside and grab the shotgun and ammo behind the chair.

3. **Make your way out of the execution chambers.** After taking the shotgun, get back in the control room and throw the switch on the right side of the window. Then position yourself so you can aim at the awaiting (and naturally disappointed) crowd as the curtains draw open. When everyone is dead or dying, jump over the half wall and find a narrow hallway. Run to the end of the hallway, and grab the medkit at the end.

## Inside the Room with Killer Cogs

1. **Grab the atomic health and night vision goggles.** Enter the gap left by the exploding wall. Approach the smaller rotating cog. Jump, aiming for its center. Then synchronize your turning rate so you can time a second jump and reach the narrow ledge along the west wall. Take the atomic health. Crawl south along the ledge, and open a secret compartment at the very corner to bag the NVG.

> ### TIP
> You start out this level completely unarmed. And what else would you expect? You're in the big house, after all. But even worse, you start out sitting on the electric chair. If your health is failing from the beating you may have taken in The Red Light District, you might not be able to withstand more than a single charge at the chair. So get off the hot chair as quickly as you can, and not an instant too soon.

2. **Collect the blue keycard and an RPG.** Jump directly onto the larger cog. Then execute a second jump onto the southeast corner. Landing on a control area, grab the RPG and the blue keycard behind the wall compartment.

3. **Get out of the cog room.** Execute a series of well-timed jumps, first onto the large cog and then onto the smaller one. Finally, at the right moment, jump back into the room's entrance and exit.

## In the Central Room and Jailhouse Courtyard

1. **Take the yellow keycard.** Enter the small circular room on the north side of the central control room. As you reach for the keycard, the side mounted light panels slide open to reveal trip bombs. Duck under the light beams and leave the room.

2. **Go after the red keycard.** Enter the large control room, and head for the yellow latch at the north end. Unlock the gates to the jailhouse courtyard and turn westward. You will find the red keycard at the southwest corner. Unfortunately, you will be under fire from roving pig cops in their

RPVs. And if that isn't enough, you're a wide open target to the turrets strategically mounted along the north end of the courtyard.

3. **Unlock Cell Block 2.** Back in the main control room, climb the ramp and unlock the red latch on the southwest corner. Push a second switch and gain access to the hologram room. Grab the ripper chain-gun on the central platform. Then push either of the switches on the circular rotating walls of the room. When the room stops, enter the small opening along the southwest side. Ascend a small ramp and enter the small room containing the switch that deactivates the force field to Cell Block 2.

**DISC DEMO**

Because a picture sometimes isn't enough, look at the demo on the CD-ROM for the Death Row level in E1L4.BLZ. You can see why the steps in this sequence require you to perform nearly flawlessly.

## At the Northeast End

1. **Find the tunnel in Cell Block 2.** Take the Control West exit, ascend the ramp, and find the entrance to Cell Block 2 (northeast of the room that once held the yellow keycard). Standing at the entrance to Cell Block 2, push the switch panel until the last cell opens. Rush to the cell and look behind the poster in the corner. Be careful not to fall in; you've just found the secret tunnel.

2. **Reach the sewage line.** It turns out the tunnel is only partially excavated. You will have to drop a couple of pipe bombs to finish the job. Eventually, you will reach a toxic sewage line. Follow it northwest to an open area where you will see a submarine.

3. **Board the sub.** You will have to dive and board it from below, so score the scuba gear before diving. It's around the south stone wall of the open area. After entering the sub, throw the periscope switch and then activate the exit switch.

# ADDED ATTRACTIONS IN DEATH ROW

They say time in the slammer hardens a person. Perhaps. You decide for yourself after experiencing:

- A moment of reflection in the prison chapel
- A bruising battle in the courtyard

## Praying Is for the Weak

Even if *pious* or *spiritual* are not words anyone would use to describe you, you might consider stopping to reflect for a minute in the jailhouse's chapel. You might not become blessed or sanctified, but you are sure to uncover some unholy secrets. If you're not totally overcome with religious fervor, you could well leave the chapel with a ripper chaingun, a few pipe bombs, and an atomic health unit.

Don't let the SILENCE, DISCIPLINE, REMORSE sign at the entrance keep you from entering. Catch the kneeling troopers and captains from behind while they are facing the altar. It helps to have an RPG launcher to better your chances, but even with a shotgun, you should be able to dispose of the few faithful in there. Approach the main altar and look above you at the tall, pointed ceiling. Shoot the hanging monk and absorb the atomic health that comes out of his body as he hits the floor.

Standing at the floor of the altar, press against the podium to activate a secret door behind the stained glass. Walk to the southernmost window, and kick it in. Go into the narrow passage, and do your very best to plant three solid shotgun blasts at the floating octabrain. Then proceed to the end of the red-lit corridor where you will find a ghastly sight—nothing less than the mangled torso of a former *DOOM* marine. Put the poor soul out of his misery, and collect the ripper chaingun behind him. Do it quickly because anything you touch here is harmful. Get back to the altar, bust the window on the right side, and grab the steroids.

The next maneuver requires impeccable timing and execution. Your goal is to reach a confined space above the chapel's entry. Notice the switch high above the altar. Stand near the middle of the room, maybe even behind the pew. Aim for the switch, and shoot it with your pistol. Then turn immediately around (or run backwards if you prefer) to stand on the narrow ascending pillar. Once at the top, crouch to reach the case of pipe bombs. Jump down and be on your way. Figure 4.11 shows the chapel's layout and your route in more detail.

## Showdown at the Courtyard

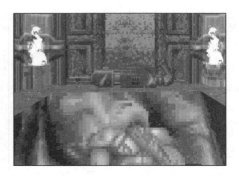

A visit to the north courtyard is inevitable. There lies the red keycard that you need to unlock Cell Block 2. However, because it is so close to the only way out, the courtyard is heavily guarded. Several pig cops patrol the area in their RPVs. A network of turrets atop an elevated area flanks the north side of the courtyard. You are also the prime target of troopers and captains inhabiting the cell blocks that look over the courtyard along its south wall. Beside the fact that you must have the red keycard, there are other good reasons to storm the courtyard. You could build a surplus of health if you can manage to reach the secret area housing four atomic health units.

When you first open the door to the courtyard, avoid rushing out. You would only serve as a target to a mob of murderers. You will have to take the courtyard in stages. First nail the pig cops by the door. Then, adjust your aim to about 45 degrees and face the west side as you sidestep to launch a grenade at the first visible firing turret. Slide back near the door and go back inside if necessary. (Do your best to avoid engaging the RPVs.) Adjust your aim and repeat the process, sliding out of the door to hit the next turret. Turn your attention to the turrets along the east side and start again.

Without the constant threat of the turrets, you will be better able to deal with the RPVs. A useful technique against an RPV in the courtyard is to simply run away from it. Then, make a sudden 180 degree turn and fire off an RPG projectile.

If you can't wipe out every RPV, don't sweat it too much. Climb the elevated north side area. Do it by first jumping onto the slanted surface beside the closed north gate. Then take another short jump onto the elevated area. Again, climb the slanted surface of the central structure in the elevated area, and you will run into a secret area. Go right through the wall to find a long corridor with a line of atomic health units and take them. Get back near the entrance to the corridor, and bombard the cell occupants with the RPG, a handgun, or

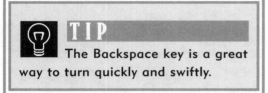
**TIP**
The Backspace key is a great way to turn quickly and swiftly.

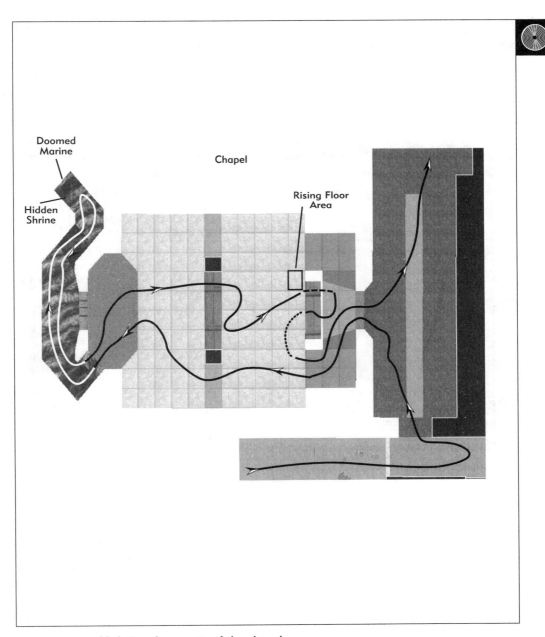

Doomed Marine

Hidden Shrine

Chapel

Rising Floor Area

**FIGURE 4.11:** Violating the secrets of the chapel.

the shotgun from your relatively safe position. Get back on the elevated surface, and run its length to either side, collecting additional ammo and weaponry.

## COVERT DETAILS

Check out Table 4.6 for a list of the stuff you might otherwise miss on Death Row.

**TABLE 4.6: THE SECRETS IN DEATH ROW**

| AREA IN LEVEL | SECRET ITEM | HOW TO GET IT |
| --- | --- | --- |
| Execution chamber | shotgun | This item is in the secret area behind and below the electric chair. The switch on the left side of the window lowers the electric chair's platform. |
| Prison chapel | ripper chaingun | This baby is in the secret shrine behind the altar. The shrine is accessible through the stained glass window to the left of the main altar. |
| | pipe bombs ripper chaingun | You'll find these in the loft area on the east side. To access this area, you must first flip a switch above the altar, so a pillar rises out of the floor near the loft. Then run and jump on top of the pillar to reach the loft. |
| The small holding cell | RPG ammo | It's in the secret tunnel behind the cot. |
| The central control area | atomic health unit pipe bombs | These are in the small chambers to the right and left (respectively) of the central totem-like structure. |
| The cell blocks | secret tunnel | This is behind the pin-up poster in the easternmost cell. |
| | exploding wall | This is at the westernmost wall of Cell Block 1, which connects to the prison courtyard. |
| The prison courtyard | multiple atomic health units | These are found inside the central structure, above the north side gate. |

# TOXIC DUMP

The small cargo submarine you hoped would carry you out of Death Row and into freedom took a nose dive. Needless to say, it was booby-trapped. It now resembles a giant cigarette butt sticking straight up from a sand ashtray. This is a fitting entrance to the Toxic Dump, an austere rock, concrete, and metal installation for the disposal of dangerous chemicals and radioactive substances. The Toxic Dump dominates over a large expanse of territory with interconnected bodies of water and small canyons.

Structures like the multi-level treatment plant, at the north end, foreshadow the increasing sophistication of later levels.

There are basically two ways to clean up the Toxic Dump. One is significantly more efficient, circumventing the treatment plant and the sewage lines. But it requires you to have a jetpack. If you don't have one, slip on those protective boots. You will be knee-deep in toxic sludge sooner or later. The key to surviving in a dump like the Toxic Dump is to boost your immune system. Cherish and seek atomic health. They are bountiful in this level. And one last thing: In this level you have to literally become small to reach key switches and passages. How do you get small? You simply stand in front of the flashing lens and look at the birdie. Get the red keycard and then learn to crawl.

## MAPS AND ROUTE

Try not to be overwhelmed when you look at Figures 4.12 and 4.13. The Toxic Dump is a sprawling structure of varied and complex architecture.

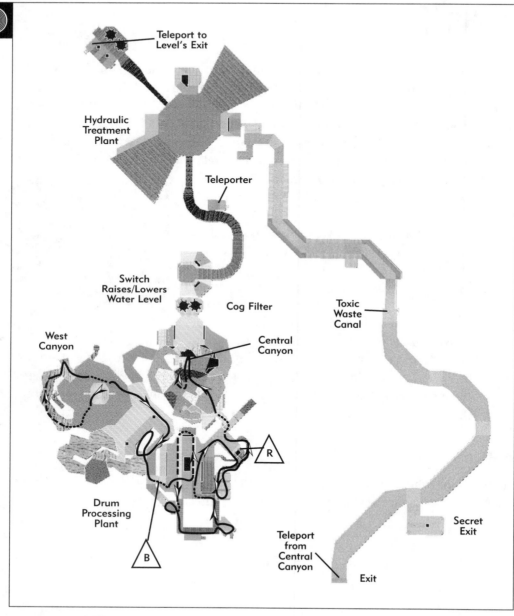

**FIGURE 4.12:** The general surgeon wants you to know that entering the Toxic Dump is hazardous to your health. Proceed at your own risk.

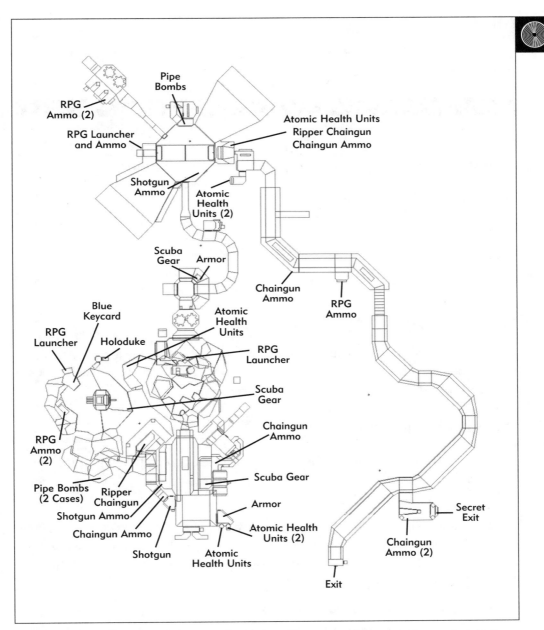

**FIGURE 4.13:** You best don your protective boots, for you are about to make a splash in the Toxic Dump.

## THE GOODS

Toxic materials, notwithstanding, not everything stinks in the Toxic Dump. Check out the goods you can collect and covet on this level in Table 4.7.

| TABLE 4.7: THE GOODS IN THE TOXIC DUMP | | |
|---|---|---|
| **WEAPONS** | **AMMO** | **POWER-UPS** |
| 2 shotguns | 2 cases | 4 portable medkits |
| 2 ripper chainguns | 1 case | 9 atomic health units |
| 3 RPG launchers | 1 case | 3 armors |
| 2 pipe bombs | 3 cases | 1 steroid flask |
| | | 4 scuba gear sets<br>2 jetpacks<br>1 NVG<br>1 holoduke<br>1 pair of boots |

## BLAZING THROUGH THE TOXIC DUMP

Do you want to avoid heartache? Are most of your limbs valuable to you? Any third-rate genius will agree that your chances of survival in the Toxic Dump will rocket if you can cut your stay there in half.

### In the Southwest Canyon

1. **Get out of the sub.** Submerge in the water-logged sub and find the vertical row of switches. Activate the top and bottom ones. Then turn around and go out of the sliding doors.

2. **Snatch an RPG and the blue keycard.** Emerge to the surface level along the rocky shore on the southwest side. Run up the rocky incline and take possession of the RPG launcher. Then grab the blue keycard and dive into the water hole, heading for the far shore.

3. **Wrestle a ripper chaingun.** Enter the Toxic Dump through the red door. A step or two after the first turn, push the wall on the right side to access a secret passage. Push a dark metallic wall to enter the narrow room that overlooks the canyon from the southeast corner. The ripper chaingun is in there, but so are a few troopers who are packed like sardines.

## In the Drum Processing Plant

1. **Take the red keycard.** Make your way to the small platform at the end of the conveyor belt near the southeast corner. Let the mechanical crane pick you up and drop you at the opposite end. Climb a second platform, and let another crane take you back to the south end. As soon as you are dropped, look for a glass door on the right side and bust in. The red keycard is inside the small compartment on the south wall, next to the computer panel. (See Figure 4.14.)

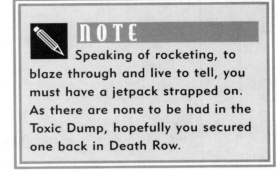

> **NOTE**
> Speaking of rocketing, to blaze through and live to tell, you must have a jetpack strapped on. As there are none to be had in the Toxic Dump, hopefully you secured one back in Death Row.

2. **Get small and open the way to the north section.** Use the red keycard on the panel at the northeastern room. Wait for the shrinkage device to blast you. Then run under the small opening on the right side. Make a right and a hard left into a metallic room equipped with its own shrinkage device. Activate the switch on the far side of the room. (It unlocks the red latch in the previous room, thus granting you access to the rest of the level.) Take another shrinkage dose, and leave the same way you crawled in.

## In the Central Canyon

1. **Reach the central canyon.** Leave the drum processing plant through the red gate, heading northeast. Go underwater and veer to your left to reach a submerged control room in ruins.

2. **Get high and head straight.** Swim out of the room toward the northwest. Activate the jetpack and soar slightly below the tallest hanging rock formations. Look for a slight indentation on the northeast rock wall, midway between the large cavernous entrances on both sides.

3. **Beam to the end.** If you found the spot, you are inside a small teleporter cabin. To activate it, turn off your jetpack. Then walk away from the beam booth and re-enter. You will find yourself a few paces from the exit switch, at the very end of the perilous sewage tunnels.

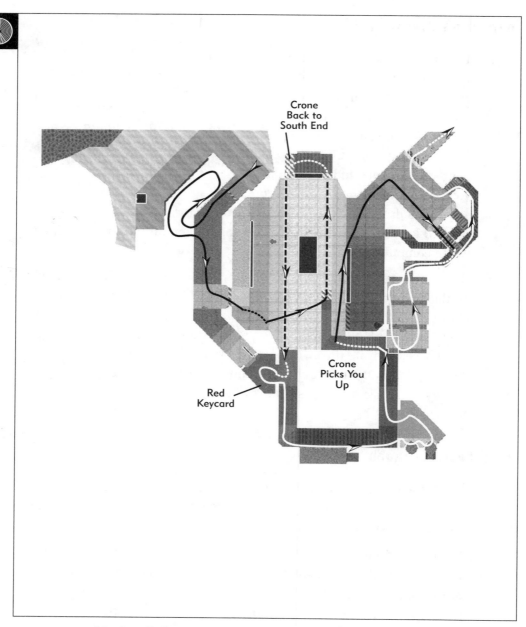

FIGURE 4.14: You literally have to crawl to solve the riddle of the drum processing plant.

## ADDED ATTRACTIONS IN THE TOXIC DUMP

There are plenty of reasons why you would want to check out the added attractions the Toxic Dump has to offer. But, most likely, you don't have a jetpack, so blazing out is not an option. Or perhaps your craving for adventure leads you to want to know what it's like to be:

- Northbound and determined
- Mistreated at the treatment plant

### Head North, Young Duke

Without the jetpack, your exposure to the Toxic Dump might be much longer than is healthy for anyone. You have no choice but to head north. But as you emerge into the sunken office in the central canyon, you notice the heavy metal door labeled "Gate 2." It bars you from reaching the treatment plant and any chance of escaping. Opening gate 2 requires a series of orchestrated maneuvers and techniques. With a bevy of octabrains swimming and hovering around the canyon, it's nothing short of risky.

Press the switch at the corner of the window to raise the canyon's water level. Stand your ground in the sunken office for a few seconds, and meet the circling octabrains with the rapid fire from your ripper chaingun. Use the floating mines as targets when an octabrain is near one.

Swim out of the sunken office, hugging the wall on your right side. Surface by the rocky shore near the northeast part of the canyon, and climb the sloping rocks around the curve. Make short work of floating octabrains with well-guided rocket propelled rounds. When the action lessens somewhat, take a running start from the bottom of the rock outcropping on the left side, and jump across to the nearly level ground on the northwest side. Follow the curving, sloping terrain to reach a small control room tucked away in a fold of the rock at the very top. Spray the troopers with a generous dousing of lead. Then step in, grab an RPG launcher, and, most importantly, press the switch by the monitor. In fact, look at the monitor after throwing the switch. Gate 2 will yield. Run back to the water and dive down. Pass right through the gate. Figure 4.15 summarizes the route graphically.

You'll emerge in a yet another confined underwater area. Reach yet another sunken office and throw the switch found in there. The next heavy gate will clear the way to the north. However, upon reaching the gate, you might be initially discouraged by the

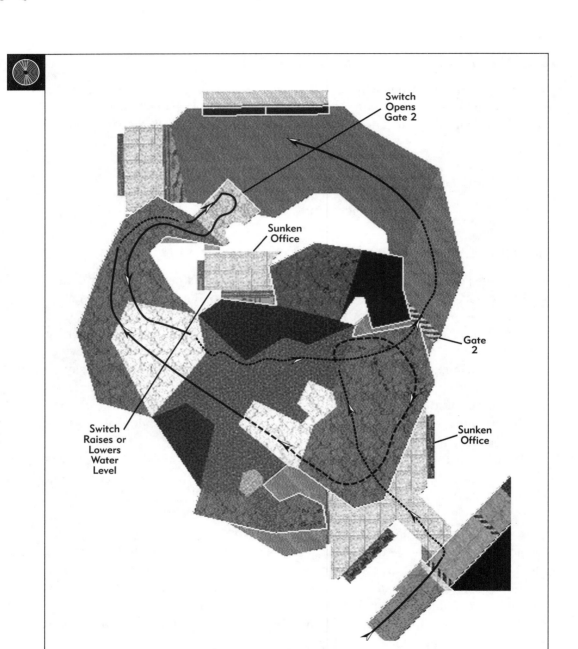

**FIGURE 4.15:** You need to reach the switch to unlock gate 2.

sight of two massive cogs, churning and spinning steadily. To clear this next obstacle, you must time your movement forward with a section of the cogs that appears metallic gray. Wait for the cogs to turn a few times. When you think you have the timing down, venture forth slowly but with determination. If you fall in right in time, the cogs will simply deposit you into the next underwater chamber. Say hello and good-bye to a couple of octabrains. And get ready for a showdown with aliens who have deplorable manners at the treatment plant.

## Blooming Violence at the Treatment Plant

The treatment plant is an impressively large, funnel-like structure with high currents of slopping waterways. It is also a veritable octabrain nesting ground. Besides wrestling with their wrath, you must also solve the riddle of the plant to reach the toxic sludge canals, which lead to one of two exits. Stepping into the fast moving sludge, you are pushed forward by the sheer mass and quantity of the thick goo. Land a shot with your RPG launcher near the visible crack along the wall on the right side. Then fight the current to reach the small room behind the blown-up wall. Mount the teleporter and materialize in the remote enclosure at the northwest side of the plant. Slide out of the teleporter booth carefully, and pelt any captains and their troopers. Then grab the cases of RPG ammo. With your RPG aiming forward, slide down into the narrow canal to reach the plant's center.

As you enter its spacious dimensions, aim and fire with precision. Chances are that some octabrains will chase you to the bottom of the plant's main tank. Work your way to the small control area at the north end of the main pool. Climb around the ramp and press the switch in front of you. Watch above and to the right as a small wall opens to reveal an elevated chamber on the south end.

Get back in the water, and climb the southwest ramp against the current. Jump onto the small ledge near the top, on the right side, and follow it to the front, once again overlooking the pool below. Climb over the separate and narrow floor section. Then aim your weapon and fire to hit the switch due south of your position. The column you stand on will move toward the center of the pool. A similar column will approach from the opposite end. Board the approaching column, and ride it back to the east side. Go around the dividing wall with the ripper chaingun handy. Pour it on the implacable octabrain, and push on into the toxic sewage network. It leads to the secret exit and the more obvious level exit.

## COVERT DETAILS

It might be a dump, and a toxic one at that; but, as shown in Table 4.8, it certainly has no shortage of interesting secrets.

| TABLE 4.8: THE SECRETS IN THE TOXIC DUMP | | |
|---|---|---|
| **AREA IN LEVEL** | **SECRET ITEM** | **HOW TO GET IT** |
| The western canyon | two RPG ammo cases | The ammo is in the secret compartment behind the turret recess in the elevated rock wall, directly east of the sunken submarine. |
| | holoduke | This item is in a similar chamber behind the turret recess on the opposing rock formation. |
| The drum processing plant | ripper chaingun | This weapon is in the chamber behind a secret door along the right wall (found a few steps into the hallway leading to the plant). |
| | ripper chaingun ammo | This is in the secret compartment at the south end, which you can access by catching a ride on the mechanical crane. |
| | atomic health units | These are inside the cylinders in the small chamber at the southeast corner. |
| The central canyon | a series of exploding walls | These dig a tunnel connecting the two canyons. |
| The treatment plant | teleporter | This is hidden behind an exploding wall in a descending canal to the south of the plant. The teleporter leads to a chamber located just northwest of the main treatment plant, where two RPG ammo cases can be found. |
| | atomic health units | Two of these are in the elevated toxic duct in a chamber just east of the plant. |
| | exploding wall | This is near the south end of the sinewy canal. It leads to the exit switch that will transport you to the secret level, The Launching Facility. |

# THE ABYSS

Was it Nietzsche who said he stood defiantly staring at the abyss, and the abyss stared back? If you feel compelled to say "gesundheit" when you hear "Nietschze" and philosophy is at best an amateurish pursuit, you might still share Nietzsche's awe when you confront your own abyss. Welcome to The Abyss and to the end of L.A. Meltdown, the first *Duke Nukem 3D* episode. (There is of course the secret level, The Launching Facility, provided you found it back in the Toxic Dump.)

The Abyss will tax not just your strength and ability but also your character and mental fortitude. Among the jagged cliffs, rocky roads, mountain sides, lava lakes and waterfalls, and fast running, toxic sludge canals, you'll find just how far the alien infiltrators have gone in their quest to possess the Earth. After exploring their bizarre temples, carved into the flanks of hanging peaks, you will be forced to conclude that the aliens' mythology combines mysticism and technology in equal measures. But you aren't here for an anthropological assessment. You're here to put an end to whatever the hell is going on. Your entire mission in The Abyss is to find the giant alien ship lying dormant in the stinking bowels of the Earth. You must then descend into a veritable inferno and face off against the gigantic Battlelord.

Bridging The Abyss requires you to blow key sections of mountain sides. The only route to the alien ship is through a net of cavernous tunnels running like veins encased in rock. Set out to find the San Andreas Fault marker, an unassuming slab of concrete. Then penetrate the mountains' temples and uncover their secrets. In the major and larger of the temples, set off a key trigger and blow open an entrance into the solid burrow where the alien craft is nestled. Gain entry to the ship and best of luck. Humanity is counting on you.

## MAPS AND ROUTE

No, you're not looking at the latest mutation of the virus of the week. Figures 4.16 and 4.17 show you maps of the best route out and all the goodies, respectively, in The Abyss and all its glory.

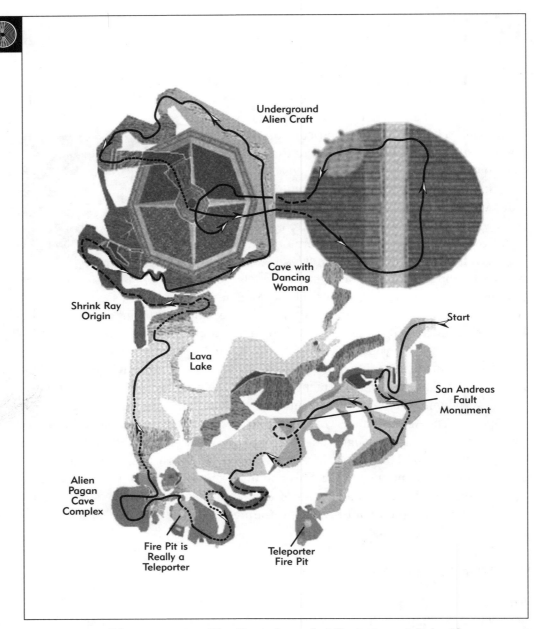

**FIGURE 4.16:** When you stare at The Abyss, do you feel like it stares right back?

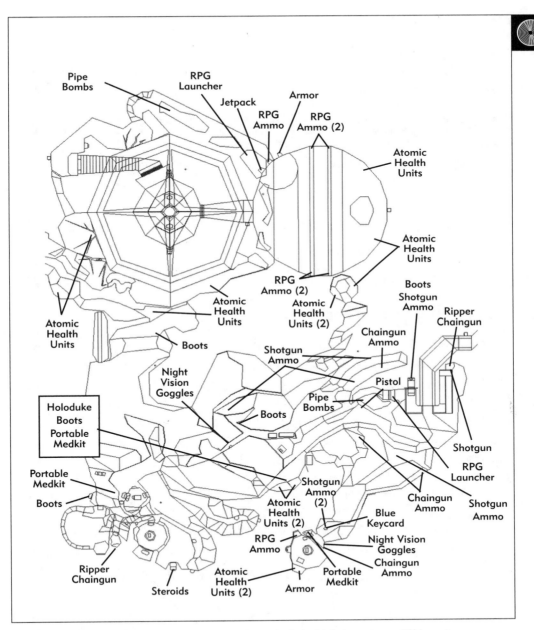

**FIGURE 4.17:** The Abyss brings your experience in L.A. Meltdown to a cliff-hanging consummation.

## THE GOODS

Considering the caliber of the opposition—after all this is the level in which you will find the Battlelord, the episode's boss—The Abyss is well stocked in the goods department. Table 4.9 shows the entire cache.

| TABLE 4.9: THE GOODS IN THE ABYSS | | |
|---|---|---|
| WEAPONS | AMMO | POWER-UPS |
| 2 shotguns | 1 case | 1 portable medkit |
| 3 ripper chainguns | 1 case | 1 atomic health unit |
| 4 RPG launchers | 1 case | 2 armors |
| | | 1 steroid flask |
| | | 1 jetpack |
| | | 1 NVG |
| | | 1 holoduke |
| | | 3 pairs of boots |

## BLAZING THROUGH THE ABYSS

*Blazing* might actually be an inaccurate verb for getting through The Abyss. Even the shortest of routes puts you at serious peril and forces you to overheat your thinking cap. The underlying assumption to blaze through is that you have a jetpack that can give you a short burst of air time. (If that isn't the case, you must find a blue keycard before you can reach the San Andreas Fault marker.)

### Along the Sludge Drain and Surrounding Mountain Paths

1. **Get the boots and RPG launcher.** Run out of the narrow toxic sludge tunnel and turn a quick right. Open the door on the rock side, and grab the protective boots. Jump into the floor below by the blue keycard door and take the RPG launcher.

2. **Reach the San Andreas Fault marker.** Jump into the sludge, letting the current carry you down a short distance to a rocky formation. Take the middle mountain path, and veer to the right at the "Y." Hop over the canal to reach the ledge on the north side. Run along the ledge until it narrows. Then drop onto a large, slightly inclined open surface. Turn on the jetpack, and hover a very short distance straight up. Land on the small rock outcropping next to the marker.

3. **Cause a major shock.** Bump against the marker and steady your footing, as tectonic plates rearrange to change the scenery somewhat.

4. **Collect two atomic health units.** Jump onto the newly accessible slanted surface. Take the first atomic health. Hopscotch onto the next surface, and take the second atomic health before heading toward the caverns.

## In the Eerie Alien Caverns

1. **Enter at your own risk.** Jump back over the canal, and run around the rock formation to reach another area fallen by the quake. From here, work your way down until you reach the level ground with the canal, which is now the size of a gurgling brook. Cross over the canal again, and reach the gaping entrance to the network of alien caverns.

2. **Reach the pit of rituals.** Crawl up the steep, rocky ground to reach a level opening where the path divides. Turn a hairpin left onto yet another tunnel that ascends all the way to the pit of rituals. Drop into the pit and activate the alien hand print on the south wall to uncover a hidden area where you can get another RPG launcher.

3. **Uncover a hidden tunnel.** Touch the alien hand print on the north side of the pit. When the nearby rock slab slides, go into the connecting tunnel.

4. **Blow up a critical mass of rock.** Come out of the connecting tunnel into the threshold of the largest of the alien caverns. Use your jetpack to hover into the chamber, hugging the wall on your right. You will come upon a ledge where you can shut off your jetpack. Through an opening in the shape of a cross, you will see the telling sparkle of the

 **DISC DEMO**  As if the creepy chanting reverberating in the alien caverns isn't enough to infuse fear into the heart of any adventurous soul, you must still keep your wits about you, and move quite deliberately to get through this particular passage. Watch the demo for The Abyss, which is stored on the CD-ROM in the file E1L6.BLZ. It will reaffirm your faith and get you through.

mysterious shrinking device. Walk up to the wall as you look out through the cross to set off another massive blast. Through the opening, you should be able to see a big rocky boulder collapse into a lava pit below.

5. **Hover toward the downed boulder.** Activate the jetpack, and exit the chamber the same way you hovered in. Get back to the ritual pit and climb out of it. Head westward. The path will lead you by a sunken fountain. Continue up the path that steers westward. As you emerge into crimson outcroppings, walk to the edge, and, assuming your jetpack has enough juice, hover straight north toward the buried alien ship.

## In and about the Alien Ship

1. **Find the entrance.** Begin a long and perilous ascent inside a red glowing tunnel. Follow the hairpin turn into a space where the ground is marred by major cracks. (Through a small opening in the wall, you should be able to catch sight of the alien ship.) Continue the downward path around the lower circumference of the octagonal vessel. Leap-frog the series of narrow rocks to reach a very steep series of rocks serving as steps. These give you access to the north side of the ship. Straighten your tie and knock on the door.

2. **Drop in for a short visit.** Open the massive door to the alien ship and walk inside. At the end of the walkway, enter through a second, even larger door. Turn to the right immediately, and activate the alien hand switch on the wall. Slide down into the funnel-like floor. You're now on the main floor of the alien craft.

3. **Exchange pleasantries with the boss.** Open the door on the east side. Enter through the green metallic tunnel. Collect all the RPG ammo you can hold before the Battlelord makes his presence known. When he emerges from an underground holding tank, manage to hit him 25 times with your RPG launcher and claim a righteous victory.

# ADDED ATTRACTIONS IN THE ABYSS

If somewhere along the blazing route your jetpack gives out, or if you're just wild about caves, perhaps you should look at these added attractions:

- ❊ The proper way to work a room
- ❊ Going to a go-go cave
- ❊ Facing off with the boss

## The Proper Way to Work a Room

When you reach the largest of the alien caverns, if your jetpack isn't up to the task, you will have to trigger specific events to be able to get out. Dropping into the chamber, look for the alien hand print along the north wall. Activate it and run along the steps emerging from the ground and going up and around the periphery of the room. Reaching the platform at the top, look through the cross opening on the wall. Your proximity to this area triggers an explosion you can clearly see from this position. The boulders sinking to the ground will allow you to access the north region of The Abyss, where the alien ship lies encrusted in the Earth.

Jump onto a narrow ledge on the east wall, and activate yet another hand print switch. Losing not a second, jump off the platform and run directly south to catch an ascending pillar. Turn to face the sparkling emanation from the shrinking device flowing across the boulders and through the cross-shaped opening. Let it catch you smack in the face and turn you instantly small. Jump off the pillar, and head for the narrow width at the base of the north wall. You will emerge right by the sunken fountain, but there might be an octabrain or two waiting. So be warned.

## Going to a Go-Go Cave

After wrecking large boulders and rock outcroppings in the northern lava region of The Abyss (by setting off a trigger in the larger alien cave), you can go for a final showdown with the ever-so-jealous-of-his-job Battlelord. Or, you could take the low moral road to visit a not-so-nearby cave for a bit of, shall we say, licentious amusement? Here, we opt for the latter.

Make sure your protective boots are adequate before visiting the northern hemisphere. The Abyss is an eroded land with flowing lava lakes, scorching waterfalls, and perilous cliffs. The setting couldn't be more appropriate for octabrain spawning grounds. They swim freely all around the lava. They can also hide behind rock outcroppings and burrow within large crevices. Watch out.

Jump into the lava hoisting your RPG launcher and aiming slightly above the lake's horizon. The second you spot three eyes in a giant gelatinous head, pull the trigger. While they are at a safe distance, you should be able to pick your targets. At the same time, you want to become an elusive target yourself, darting left and right, while struggling against the current to keep a safe distance. If your jetpack isn't depleted, you can also hover and rain upon the octabrain parade below.

Find the passage flowing eastward. Head northeast, staying near the wall on your right side. What will seem like legions of octabrains swimming upstream to spawn will do their damnedest to stop your progress. Persevere undeterred. Find the small platform with the alien hand print and activate it. Then climb over the opening above the flowing lava. Fight upstream until the ground levels and then suddenly drops into a small circular cave. Enter the cave, grab the atomic health, and don't attempt small talk with the dancing woman. She's apparently entranced by the deep beat of a primeval alien rave.

## facing Off with the Boss

This is the moment of truth. You've demolished mountains to reach the alien ship, which is encrusted deep in California mountain rock like a metallic seed of unreal proportions. Now, standing on its imposing bridge, you're suddenly aware you've entered truly alien territory. The ship's controls, engineering, and architecture were never meant for human occupants. The atmosphere is still and eerie, and you can't stop feeling imminent danger and dread. You've come very far, but not far enough. You have an appointment to keep with the Battlelord, and he hates to wait.

Armed with all the RPG ammo you can hold, walk toward the only door on the east side of the bridge. Activate the alien hand print switch to look behind the green door. Start into the room. Just before an overhead beam crosses the hallway, stop and activate your jetpack to hover into the room. You want to avoid running over trigger 1, near the chamber's entrance. This trigger causes the door at the start of the hallway to shut permanently.

The idea is to leave yourself an out if the idea of standing toe-to-toe with the Battlelord is not even halfway appealing. Hover onto the circular platform on the northwest side.

Don't let the ghastly sight of the women in cocoons distract you from your task. Take the additional RPG ammo. By this time, the Battle-lord should be emerging from his slumber. Seize this moment when he's vulnerable, and pound him with all the rocket propelled grenades you can possibly launch. If you've got the tempera-

**WARNING**

Avoid locking yourself in the sentry's chamber by hovering over trigger 1. You can also hop over it.

ment for it, you can attempt to fight the Battlelord on his grounds. The first thing you must do is maintain a safe distance while you make him chase you from one half of the chamber to the other, over the elevated lava canal. You will have a few precious seconds to act as he starts to cross the canal, leaving the top of his ferocious face exposed. You stand to sustain some damage, so make it a point to pick up the two atomic health units in this room.

If you can maintain a sustained attack before you're really hurt, you're a better Duke than most. But even so, remember that you can get back to the bridge area—if you remember not to cross over trigger 1. Bet as sure as daylight the Battlelord will follow. Unfortunately for him, his corpulent frame might prove too much for the door frame. This is your perfect opportunity to punish him with impunity.

## COVERT DETAILS

Labyrinthine and enormous in its sheer proportions, The Abyss cradles many a secret, as shown in Table 4.10.

### TABLE 4.10: THE SECRETS IN THE ABYSS

| AREA IN LEVEL | SECRET ITEM | HOW TO GET IT |
|---|---|---|
| The alien caverns | fire pit that is really a teleporter | This device sends you to the otherwise inaccessible circular chamber, due directly east of the cavern complex. Loot abounds in this area, including RPG ammo, atomic health units, and armor. |
| The rocky outcroppings | atomic health units | These vital items can be found in the northeastern chamber, the home of the dancing cavewoman. |

*(Continued on next page)*

*(Continued from previous page)*

| AREA IN LEVEL | SECRET ITEM | HOW TO GET IT |
|---|---|---|
| | shotgun and ripper chaingun ammo | The ammo can be found in the rocky tunnel that looks like an appendage near the eastern end. The tunnel is only accessible through an exploding wall on its north side, across from an alien hand print. |

# THE LAUNCHING FACILITY

Why are you here? Don't look for really deep answers. Either you stumbled upon the secret exit back in the Toxic Dump, or you purposely sought it out. But all that's irrelevant now. Your mission here, if you can accomplish it, is nothing less than to sabotage a rocket to the Moon. The rocket carries helpless female specimens wrapped in leathery green cocoons. (God only knows for what purpose.)

Destroying the rocket is a two-stage proposition. First you must get onboard to activate the self-destruct mechanism with the aid of the red keycard. Next, you have to find and push the remote detonation switch. But this seemingly straightforward task is anything but that. To begin, the rocket might as well be invisible until you cause it to surface from its underground silo. To do that, you must first secure a blue keycard, without which the security switch will not work. And just as important, you also must find a way to open gate 2 to access the northern half of The Launching Facility.

## MAPS AND ROUTE

The Launching Facility's layout, as shown in Figures 4.18 and 4.19, consists of medium-sized chambers connected by a network of corridors and passages at right angles. And as the route makes it painfully obvious, you have to run its entire length to accomplish your goal.

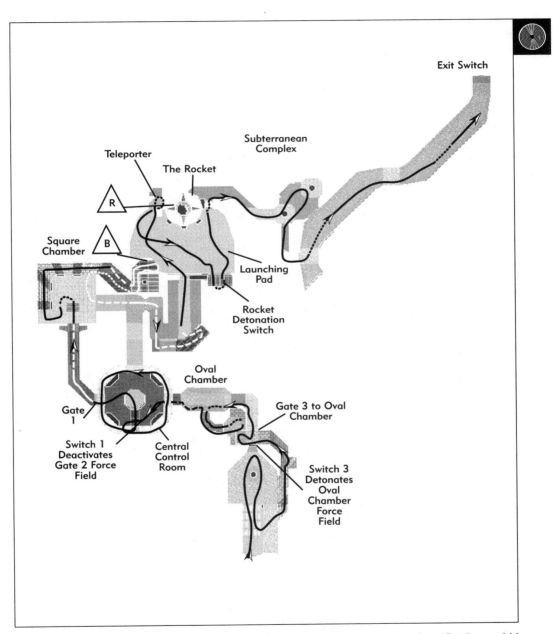

**FIGURE 4.18:** Ten, nine, eight, seven, six . . . Can you penetrate the Launching Facility and blow up the rocket before it's too late?

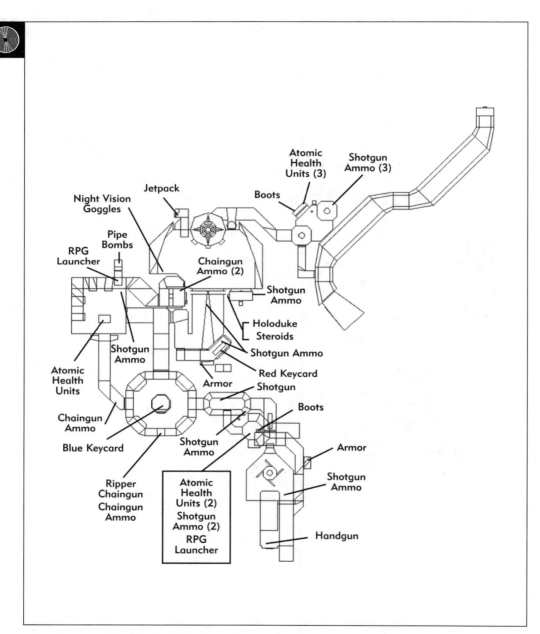

**FIGURE 4.19:** Don't lose sight of your mission in the narrow confines of The Launching Facility; but above all, don't lose your head.

## THE GOODS

While not particularly overflowing with goods, The Launching Facility has a respectable number of atomic health units—and you know you can never be too healthy (see Table 4.11).

| TABLE 4.11: THE GOODS IN THE LAUNCHING FACILITY | | |
|---|---|---|
| WEAPONS | AMMO | POWER-UPS |
| 2 shotguns | 1 case | 5 portable medkits |
| 3 ripper chainguns | 1 case | 1 atomic health unit |
| 4 RPG launchers | 1 case | 2 armors<br>1 steroid flask<br>1 jetpack<br>3 NVGs<br>1 holoduke<br>1 pair of boots |

## BLAZING THROUGH THE LAUNCHING FACILITY

How do you cause a rocket to rise from its out-of-reach silo, board it, get out of it, and then cause it to blow up? You're about to find out (but maybe not in one breath).

### Before Entering the Central Control Room

1. **Gain access to the middle, oval chamber.** Reach the north side of the toxic pit on the opposite side of the churning blades. Activate switch 3 to deactivate the force field barring access to the oval chamber. Run back to the ramp, and cross over the elevated ooze canal into a green corridor. Grab the protective boots from the compartment next to the monitor. Then follow the corridor as it turns westward into the oval chamber.

2. **Dive for pearls.** Dive right into the ooze and grab a shotgun. (The ooze in this pool is completely harmless.) Find the circular openings to a connecting underground tunnel to access a smaller sunken chamber. Then surface to claim two atomic health units and two cases of shotgun ammo.

3. **Go kick butt in the central control room.** Beaming with health and more ammo, get back to the oval chamber.

## In the Central Control Room

1. **Reach the top level.** As you enter the room, run toward the southwest corner. Run up the platform that circles the entire area until you reach a row of four circular switches.

2. **Gain entry to the control column.** Activate the first, second, and fourth switches (starting on the left side). Cross the metal bridge to the central column. Grab the blue keycard and activate the switch labeled "1." It deactivates the force field in gate 1, so you can reach the next chamber.

## In the Square Chamber

1. **Get more health.** Run up the corridor leading to the largest chamber in The Launching Facility. With a short running start, land on the central pillar to claim an atomic health.

2. **Reach the rocket control switch.** Climb along the ramp and over an irregular patch of ground to emerge in a small chamber with a few monitors and other control panels. Go into the small connecting division on the east side to use the blue keycard on switch 2, and then watch the rocket emerge from its underground storage base. This same switch also opens a door to the warehouse. The warehouse, of course, is adjacent to your target, the rocket.

## In and around The Launching Pad

1. **Get the red keycard.** Go back to the large square chamber, and enter the hallway on the east side. Go straight through a raised door, and climb the steep walkway, heading south, to come upon a set of swinging doors. Open the doors, enter, and reach the top area to grab the red keycard. Also, throw the switch along the half wall to open the large metal doors.

2. **Board the rocket and drop the card.** Get out onto the launching pad. Take the elevator on the west side to the very top. Emerging in a small and dark control room, grab the jetpack by the console before jumping into the teleporter. Open your eyes to see you are now inside the rocket.

Walk over to the key switch and drop the red keycard. As the lights turn red, get back on the teleporter and ride the elevator back to ground level.

3. **Detonate the rocket.** Crawl into the narrow opening east of the warehouse gates. Find a simple toggle switch and push it. Watch the once proudly erect structure come crashing down in a smoldering heap.

4. **Reach the underground.** Take the elevator on the east side of the fallen structure a good distance into a subterranean complex.

## In the Subterranean Complex

1. **Grab the boots and push the switch.** Follow the corridor eastward. Coming upon another computer console area, take the boots on the northwest panel. Then push the adjacent switch to open a wall at the end of the short southern corridor.

2. **Ride the ooze to victory.** Get out into the ooze and let it lead you to the exit switch.

3. **Give yourself any form of kudos you prefer for your conquest of the L.A. Meltdown episode.**

## COVERT DETAILS

As the secret level, it's only natural that the Launching Facility contains quite a few secrets. Witness them in Table 4.12.

**TABLE 4.12: THE SECRETS IN THE LAUNCHING FACILITY**

| AREA IN LEVEL | SECRET ITEM | HOW TO GET IT |
| --- | --- | --- |
| The toxic tank room (east of the central control area) | RPG launcher shell cases atomic health units | These items are in a sunken chamber, which you can get to by diving into the sludge and swimming through a narrow passage. |
| The cubic green chamber | pipe bomb case | This item is tucked away in a duct above the ceiling fan. |
| The hangar area | armor | This item can be found in a secret compartment in the elevated control area at the south end. |
| The underground chamber | atomic health unit | The item is behind the computer panel. |

# CHAPTER

# 5

# Lunar Apocalypse

At the conclusion of the L.A. Meltdown episode, you found an alien craft embedded in the Earth's rock mantle. Undaunted, you entered the strange vessel and faced off with a fearless Battlelord, pulling quite a job on his head. Using the ship's monitors, you also learned that the aliens were loading scores of women in cocoons into one of their huge interstellar ships. You vowed to not let this intergalactic kidnapping continue unabated.

Lunar Apocalypse, the nether region between L.A. Meltdown and Shrapnel City, marks the second episode in Duke's quest to undermine the alien's evil plot. As the level of the opposition rises, your arsenal also undergoes a considerable face-lift. In this level, you get to measure your might and wits against new adversaries, including the hovering sentry drone, the leaping enforcer, and the single-minded assault commander.

## SPACEPORT

You proved your mettle in L.A. Meltdown, and now you are back for more. Spaceport is your first stop along your tour of duty in Lunar Apocalypse. Spaceport sees you aboard a hovering, man-made station in lunar orbit. The place is obviously infested with aliens, and the blood trail flows ever so freely. Your job is to board the docked shuttle and reach The Incubator, the next station in the maddening Lunar Apocalypse episode. Commensurate with the higher level of the opposition, you will also find nifty new weapons of awesome destructive power. Witness the shrinker and the devastator, yours only for a few quarts of blood.

Reaching the elusive shuttle involves fighting through walls of enemies and working the installation's secrets to unlock the path. Be especially careful when confronting chaingun-wielding enforcers because this might be the first time you confront them. The shuttle you must board is behind a door that won't yield unless you have the red keycard. However, getting the red keycard involves first finding the blue keycard and then deactivating the force field around the central shaft; to do this you must use the right combination on a panel of switches.

## MAPS AND ROUTE

The layout of the Spaceport level, as you can see in Figures 5.1 and 5.2, is a no-frills, utilitarian docking station. Because there are two completely overlapping floors in the main central area, Figure 5.2 shows views for both the lower and the higher floors.

## THE GOODS

Table 5.1 displays the bountiful weapon and power-up cache to be had in Spaceport.

### TABLE 5.1: THE GOODS IN SPACEPORT

| WEAPONS | AMMO | POWER-UPS |
| --- | --- | --- |
| 1 shotgun | 3 cases | 1 portable medkit |
| 1 ripper chaingun | 2 cases | 5 atomic health units |
| 1 RPG launcher | 5 cases | 1 armor |
| 1 shrinker | | 2 steroid flasks |
| 1 devastator | | 2 jetpacks<br>2 NVGs<br>1 holoduke |

## BLAZING THROUGH SPACEPORT

The steps in this section will help see you through the mayhem in Spaceport and, thus, limit your exposure to space madness.

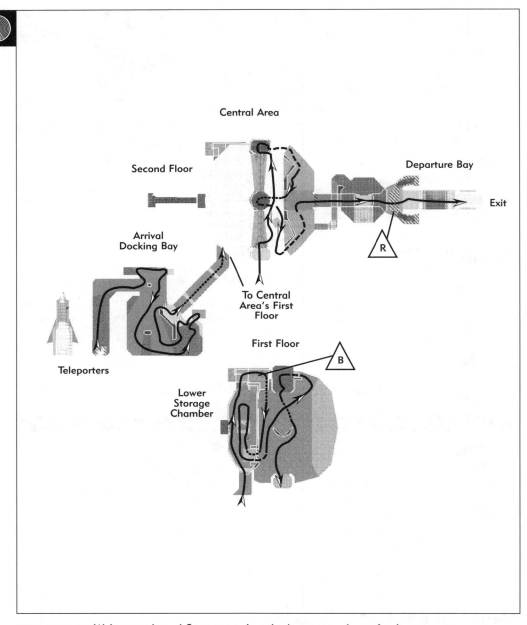

**FIGURE 5.1:** Welcome aboard Spaceport, but don't expect a bag of salty peanuts.

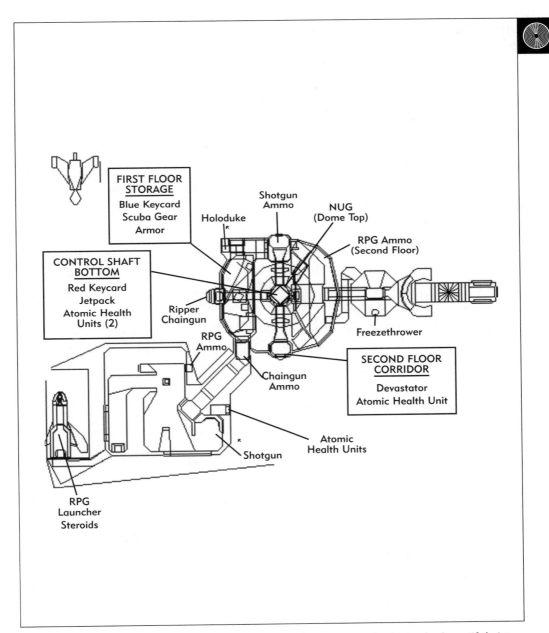

**FIRST FLOOR STORAGE**
Blue Keycard
Scuba Gear
Armor

**CONTROL SHAFT BOTTOM**
Red Keycard
Jetpack
Atomic Health
Units (2)

Holoduke

Ripper
Chaingun

RPG
Ammo

Shotgun
Ammo

NUG
(Dome Top)

RPG Ammo
(Second Floor)

Freezethrower

Chaingun
Ammo

**SECOND FLOOR CORRIDOR**
Devastator
Atomic Health Unit

Atomic
Health Units

Shotgun

RPG
Launcher
Steroids

**FIGURE 5.2**: Don't be afraid to wander around the Spaceport and take in the beautiful vistas, as you collect what you need.

## Around the Arrivals Docking Bay

1. **Get an RPG launcher.** Hop onto the teleporter behind you to board the inoperative docked shuttle. (This is not the shuttle you need to reach the next level.) Grab the RPG launcher and the steroids near one of the wings. Then, teleport back to the station.

2. **Take stock of the situation, and beef up your arsenal.** Reach the monitor behind the dividing wall at the northwest corner. As you turn the corner, listen for the hissing sound of the secret compartment behind you (directly facing the monitor). Turn around quickly and jump inside the slightly elevated compartment to grab a case of RPG ammo.

3. **Activate a switch to gain access to the central area.** Work your way to the southwest corner, disposing of the troopers and their captains along the way. Crouch in front of the computer panel as you take a shotgun, and push the broken computer monitor to enter a small secret area. Grab the atomic health unit and get out. Finally, throw the switch to the left of the computer panel to deactivate the force field that is barring entrance to the central area.

## On the Central Area's First Floor

1. **Get the blue keycard and a few other necessities.** Descend the long ramp, past an intermediate chamber, and make a hairpin turn into the wide open space of the central area's first floor. Although you will have a very nice view of the blue planet, you should be more interested in the blue keycard for now. (This is a good time to use the RPG launcher on the leaping enforcer.) Enter the storage compartment behind the door on the west wall. Climb on the crates to get the blue keycard, the scuba gear, and the armor.

2. **Access the second floor of the central area.** Get out to the main floor and find the narrow lift on the north side. Ride the lift to an elevated control area where you can use the blue keycard on the switch next to the opening. Activate the switch. It makes an elevator accessible at the

south end of the floor. This elevator is your only way of reaching the second floor. Go get on it.

## On the Central Area's Second Floor

1. **Uncover the panel of combination switches.** When properly configured, these switches deactivate the shield around the central shaft. (The red keycard lies at the bottom of this shaft.) Switch 2 is inside the out-of-order elevator at the north end of the floor. Blow up the C-9 canisters next to the elevator to create a gaping opening you can walk through. Step in and push switch 2.

2. **Push the right combination of switches.** Run out of the elevator and climb the short ramp to the green metallic chamber. Walk up to the panel of switches, and push them in the same configuration as shown in Figure 5.3.

3. **Take a dive down the shaft.** With the shield no longer barring you from the main shaft, dive right in and touch bottom. Grab the red keycard, and, while there, open the small compartment to take a jetpack and an atomic health unit. Climb out of the shaft and head back to the metallic chamber.

4. **Board the shuttle and wave good-bye.** With red keycard in hand, cross over the heavy blue door and enter a chamber connecting the central area to the docked shuttle. Walk right up to the switch, and use your red keycard to open the circular door. Fend off the sentry drone, walk in, activate the exit switch, and catch a ride to The Incubator.

## ADDED ATTRACTIONS IN SPACEPORT

Although you can get through Spaceport expeditiously, why not prolong your stay and claim two awesome weapons? Once you try them, you will agree that the devastator and the freezethrower are worth the extra time.

**DISC DEMO**
You can view this fast and furious sequence in the demo for Spaceport. Look in the CD-ROM for E2L1.BLZ. Then try to do even better if you can.

FIGURE 5.3: Activate the correct combination of switches to gain access to the main shaft.

## In Search of the Devastator

The only way to get the devastator is to reach an elevated hallway through the central shaft. If you haven't scored a jetpack yet, that should be your first priority. There are two jetpacks in this level. One is at the bottom of the central shaft; the second is on top of a small platform along the west wall of the second floor in the central area.

After deactivating the force field around the central shaft, simply step in it and activate the jetpack. Fly straight up until you come upon a hallway that runs north and south. Take the hallway south, and grab the devastator at the very end of the hallway. Then turn around and get back in the shaft. If you like, you can continue climbing all the way to a small top dome where you can also collect a pair of NVG.

## Scoring the Freezethrower

As you take the final straightaway toward the awaiting shuttle, notice a roughly oval area along the middle of the floor. It is in reality a platform that lowers automatically as you enter the anti-chamber to the shuttle. If you jump into the open pit, you will come upon an octagonal chamber where the freezethrower is hibernating. Grab it quickly and then make your way out of the sunken chamber by crawling into the narrow duct on the northwest wall. The duct starts a steep ascent and lets you come out through a one-way secret wall in the green metallic chamber.

## COVERT DETAILS

Table 5.2 airs out every secret in the Spaceport level.

| TABLE 5.2: THE SECRETS IN SPACEPORT | | |
| --- | --- | --- |
| **AREA IN LEVEL** | **SECRET ITEM** | **HOW TO GET IT** |
| The arrivals docking bay | atomic health unit | You'll find it in a secret compartment at the southeast corner. Crouch and press the broken monitor to access the secret area. |
| | RPG ammo | It's inside the elevated compartment at the northeast corner, directly across from the monitor. A sensor near the monitor triggers the compartment open. |
| Central area, first floor | pipe bombs | These are tucked away inside a duct. The duct is accessible in one of two ways: through the duct opening inside the small storage chamber at the west side or by jumping through a secret place from the small chamber that leads into the central area. Take a running start and jump directly at the sign that reads "Authorized Personnel Only." |
| Central area, second floor | devastator | This item is at the south end of an elevated tunnel. Once you have deactivated the shield, access the central shaft and hover to the tunnel's opening. Head southward to take the devastator. |
| Anti-chamber to the shuttle | freezethrower | This is at the bottom of a chamber that connects the central area to the exiting shuttle. |

# THE INCUBATOR

Why this installation is called The Incubator will become painfully obvious very soon. Another station orbiting the moon, The Incubator is literally infested with alien folk and their ghastly young. Organic, web-like formations grow wildly along metallic walls and computer panels. The basic layout of The Incubator consists of two chambers joined by a single doorway. The southern half of The Incubator is littered with dozens of eggs ready to spew a new member of the alien race—a crawling, bouncing, formless protozoid slimer with vicious serrated teeth in its underside. Could these eggs be the next progression along some aberrant evolutionary path crafted by alien intelligence? Is this what's become of human females? You shudder to think.

Your main concern in The Incubator is to reach the southern chamber, where the exit door is found. But the southern half will remain inaccessible unless you can deactivate the force field blocking the entrance. Once you make it to the southern chamber, you need only get past a few formidable adversaries and a barrier of hatching eggs to grab the yellow keycard. With this keycard, you will be able to access another chamber where a special switch opens the alien egg nest. After experiencing The Incubator, you will never think of poached eggs in quite the same way.

## MAPS AND ROUTE

As you can see in Figures 5.4 and 5.5, The Incubator is basically composed of two sections joined by a single doorway.

## THE GOODS

Table 5.3 lists the booty you can amass in The Incubator.

| TABLE 5.3: THE GOODS IN THE INCUBATOR | | |
|---|---|---|
| **WEAPONS** | **AMMO** | **POWER-UPS** |
| 1 shotgun | 3 cases | 3 portable medkits |
| 1 ripper chaingun | 2 cases | 3 atomic health units |
| 1 RPG launcher | 2 cases | 1 armor |
| 1 devastator | 3 cases | 2 steroid flasks |
| 1 shrinker | 4 crystals | 1 NVG |
| 3 laser trip bombs | | 1 holoduke |
| 1 freezethrower | | |
| 3 pipe bomb cases | | |

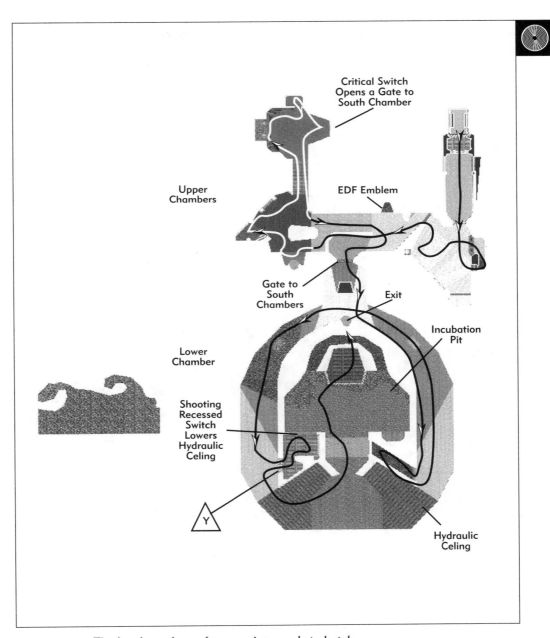

**FIGURE 5.4:** The Incubator has a few surprises ready to hatch.

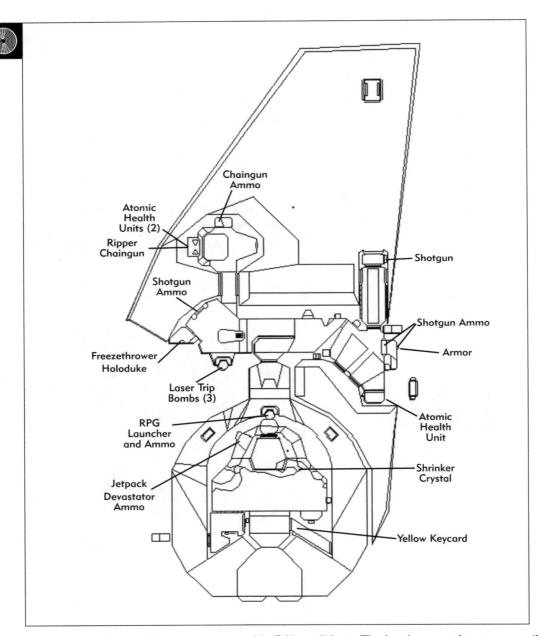

**FIGURE 5.5:** Do you like your eggs scrambled? You will fry in The Incubator, and not necessarily from the excess cholesterol.

# BLAZING THROUGH THE INCUBATOR

Alien eggs by the dozens, sentry drones, and a few vicious enforcers are only a few of the reasons why you might want to blaze right through The Incubator. Stick to the plan below, and you will live to earn bragging rights.

## In the Northern Chamber's East Wing

1. **Reach the computer room at the southeast corner.** Open the door in front of you and enter a small chamber. Take the shotgun from a hidden compartment to your left, before opening the door into the rectangular room to the south. You will become the target for a couple of sentry drones. Knock off the sentry drones, and enter the dark computer chamber to the south.

2. **Reap the secret booty from a computer room.** Step into the computer room and grab the case of shotgun shells from the computer panel on the left. Then push the square metallic panel to the right of the computer terminals to open a secret compartment. Grab the pipe bomb case and hop inside. Then push a second secret panel to access a narrow room behind the terminals. Take the case of shotgun shells and the armor before you jump back inside the room through the one-way wall.

> **TIP**
> The moment you spot a sentry drone, back off to put some distance between you and the enemy and then begin firing. Once a sentry drone gets too close to you, you can count on suffering a hard concussion, at the very least, from the sentry drone's diving attack and ensuing explosion.

3. **Get healthy quickly.** Cross the room and throw the switch in the middle of the wall on the southwest side. Two large metal panels open to reveal a view of the southern chamber. At the same time, an elevated compartment on the east side gives way to unleash a couple of sentry drones, and a secret door gives way to the remainder of the northern chamber.

## In the North Chamber's Middle Section

1.  **Get a large medkit.** Run right into the Earth Defense Forces emblem on the north side wall, and take the medkit in the small space behind the wall.

2.  **Get the freezethrower.** Continue up the ramp to a double door that appears to be locked. Your presence will trip a sensor, and the doors will lower as the computer room is being automatically assembled inside. Enter the dark computer chamber and head for a set of tall panels at the west side. The one on the right yields to let you inside a small enclosure where a holoduke and a freezethrower are your rewards (see Figure 5.6).

## In the Small Northwest Computer Room

1.  **Take more loot.** Follow the short ramp up to a small, dark computer room in the northwest corner. The sunken floor in this chamber will rise

**FIGURE 5.6:** The lovely sight of two of your favorite items.

as the sensors detect your presence. This is a good time to drop a pipe bomb onto the rising floor and wipe out the troopers before they reach the ground level. Along the west wall, you can grab a ripper chaingun and two atomic health units. The panel on the north wall hides a case of chaingun ammo.

2. **Throw the force field switch.** Walk to the wall on the east side and throw the switch that deactivates the force field connecting the northern and southern chambers.

## near the Southern Chamber's Entrance

1. **Take the RPG before going too far.** Standing at the threshold of the southern chamber, dart in to the weapons armory and grab the RPG and the two ammo cases before retreating.

2. **Bust in and get the yellow keycard.** Open yourself a path into the east wing (on your left). Enter the small door at the end of the half-circular hallway. Grab the yellow keycard near the bottom of the ramp, and run back out.

3. **Proceed to the right wing.** Once you have scored the yellow keycard, circle all the way around the southern chamber to reach a small chamber on the west side. Use the keycard to enter the chamber. Look for a small indented switch along the metallic wall, and fire a single bullet to activate it. This switch lowers the entire southern wall, thus granting you access to The Incubator's egg nest.

> **TIP**
> You don't want to stand inside the southern chamber for very long. Hatching eggs to the left and right and a meandering octabrain can easily overwhelm you. It is best to drop pipe bombs or pick off the protozoid slimers that come after you. After thinning out their numbers, run straight for the left wing of the southern chamber and pluck off the octabrain in mid air with a single shot from the RPG launcher.

## In the Egg Nest

1. **Penetrate the egg nest.** Hop onto the lowered southern wall, and dive into the racing water to reach the circular egg nest. You will come to rest on a solid platform overlooking a ghastly sight indeed. Before you risk more injury to yourself, walk over to the small compartment on the west side and take the large medkit.

2. **Unlock the exit and get away.** Hop into the uninviting water, and swim quickly across to the mess of organic matter that carpets the entire northern half of the chamber.

3. **Throw the organic switch.** Find a circular, organic switch along the middle part of the organic mess, and stand back as the middle section of the organic formation is lifted to reveal the exit switch. If your devastator is up to the task, pop any remaining eggs and throw yourself toward the switch.

> **TIP**
>
> You can detonate multiple pipe bombs at once. Throw your first pipe bomb. The detonator button appears in your hand. Press **6** on the keyboard to put away the detonator and grab another pipe bomb. Throw the second bomb as well. Again, press **6** to grab a third pipe bomb. Repeat this process as many times as you like, so long as your supply of bombs doesn't run out. After throwing the last bomb, stand a good distance away and punch the detonator switch for an explosion equal in proportion to the number of pipe bombs you deposited.

## ADDED ATTRACTIONS IN THE INCUBATOR

By the time you reach the southern chamber and its gruesome alien egg nest, you might be ready to get out screaming. However, on a more rational level, consider checking out the sizable loot to be had there. It can only make you stronger over the long haul.

### Padding Your Arsenal in the Egg Nest

After unlocking the entrance to the nest egg, you can potentially score a devastator and a shrinker and even ammo for these formidable weapons, in addition to a jetpack. The devastator and its ammo are found underwater. Because octabrains and protozoid slimers swim freely in the water pit, drop four or five pipe bombs in succession into the water; then detonate them all at once.

Feeling a bit more confident, jump into the tepid waters and look for an indentation along the submerged organic wall on the north side. The indentation on the right side takes you directly to three devastator ammo cases. The indentation on the left side leads to an actual devastator.

Ascend from the depths and reach the east side of the organic formation. Climb along the series of rocks along the west side until you come upon the entrance to a tunnel that burrows right through the organic structure. Near the eastern side of the tunnel you will find a jetpack behind a slightly translucent area in the wall.

## COVERT DETAILS

Secrets abound in The Incubator, and Table 5.4 summarizes them for you.

### TABLE 5.4: THE SECRETS IN THE INCUBATOR

| AREA IN LEVEL | SECRET ITEM | HOW TO GET IT |
| --- | --- | --- |
| North chamber, east wing | pipe bomb case<br>armor<br>shotgun shells | The pipe bombs are hidden behind a small metallic plate next to a small bank of computers. Stepping inside the enclosure, a second secret panel gives way into a hidden chamber lined with electronic circuitry. The chamber hides the armor and a case of shells. |
| North chamber, west wing | freezethrower<br>holoduke | These are tucked away behind a small closet-like enclosure. |
| Computer room, northwest end | ripper chaingun<br>ammo | This item is behind the panel on the north wall. |

# WARP FACTOR

Appearing more like a spaceship than a sedentary orbital station, Warp Factor is light years more complex than the previous two levels in this episode. Expect the unexpected in Warp Factor. Opportunity and danger lurk around every nook and cranny. This level also introduces yet another menacing figure, the rocket-spewing assault commander. And if that isn't enough, how about a cameo by the nemesis you thought you demolished back in L.A. Meltdown, none other than the Battlelord.

A multilevel structure, Warp Factor is characterized by long, wide hallways and a wide variety of utilitarian chambers. Near the main observation deck at the north end, you will see some telling clues as to the aliens' plan to crack Earth like a walnut by targeting California's San Andreas Fault. In a humorous way, Warp Factor is also a tribute of sorts to a staple American science-fiction television show. If you persevere, you might be able to pay a visit to not just a famous captain's ready room but to a "really ready room."

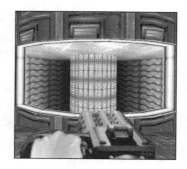

Making it in Warp Factor is all about picking your battles and being completely aware of your surroundings. You must traverse the totality of this installation before you get rightful access to the level's exit. The path to the exit is barred by a deflecting shield. The critical switch is in a secret area at the north end of Warp Factor. But to get to that area, you must first find both the blue and then the yellow keycards, and in just that order.

## MAPS AND ROUTE

If the general shape of Warp Factor reminds you of anything, your imagination is definitely engaged. Your number one priority is to get familiar with every aspect of Warp Factor. Logically, Figures 5.7 and 5.8 are good places to start.

## THE GOODS

It's only fair that such a complex structure as Warp Factor delivers on the goods too, and Table 5.5 proves that it does.

| TABLE 5.5: THE GOODS IN WARP FACTOR | | |
|---|---|---|
| **WEAPONS** | **AMMO** | **POWER-UPS** |
| 1 shotgun | 3 cases | 4 portable medkits |
| 2 ripper chainguns | 2 cases | 7 atomic health units |
| 1 RPG launcher | 1 case | 1 armor |
| 2 devastators | 4 cases | 1 steroid flask |
| 1 shrinker | 2 crystals | 1 NVG |
| 1 freezethrower | 1 charge | 1 holoduke |
| 1 laser trip bomb | | |

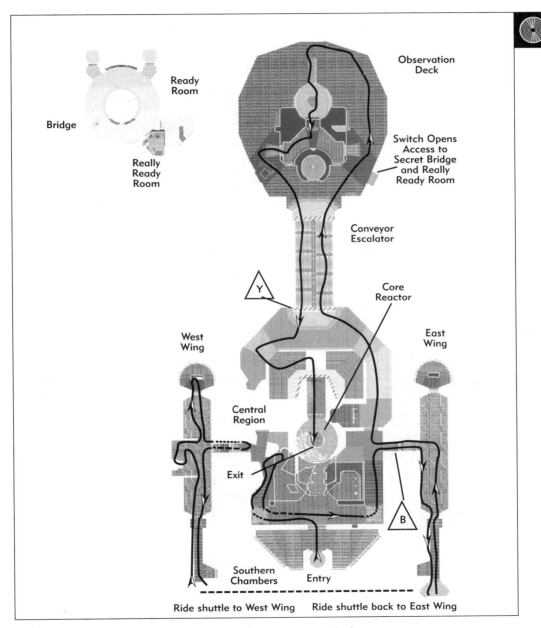

Bridge

Ready Room

Really Ready Room

Observation Deck

Switch Opens Access to Secret Bridge and Really Ready Room

Conveyor Escalator

Y

Core Reactor

West Wing

East Wing

Central Region

Exit

B

Southern Chambers

Entry

Ride shuttle to West Wing    Ride shuttle back to East Wing

**FIGURE 5.7:** This is Warp Factor, where no Duke has gone before.

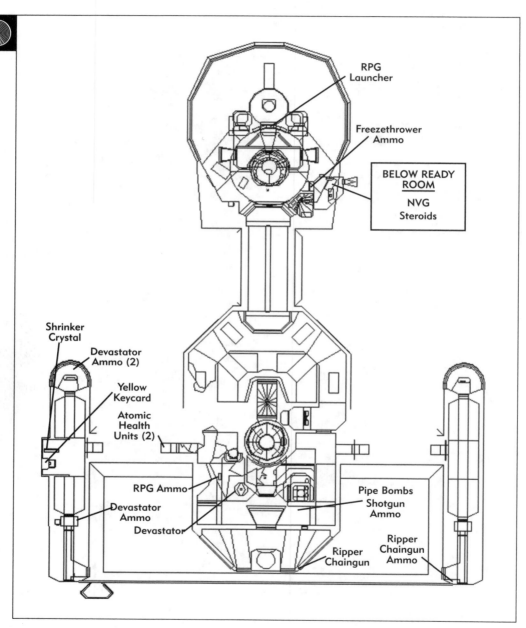

**FIGURE 5.8:** Don't look for anyone to beam you out of Warp Factor.

# BLAZING THROUGH WARP FACTOR

The pace in Warp Factor is nothing short of frantic. Even if you wish to blaze through this level, you will still have to cover the entire length of this installation.

## In the Southern Chambers

1.  **Get a ripper chaingun.** Make a hard right stepping out of the elevator to claim the ripper chaingun on the floor.

2.  **Lay your hands on a devastator.** Proceed into the chamber to the north, dashing across to the armory closet on the left side of the green metallic chamber. Open the semicircular door and nab the devastator. Turn around as soon as possible, and use your new weapon on the enforcer and the sentry drones that were automatically released from the dark chamber on the right side.

3.  **Get down and claim the blue keycard.** Step on the platform to the left side of the chamber. It will immediately collapse to a lower level area where the blue keycard is found. Search along the rubble, sticking to the left side, and crouch along the northwest corner to reach the blue keycard.

**TIP** Before stepping out of the small elevator, be aware that a sentry drone flanks you on each side. Therefore, when you step out, be ready to fire on a sentry drone or to back up into the safety of the elevator enclosure. Of course, you can also run to a far corner of the room to get a bit more breathing room so you are able to aim squarely at them.

**TIP** To better your odds of making it to the bottom floor, try going down once and shooting the enforcers from the dubious safety of the elevator. Then, with the enforcers out for good, drop one or two pipe bombs and activate the elevator to get out of harm's way. As the elevator begins ascending, detonate the switch. Now you are clear to go down again and proceed into the hallway, with the laser trip bombs safely exploded.

4. **Reach the lower floor on the east side.** Having obtained the blue keycard, get back to level ground and then head toward the platform on the opposite side. The platform will lower into a wide hallway, but further progress will seem unlikely because, not only are you dealing with a couple of enforcers, but the threshold of the hallway is lined with laser trip bombs.

## In the East and West Wings

1. **Access the east wing.** Having cleared the laser trip bombs, head north and take a quick right into a small door where you will need to use the blue keycard. Step inside the small enclosure, and activate the elevator to reach the long and narrow east wing. Deal with the sentry drones, and travel southward along the east wing.

2. **Ride the shuttle to the west wing.** When you reach the southern end of the east wing, activate the switch near the observation deck. Notice how the shuttle travels across from the west wing to where you are (see Figure 5.9). When the shuttle arrives, hop on it and activate the transport switch.

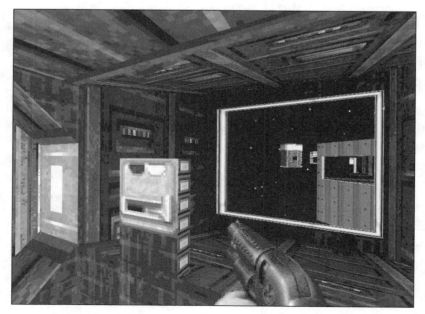

**FIGURE 5.9:** The shuttle is your ticket to the west wing and the yellow keycard.

## In the West Wing

1. **Go for the yellow keycard.** Forge northward along the west wing. Near its middle section, you will see the yellow keycard locked behind a seemingly impenetrable barrier. Throw the middle switch in a nearby switch panel, and the barriers blocking the yellow keycard will yield.

2. **Ride the shuttle again.** Get back to the southern end of the wing, and push the button to beckon the shuttle. Get on it and get back to the east wing.

## Toward the Critical Switch

1. **Meet an old acquaintance.** Stepping down back into the main level, you will run into the Battlelord. Remember him? If your health, armor, and weaponry allow it, you might be able to pepper the Battlelord with a combination of your devastator and RPG launcher. You can also retreat into the small elevator, and close the door in front of you.

2. **Probe beyond the yellow door.** Run all the way to the north end, where a massive metal barrier cuts you off from reaching the very large, semi-circular observation chamber at the north end of Warp Factor.

3. **Reach the observation deck, and get the freezethrower.** Use the yellow keycard to gain access and press past the yellow door, and ride the conveyor escalator to the observation deck's entrance. At once, run directly across to the cylindrical enclosure and push the door open. Step inside and grab the freezethrower; you have earned it.

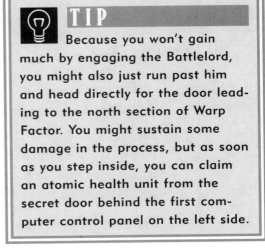

**TIP** Because you won't gain much by engaging the Battlelord, you might also just run past him and head directly for the door leading to the north section of Warp Factor. You might sustain some damage in the process, but as soon as you step inside, you can claim an atomic health unit from the secret door behind the first computer control panel on the left side.

## On the Observation Deck

1. **Reach the circular control chamber.** Run to the very north end of the observation deck, and notice that there really isn't much to observe yet. Ascend the short ramp into the circular control chamber, and activate the switch behind the 3D model of the Earth. The shields around the observation deck will raise to reveal a breathtaking view of our home planet.

**TIP**

As you head for the yellow door, you might engage the curiosity of the assault commander. If he comes after you, keep a safe distance between you and him, leaving yourself the ability to find shelter from the rapid-fire rockets he is so fond of expelling in your general direction. Then retaliate with sustained fire from the devastator, or score one direct hit with the RPG launcher.

2. **Access the secret area.** Walk directly to the large map depicting the point of impact along the North American continent, and open a secret door behind the map. Step inside and claim the RPG launcher along the elevated ledge. Also, the middle section of the computer banks has a holoduke behind a small secret compartment.

3. **Activate the critical switch.** Look for the switch near a monitor on the west side. Turn on the switch to lower a shield barring access to the core reactor.

## Back in Warp Factor's Central Region

1. **Retrace your steps.** Get back to the middle area, just south of the yellow door.

2. **Find the back door to the core reactor.** Proceed to the large cubic chamber located right smack in the center of Warp Factor. Open the large metallic door, and race across the empty, but highly harmful, chamber. Radiation contamination in this chamber is quite high.

3. **Time your move and go for it.** Wait for the moment when the rotating, incandescent shields leave a gap through which you can actually see a clear path to the central core, and then rush in. (See Figure 5.10.)

4. **Ride up and away.** Activate the core (it acts like an elevator), and you will come upon an elevated circular enclosure, with the exit switch prominently displayed on the east side. Push the switch and you're gone.

Count your blessings; not everyone makes it this far and stays sane.

## ADDED ATTRACTIONS IN WARP FACTOR

Space, the final frontier, can also be highly stressful and maddening. For that reason, if no other, most mortals might need a special place to find solace and renew their energy. For the captain of the Enterprise, this place is the "ready" room. For Duke Nukem, such a place might be the "really" ready room. Here is how you can find it and take a little time to kick off your shoes.

FIGURE 5.10: Make your move at the right moment, and get in through the back door.

## Getting Some R&R

Should you decide to take a breather—and you really ought to—then the really ready room is the place to be. But reaching the really ready room is not completely an effortless proposition. Timing and execution are critical.

> **DISC DEMO**
>
> For a preview of how to get R&R in the really ready room, check out the CD-ROM for the Warp Factor walk-through, E2L3.BLZ. You will see that it's tricky getting there, but ultimately worth it.

Near the southeastern end of the observation chamber, you will notice a wall panel with small green LEDs. This panel is in reality a secret wall. Open it and aim up to fire your gun at an elevated switch inside. Without loosing a second, run around the southern end of the observation deck to reach a lowered area along the outside west wall of the circular control chamber. Step inside and ride the elevator to reach a secret area above the circular control chamber.

Notice that the secret area, too, is circular and very reminiscent of the bridge of a once maiden starship. Access the chamber with the "Ready Room" sign on its door. Walk behind the desk and activate the desktop computer. Then step into the festive, lounging atmosphere of the really ready room, and let your hair down—for awhile, anyway.

## COVERT DETAILS

Table 5.6 summarizes the secrets in Warp Factor.

| TABLE 5.6: THE SECRETS IN WARP FACTOR | | |
|---|---|---|
| **AREA IN LEVEL** | **SECRET ITEM** | **HOW TO GET IT** |
| Northern observation deck | starship bridge | This area is accessible only after you activate the switch along the southeast wall (behind the computer panel with illuminated green LEDs). The switch lowers a panel on the west side of the central structure. |
| | really ready room | This area becomes available after you enter the "ready room" and activate the computer on the desktop. |

# FUSION STATION

Essentially, the Fusion Station is nothing more than an oversized instrument for spewing forth massive power loads to juice up all the lunar stations. Circular in shape and strictly utilitarian, the Fusion Station is an impressive structure of gargantuan proportions. Standing erect and dominating its central area, a very wide cylindrical column reaches up to the black heavens. This central core reactor houses three floor levels inside, each one posing a clever puzzle.

The north and west side periphery of the Fusion Station is crowned by another series of chambers and a long tunnel. Orgiastic in its unbridled decor, the Fusion Station is far from *Home & Gardens* fare. Your mission in the Fusion Station is to reach the head of the reactive column and blow it completely off.

To reach the head of the reactor, you will need to traverse the four corners of the Fusion Station and confront more sentry drones, enforcers, and assault commanders than ever before. If your current arsenal includes a devastator, an RPG launcher, or a more exotic weapon like a shrinker or a freezethrower, things might not be as dire.

The Fusion Station paces your progress because, as you reach a major area, you have to solve a puzzle before moving onto the next place of interest. This means you should pay particular attention to secret passages, switch-controlled doors, and other installation features. You would be surprised what you can find and where you can find it in the Fusion Station.

## MAPS AND ROUTE

The seemingly straightforward layout of the Fusion Station belies the fact that its multiple levels and secret passages make it a very hard level to crack open. Study Figures 5.11 and 5.12, and refer to them as often as necessary.

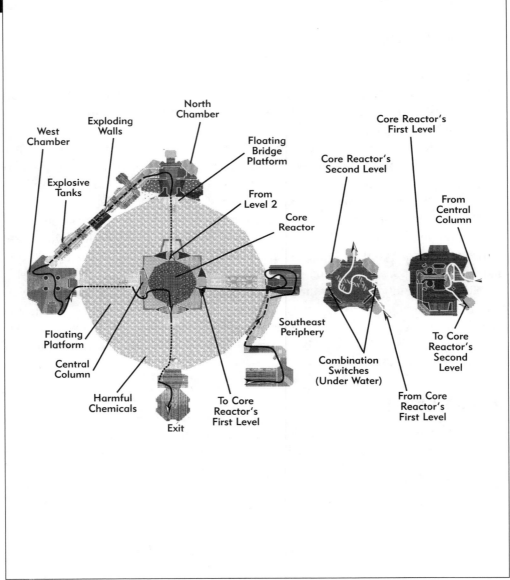

**FIGURE 5.11:** You are bound for an electrifying and maybe somewhat shocking experience in the Fusion Station.

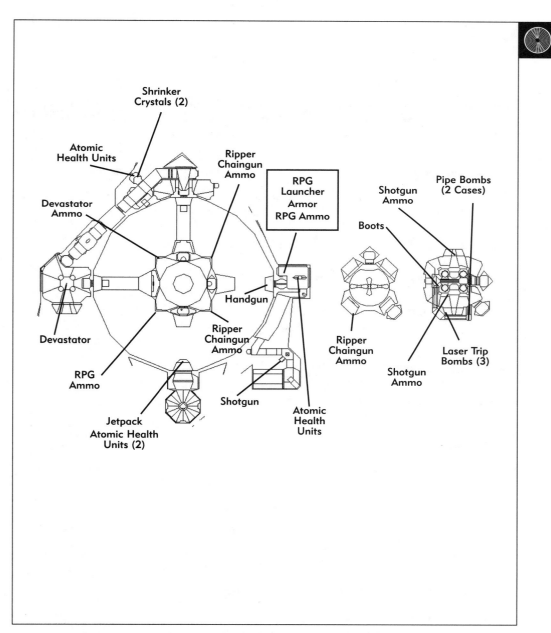

**FIGURE 5.12**: As you solve the Fusion Station's puzzles, you can collect from its sizable cache of weaponry and power-ups.

## THE GOODS

As you can see in Table 5.7, the goods in the Fusion Station are commensurate with its physical proportions.

### TABLE 5.7: THE GOODS IN FUSION STATION

| WEAPONS | AMMO | POWER-UPS |
| --- | --- | --- |
| 2 shotguns | 2 cases | 1 portable medkit |
| 1 ripper chaingun | 1 case | 3 atomic health units |
| 1 RPG launcher | 1 case | 2 armors |
| 2 pipe bomb cases | | 2 steroid flasks<br>1 NVG<br>1 holoduke |

## BLAZING THROUGH FUSION STATION

Getting from point A to point B in the Fusion Station level is never as simple as it might seem. Let this section be your pocket guide along the way.

### In the Southeastern Periphery

1. **Pick up a shotgun.** As you come around the second turn, take the shotgun behind the female in a cocoon.

2. **Take out the turrets.** Proceed up the long hallway, and duck to avoid direct turret hits. Stand up with the RPG launcher at the ready, and take out one of the turrets. Still ducking, move a few feet, stand up, and repeat the process with the second turret.

3. **Reap the goods in the eastern chamber.** Take the RPG and armor at the northwest corner of the chamber, by the Earth Defense Forces (EDF) monitor. Then claim the atomic health unit below the rising pillar. (A sensor near the monitor triggers the pillar.)

4. **Reach the central column.** Throw the switch near the door to open a small chamber leading to the exit. Throw the second door open, and be ready to back up and pound the diving sentry drone. Cross the hand rail bridge to reach the central column.

## On the Core Reactor's First Level

1. **Pick up a few shotgun shells.** Enter the chamber and follow the path to the north side. Hop onto the elevated platform, and grab the case of shotgun shells.

2. **Activate the switched door.** Hop down from the platform and onto the first pumping pillar. Crouch and scoot southward into the small space between the two pillars. Then look the length of the glowing tunnel, and aim directly at the alien hand switch (see Figure 5.13). It causes the switched door on the southeast corner of the chamber to give way.

3. **Reach the second-level floor.** From your precarious position between the pumping pillars, sneak into the second pillar's hole. Then immediately jump out onto the main floor of the chamber, and race for the door at the southeast corner. Get on the elevator and ride it up to the next floor.

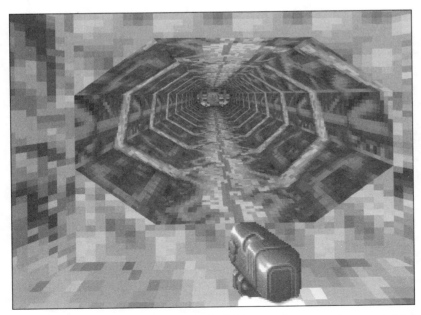

**FIGURE 5.13:** The switch at the end of this tunnel opens up access to higher floors and many more possibilities.

> **TIP**
>
> Jumping into a pillar hole is extremely dangerous. If your timing is anything but perfect, you could be the thickness of a silver coin in two or three seconds flat. Therefore, getting into the hole should be a two-stage procedure. First, jump up right next to the pumping column. Then, as soon as it reaches bottom and starts its upward motion, slip right through. Immediately crouch and move into the cubbyhole just south of the first pillar.

> **TIP**
>
> It's always a good idea to save a game before you attempt to do something that could damage you seriously or kill you. That way, if the worst should happen, you can pick up the game from the place where you last saved it.

## On the Core Reactor's Second Level

1. **Activate the combination switches.** There are two switches that activate a door in this chamber that opens in stages. You can only access the door after you activate both of the switches. Each switch is located inside the pool at the east and west ends, and each raises a portion of the door on the north end. You must time your movement in and out of the pool to avoid the heavy, churning arms of the central mill-like asps.

2. **Reach the third floor.** When the door is fully open, step out to view a wide chasm and the north end of the station.

## On the Core Reactor's Third Level

1. **Cross the chasm.** Activate the switch at the end of the observation deck to beckon the floating platform from the north side. Get on top of the platform, aim your gun at the alien hand print switch, and fire. The floating platform will take you across the chasm and deliver you to the entrance of the north chamber.

## In the North Chamber

1. **Get more stuff.** Grab the pipe bomb cases and any other weaponry strewn about.

2. **Head southwest.** Proceed along the west side to find a door yielding into a long tunnel that connects you to the west side chamber.

## In the West Side Chamber

1. **Collect the devastator.** Quell the opposition in the square side chamber on your left and then take the devastator weapon from the oscillating floor in the middle of the room. If your shrinker has been under used, feel free to pour its frigid might onto the assault commander guarding the devastator.

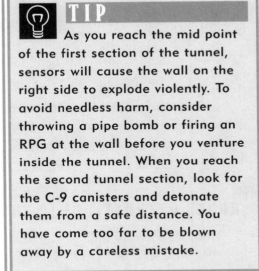

**TIP**

As you reach the mid point of the first section of the tunnel, sensors will cause the wall on the right side to explode violently. To avoid needless harm, consider throwing a pipe bomb or firing an RPG at the wall before you venture inside the tunnel. When you reach the second tunnel section, look for the C-9 canisters and detonate them from a safe distance. You have come too far to be blown away by a careless mistake.

2. **Reach the central column's west side.** Find the hand print switch behind a dividing wall on the south side of the chamber and activate it. Without skipping a single beat, turn around and race for the door on the east side before it is shut down automatically. Standing on the deck, beckon another flying platform as before and reach the central core reactor.

## Back in the Core Reactor

1. **Blow up the reactor's head.** You are now at the top level of the core reactor, and the massive pillar in the middle of the room will descend shortly to reveal a claw-like head buzzing with energy. Run around the four corners of this floor, collecting all the ammo to be had. Then stand near the point where you entered, fire an RPG round or two, and seek protection behind the dividing wall. You will need it. The reactor will blow in a big way.

2. **Ride the floating platform.** The otherwise impenetrable door at the south end of the core reactor should now be cracked open. Go through the hole. Now you must bridge another chasm to reach the southern

chamber. If you have a jetpack, you are set; if not, don't despair. If you look down, you will see a small platform below the entrance to the southern chamber. Take a running jump and land on the platform. Replenish your health with the atomic health units while you are there. Notice also that there is a jetpack waiting for you. Strap on the jetpack and rise straight up.

3. **Defeat the assault commander and adios amigo.** Go through the final gate. Sensors will cause the exit switch to rise from the floor. But, unfortunately, a sentry drone will be released at the same time. If you have some devastator charges left, this is the time to put them to use.

## ADDED ATTRACTIONS IN FUSION STATION

Although mostly utilitarian, the Fusion Station is not totally without its charm and beguiling surprises. Don't expect creature comforts, but you owe it to yourself and future generations to investigate a couple of the Fusion Station's elusive secrets.

### Life at the End of the Tunnel

The first floor of the core reactor is an interesting structure in more ways than one, and there are nice perks to be had on the side. To begin, the core's heavy, industrial quality is reinforced by the lattice of wiring and pipe work lining the walls. Four pumping pillars dominate the main area of the chamber, pounding away incessantly like well-tuned high performance pistons.

The poor lighting of this chamber makes you slightly more vulnerable if you don't have a pair of NVGs. Upon entering you are beset by overzealous enforcers. Choose your favorite weapon to put down the reptilian menace. Jump right next to the pillar, and drop into the gaping hole as the pillar begins its upward motion. Crouch and move into the small cubbyhole so you're actually sitting right between the two opposing pillars. Look eastward for a long but narrow crimson tunnel. Aim a bullet directly at the hand print switch to unlock the exit to the chamber. Notice the atomic health units at the end of the tunnel. You will make them yours very soon.

**DISC DEMO**

Witness the delicate timing and swift movement required to activate the hand print switch. Watch as Duke eludes the pumping pillar to position himself at the mouth of the crimson tunnel. Check out the CD-ROM for E2L4.BLZ.

Time your next jump into the hole for the second pillar and, just as quickly as possible, jump out onto the main floor of the chamber. Take care of the enforcer and trooper parade, and jump onto the elevated platform on the south wall. Pick up the laser trip bombs in the corner. Then look for a slightly brighter panel along the south wall and push it open. You have reached a secret duct. Follow it as it turns westward to pick up two cases of pipe bombs. Retrace your steps, follow the duct to the west, and then go on a very steep incline as the duct turns northward. You will come upon those precious glowing objects otherwise known as atomic health units.

## COVERT DETAILS

The Fusion Station's secrets are listed in Table 5.8. Your job is to find them all.

### TABLE 5.8: THE SECRETS IN FUSION STATION

| AREA IN LEVEL | SECRET ITEM | HOW TO GET IT |
| --- | --- | --- |
| Central core reactor, first floor | atomic health units | You'll find these at the end of a long crimson tunnel nestled between two pumping pillars. Because the tunnel is too narrow, you must find the secret duct leading to the end of the tunnel. The duct's entrance is through a metal panel on the southern wall, on top of the large platform. |
| | pipe bomb cases (2) | These are at the eastern end of the secret duct. |
| | ripper chaingun | This weapon is in the cubbyhole between the two pillars on the east side of the chamber. You must time your jump inside the hole of either pillar and then rapidly scoot into the narrow space between the pillars to claim the ripper chaingun. |
| Along the northeastern bridge | atomic health unit shrinker crystals (2) | These items are in a secret area above the air ducts. The exploding wall in this segment serves as a guide post to tell you where you should look up. In fact, use the rubble on the wall to climb onto the overhead duct. Go through a secret passage on the inside wall and follow it around as it comes out over the other duct. At the end of this duct, you will find a female held captive by a strange alien vine. Grab the crystals, waste the unfortunate soul, and claim the atomic health unit. |

# OCCUPIED TERRITORY

Making serious headway into Lunar Apocalypse, you are about to confront what is arguably the toughest level. If for nothing else, Occupied Territory is daunting by the sheer number and the viciousness of your co-occupants. It's as though a fearsome force of fiendish foes has come together to cause your fall and evict you permanently from Occupied Territory.

Returning to a slick and pleasantly simple geometric level design, Occupied Territory spreads from an immense central observation chamber with huge translucent panes to three extensions of various lengths and shapes. To the east, the dark Battlelord's quarters house the blue keycard. But don't count on the Battlelord handing it to you when you get there. The west wing is dominated by a wide and large open skyway, which ends right where you start your foray into Occupied Territory.

Circumventing the many perils of Occupied Territory is just impossible. So brace yourself for serious bare-knuckle action. But for the raw brutality that awaits you, there are still some important pieces of strategy you should keep in mind. First, your ultimate destination is to penetrate the tightly guarded central cage in the observation mall. That is where the exit switch is. But knowing it's there means nothing, if you can't penetrate the cage. The aforementioned blue keycard will let you in, but there is another problem. The Battlelords' chamber is beyond reach unless you have the red keycard to begin with. No problem. You can get the red keycard with your trusted ripper chaingun. This weapon excels at cleaning a path over the vicious protozoid slimers as you work your way up the ramps into the southernmost cavernous chamber. You will find the red keycard deposited at the tip, as it were.

## MAPS AND ROUTE

Figures 5.14 and 5.15 show Occupied Territory to be a simple, sleek, but quite perilous construction.

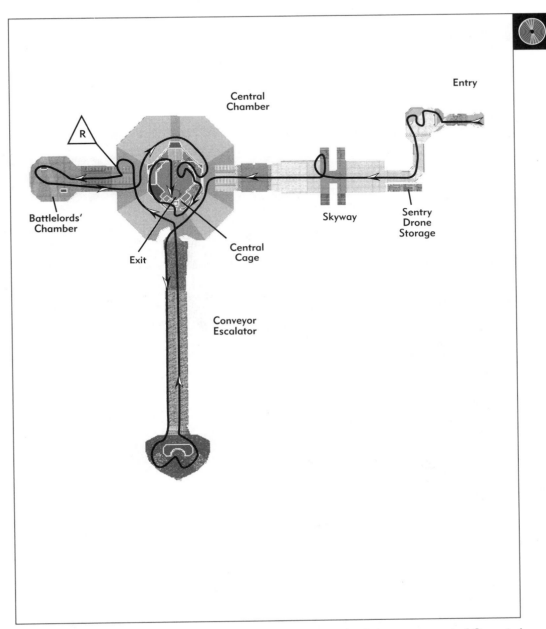

Entry

Central
Chamber

R

Battlelords'
Chamber

Exit

Central
Cage

Skyway

Sentry
Drone
Storage

Conveyor
Escalator

**FIGURE 5.14:** Squatter's rights or not, you must kick every alien's butt to get out of Occupied Territory.

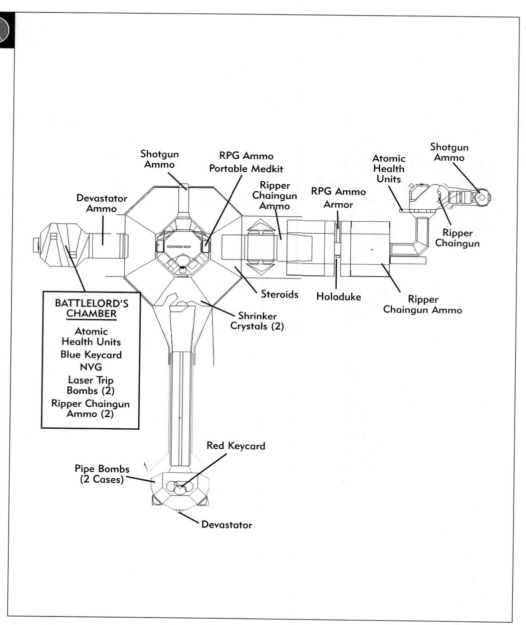

**FIGURE 5.15:** That this level is lean on the goods demonstrates further just how tough this level can be.

# THE GOODS

This level isn't necessarily overflowing with goods, but sometimes the work should be its own reward. Table 5.9 shows you the goods to be had.

| TABLE 5.9: THE GOODS IN OCCUPIED TERRITORY | | |
|---|---|---|
| **WEAPONS** | **AMMO** | **POWER-UPS** |
| 1 shotgun | 4 cases | 1 portable medkit |
| 1 ripper chaingun | 4 cases | 3 atomic health units |
| 1 RPG launcher | 3 cases | 1 armor |
| 1 devastator | 3 cases | 1 steroid flask |
| 2 laser trip bombs | | 1 NVG |
| | 2 shrinker crystals | 1 holoduke |

# BLAZING THROUGH OCCUPIED TERRITORY

Getting through Occupied Territory requires you to cover a large amount of ground and endure many fierce battles. Only your sharp skills and the wise use of your weaponry will see you through.

## In the Entryway and on the Skyway

1.  **Open the door and boost your health.** Grab the shotgun and the shells before using the switch to open the circular door. Clear the path of crawly protozoid slimers with a few pipe bombs before proceeding into the chamber behind the Earth Defense Forces emblem. Take the ripper chaingun from behind the emblem, and spray bullets at the troopers behind the diagonal partition. Enter the partition through the side door, and flick the switch on the wall to open the large door to the south. Get ready for a few more fireworks and then stop at the gate's threshold, squat down, and thrust your way into a narrow opening where an atomic health unit awaits.

2.  **Collect what you can, and reach the central observation chamber.** Stepping into the long and wide runway, you will notice gigantic metal

**TIP**

As you reach the entrance to the main chamber's foyer, a sensor triggers a door open back toward the start of the skyway. The small storage area is a veritable sentry drone hive, buzzing with frenzy. Use the long space between you and the sentry drones and put the RPG launcher to work overtime for you.

curtains recede to give way to a bold, translucent sky. But your sense of awe will be drawn short by the party assembled on the skyway. Be sure to grab the ammo for the ripper chaingun and the RPG launcher as you move westward along the skyway. When you come upon a narrow wall cutting the skyway in half, climb the north slope and kick in the duct grill. Step inside and traverse the length of the narrow duct to claim an armor and an RPG launcher. Armed with your new weapon, continue forging westward.

## In the Central Chamber

1. **Seek out the red keycard.** Upon entering the central observation chamber, head immediately southward, toward the organic growth along the south wall. Crawl inside the squishy interior, fend off creeping protozoid slimers, and grab two very indispensable shrinker crystals before moving forward. Ride the conveyor to the top of the narrow tunnel.

2. **Take the red keycard.** Push open the next door and step in to wrestle the red keycard from a less-than-compliant assault commander. Limit your exposure, and don't give the assault commander time to react as you clear the small wall partition. Be ready to aim and fire at the C-9 canisters next to the assault commander. If he survives the explosion, finish him with one or two shotgun blasts.

3. **Return to the central chamber.** Ride the conveyor escalator back to the central chamber, and then make your way over to its western wall.

4. **Greet a couple of old pals, and yank the blue keycard.** Use the red keycard on the switch along the western wall. Stand back as a slanted platform pushes its way from out of the wall. Climb up the steep platform, and be sure to pick up the devastator ammunition en route to the

top. Open the rusty metallic door emblazoned with the Battlelord's contemptuous countenance and step in a ways. It's best to draw the Battlelords out and clobber each with a shower of devastator charges or an all-out RPG shower. When they succumb, go inside the chamber to take the blue keycard. Check the secret compartment behind the broken terminal to claim an atomic health unit and a couple of laser trip bombs.

5. **Penetrate the central cage's lock.** Rush back toward the east side of the central cage. You have earned the right to enter.

## In the Central Cage

1. **Activate the switch to the side door.** As you enter the central cage, look for a switch next to a small computer bank. Activate the switch. It causes a door on the south side of the central cage to open, thus granting you access to the space between the walls of the central cage.

2. **Enter through the back door.** Get out of the cage only to find the newly opened door on the south wall that you will re-enter. Don't let the enforcers stop you from reaching what appears to be an observation deck that looks into the middle section of the cage.

3. **Take down more Battlelords before making tracks.** Press the switch to the right of the observation window, and watch a heavy shield give way to reveal two Battlelords and a holographic image of a yet-unseen alien host.

4. **Battle the two giants.** Dodging their projectiles and explosive pellets, strafe left and right and take advantage of every opening to administer unhealthy doses of devastator charges. For variety, pelt the Battlelords with RPG rounds too.

5. **Cross the planks to reach the exit.** Jump through the observation opening, and pass over the row of metal planks to reach the circular stage with the holographic horror. Push the switch to its right side, and punch the exposed exit switch.

## ADDED ATTRACTIONS IN OCCUPIED TERRITORY

Almost every step along the way in Occupied Territory is fraught with uncertainty and danger. Here, you get to examine one such moment more closely.

### Battlelord, Will You Please Hand Me the Blue Keycard?

By far the most daring maneuver in this level involves obtaining the blue keycard. There is too much at stake. Without the blue keycard, you won't be able to enter the central cage, where the final exit switch awaits. But perhaps no keycard in this game is under such tight guard as this blue keycard. Not one, but two Battlelord s are entrusted with the simple mission of annihilating anyone who even comes near.

Don't let the prospect of being rendered a slice of human Swiss cheese detract you from your quest to save humanity. Once you have obtained the red keycard from the southern chamber at the end of the long corridor with the conveyor ramps, activate the central chamber's switch on the west wall. Hop on top of the massive slanted surface pushing its way out from the wall. Halfway up the ramp, pick up the two cases of devastator ammo. Though this is far from a prize fight, every single round is crucial.

Coming upon the emblazoned mug of the Battlelord on the metallic doorway, ready your devastator. Push the door open, and venture in just enough to douse one of the Battlelords before suddenly retreating toward the entry ramp. Jump off the ramp and think quickly. You know the Battlelords are after you. Ideally, you should have enough health, armor, and ammo to pummel both Battlelords before they can even get off the ramp.

However, should they reach the chamber's main floor, you're in for a terrifying game of cat and mouse. The first thing to do is find a position where you can take shield from the chaingun and explosive pellet onslaught. The best place for that is along the northern or southern wall so you can use the central cage as a shield. You can, in fact, run around the central cage and fire upon the Battlelords when you find the slightest opening. But this is at best a tenuous proposition. Something a bit more conservative is to run into the long, webbed hallway to the south. The Battlelords' massive size will prevent them from following you. You can then unload your weaponry almost at will.

With the Battlelords in the pages of history, climb up the ramp to the west chamber a second time and secure the blue keycard.

## COVERT DETAILS

For its apparent simplicity, the Occupied Territory level houses an unusual and assorted collection of secrets. See Table 5.10 for a full list.

**TABLE 5.10: THE SECRETS IN OCCUPIED TERRITORY**

| AREA IN LEVEL | SECRET ITEM | HOW TO GET IT |
|---|---|---|
| The entry way | atomic health unit | This item is in the small recess by the threshold of the first door. |
| The skyway | RPG ammo<br>armor | These are inside a narrow duct. The duct is accessible through a grill on the west side of the wall dividing the skyway down the middle. Climb up the ramp to reach the duct grill. |
| | shotgun chaingun ammo | These are in the rocky tunnel that looks like an appendage near the eastern end. The tunnel is accessible only through an exploding wall on its north side, across from an alien hand print. |
| The Battlelords' quarters | laser trip bombs (2)<br>atomic health unit | These can be found behind the computer panel. The secret compartment is accessible through the broken computer monitor to the right of the original place where the blue keycard sits. |

# TIBERIUS STATION

You may not be the first person to walk on the moon. But at least in this adventure, this is the first time you reach the desolate planes and craters of our companion satellite. Like the orbital stations, Tiberius, too, is under heavy alien occupation. Laid out in a vertical north-south floor plan, Tiberius Station also has an extensive duct network. Starting at the southernmost point, your mission is straightforward. Get to the northernmost chamber, where an eager Battlelord Sentry will do his best to render his usual hospitality and keep you from activating the exit switch.

Unless you know about certain shortcuts, your seemingly simple task can become suddenly very complicated. It is possible, in fact, to get through Tiberius Station with a single red keycard. However, you risk missing a large part of the installation. Considering you are facing some very unforgiving opponents, you might want to explore the very generous offerings of weapons and power-ups in this level. The general key to succeeding in Tiberius Station is to blow things up, if there is any doubt. You won't need to ask questions later.

## MAPS AND ROUTE

Figures 5.16 and 5.17 show Tiberius Station to consist of a few chambers of varying sizes connected by a network of hallways and air ducts.

## THE GOODS

Few other levels in the Lunar Apocalypse episode are as generous in the goods departments, as you can see in Table 5.11.

### TABLE 5.11: THE GOODS IN TIBERIUS STATION

| WEAPONS | AMMO | POWER-UPS |
|---|---|---|
| 1 shotgun | 5 cases | 3 portable medkits |
| 2 ripper chainguns | 2 cases | 3 atomic health units |
| 2 RPG launchers | 2 cases | 2 armors |
| 1 devastator | 1 case | 1 steroid flask |
| 1 shrinker | 2 crystals | 1 NVG |
| 1 freezethrower | | 1 holoduke |
| 2 laser trip bombs | | 1 scuba gear |
| 5 pipe bombs | 2 cases | 1 pair of boots |

## BLAZING THROUGH TIBERIUS STATION

Do you want to avoid much heartache and sorrow? Reap some choice goods, and get through Tiberius Station in a mercifully short time. This section shows you how.

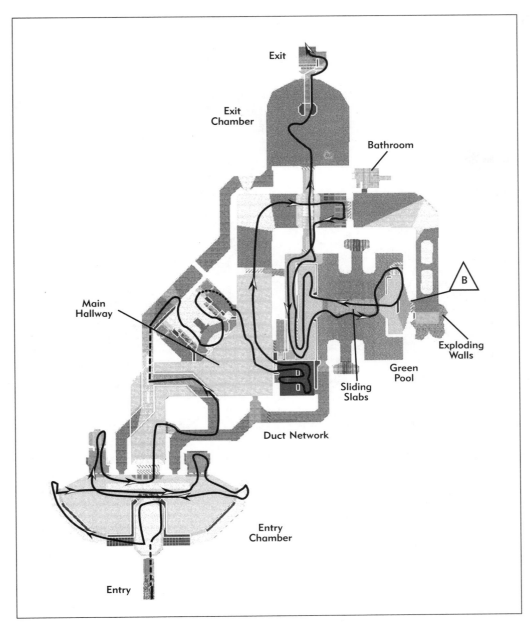

Exit

Exit
Chamber

Bathroom

Main
Hallway

B

Exploding
Walls

Green
Pool

Sliding
Slabs

Duct Network

Entry
Chamber

Entry

**FIGURE 5.16:** Welcome to the moon and sorry about the bloody mess, but after all, Tiberius Station is under siege.

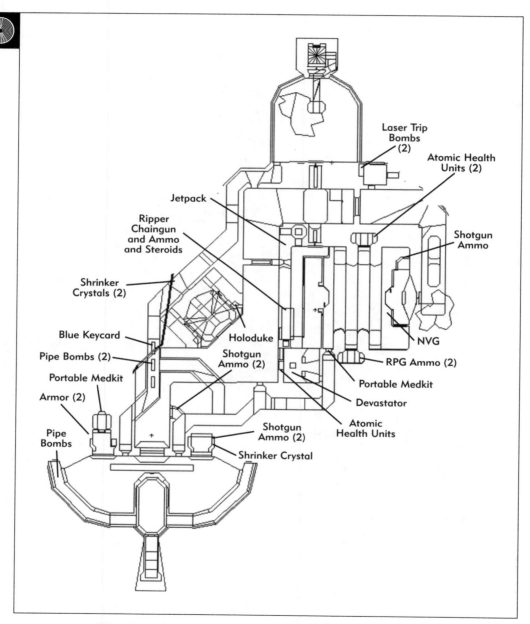

**FIGURE 5.17:** The alien infestation has reached our moon bases. Collect your fill as you liberate Tiberius Station.

## In the Entry Chamber

1. **Climb out of the goo.** Hop over the door and punch a hole through the grill to get out of the narrow and gooey entryway. Landing on an elevated control platform, find your way down through either long, narrow east or west walkway.

2. **Collect the goods in the east and west side storage rooms.** At the end of the walkway you will run into a monitor and a switch. The switch causes a small storage room at the opposite side of the chamber to open. The storage chamber on the east side has two cases of shotgun ammo and a shrinker crystal. The other storage room boasts two armors, a large medkit inside a refrigerator, and a secret panel between the two armors. The panel leads to a small back room with a portable medkit.

3. **Open the gate to the main hallway.** Get back on top of the control platform, and activate the switch overlooking the chamber's exit gate. Get down and enter the main hallway.

## In the Main Hallway

1. **Blow up a hole in the wall.** Drop a pipe bomb near the wall on the right side. Stand back and detonate the pipe bomb. Hop inside the gaping hole in the wall, and take the two cases of shotgun shells.

> **TIP**
> Look for the cracked lines on the right wall's surface as a telling sign of the correct location for placing the pipe bombs.

2. **Take the goods in the computer control room.** Continue along the duct directly due north. Follow it as it makes a couple of sharp right turns and slopes upward. You will come upon two shrinker crystals right in from of a duct grill. Take the crystals and bust through the grill. The compartment in the computer panel on the left side houses a holoduke.

3. **Go after the devastator.** Punch the switch overlooking the main hallway, and race down one of the side platforms to catch the gate across the hallway before it closes. Grab the devastator on the table, and annihilate the enforcers.

4. **Pound your way to the north hallway.** Armed with your new weapon, clean yourself a path to reach the north hallway, past the gate at its

north end. As you turn the corner, face off the rushing enforcers. Then run to the east end of the hallway to stand behind the handrail.

5. **Access the overhead bridge.** Hop onto the handrail, aim upward toward the overhead bridge, and then jump. Walk up to the door on the south side; it opens into the central ooze pit.

## In the Central Ooze Pit

1. **Work your way down to the ooze.** Two elevated areas flank the ooze pit on the east and west sides. Your entry point is at the top of the western side. While you are at the top, take advantage of the heavy walls shielding you and pepper the octabrain parade floating above the pit. Walk south along the narrow passage to reach the next lower floor.

2. **Don the scuba gear and dive for the red card.** You will find the scuba gear sitting next to a panel of computers. Slip it on and plunge into the murky toxic waters. Reach the very bottom and collect the red keycard. The keycard is directly below the middle of the flanking area you jumped from.

3. **Reach the eastern flanking area.** Once you have the keycard in your possession, swim across to the eastern area and hop onto the platform on its north side. Activate the platform and get on it to reach the elevated area.

4. **Build a bridge and get out.** Look for the switch in the middle of the elevated area and punch it at once. Four heavy metallic platforms will emerge from the north and side walls to line up in the middle of the pit and form a bridge. Cross the bridge to the west side again.

5. **Get back to the top floor.** Trace your steps back to the top side and get back out of the pit chamber and onto the bridge where you entered. Walk straight north on the bridge to reach the final chamber.

## In the Exit Chamber

1. **Greet the Battlelord with a bang.** The instant the door opens, aim for the C-9 canisters on the left side of the chamber and back away quickly. It matters not if you fall off the bridge. Keep banging at the Battlelord until you watch him crumble. (See Figure 5.18.) Occasionally the

**FIGURE 5.18:** Bang this dude hard. He won't go down any other way.

Battlelord Sentry will stay back behind the pillar in the middle of the room. If he does, you will have to go hunt him down in the reduced space of the final chamber.

2. **Find the underground passage.** Enter the chamber and look for a duct entrance on the south side of the chamber's only pillar.

3. **See you next time.** Crawl through the tunnel and then walk out onto the small enclosure with the glowing red light and the exit switch. You know what to do next.

## ADDED ATTRACTIONS IN TIBERIUS STATION

For the amount of pain, suffering, and untold psychological damage you can undergo in this level, it is only fair that you get at least a little something in

> **DISC DEMO**
> Check out these underwater scenes in the walk-through for this level. Load E2L6.BLZ from the CD-ROM and pinch your nose as you go below.

return. Isn't it? The pool area, east of the main hallway, is a place where you can be almost suitably compensated.

### This is No Pool Party

There are at least two ways to reach the green slimy pool. One involves using the blue keycard, which is found in the elevated computer room west of the hallway. With this keycard you can access the pool through a security latch at the far east side. The second way does not require you to use the blue keycard. Instead, you have to jump from the railing at the end of the north hallway onto the overhead bridge. Then you can simply go through the entrance at the northwest corner of the pool.

If you went in through the east side door, grab the protective boots along the wall overlooking the pool. Then activate the switch in the center of the platform to cause four heavy metallic slabs to line up in the middle of the pool, creating a bridge in effect. Then run over the newly formed bridge across to the east side of the pool.

If you entered through the bridge at the north end, you will find yourself on the top floor of a balcony overlooking the pool. Drop a pipe bomb a short ways into the narrow hallway. When you detonate it, it will open up a crevice in the wall large enough for you to walk into and claim a jetpack. Continue southward to reach the middle level platform. Collect the scuba gear and the shrinker near the north end of the platform. Then activate the switch to cause the heavy metallic slabs to line up in the middle of the pool. Dive into the pool on the north side of the slabs, and swim to reach the wall indenture where the second slab is normally found.

Resurface and push against the wall to uncover a small enclosure holding two atomic health units. Take the atomic health units and go back underwater. Swim to the south side of the slabs, and look for a similar enclosure along the south wall, in the place where the third slab (from the left) is normally found. In this second enclosure you will be able to grab two cases of RPG ammo.

## COVERT DETAILS

Table 5.12 shows the truly staggering number of secrets in Tiberius Station.

### TABLE 5.12: THE SECRETS IN TIBERIUS STATION

| AREA IN LEVEL | SECRET ITEM | HOW TO GET IT |
|---|---|---|
| The entry chamber | portable medkit | This is in a secret compartment behind a panel in the west side storage room. The panel leading to the secret room is between the two armors in the storage room. |
| | shotgun shells access to west side duct network | These are found through the exploding wall, right outside the main gate to the entry chamber. |

| AREA IN LEVEL | SECRET ITEM | HOW TO GET IT |
|---|---|---|
| The main hallway | pipe bomb cases (2) | These are in a secret area below the elevated computer room on the west side of the hallway. To get the bomb cases, you must walk through a fake wall right across from a small water fountain under the computer room. |
| | steroids chaingun ammo | These are in a secret panel to the left of the door labeled "Radioactive." |
| | RPG launcher | This is in an elevated secret panel at the northwest corner, to the right of the vertical light panel. This panel opens only for a few seconds after a sensor is tripped inside the duct across the way. That duct is only accessible through the exit chamber to the north. |
| The pool area | atomic health units (2) | These are in a secret chamber near the northwest side. To access this area, you must first cause the large metallic slabs to line up in the middle of the pool. Then you can jump in to reach the area, which is at surface level, push against the wall, and then enter the enclosure. |
| | RPG ammo (2) | You'll find these in a similar enclosure along the southeast side. |

# LUNAR REACTOR

Almost twice as large as Tiberius Station, and posing an even greater threat, the Lunar Reactor level sprawls its long hallways, assorted chambers, and multiple secrets over a vast expanse of lunar surface. Complete with crew quarters, working bathrooms, underground toxic disposal canals, a sealed-in courtyard, and crushing tunnels, Lunar Reactor places you in an environment where only your skill, keen reflexes, and intelligence can see you through. There are various places where you must perform difficult maneuvers under extreme pressure. Of course, the piece de résistance in this level is the core reactor chamber and the cinematic escape sequence.

Your objective is to seek out and destroy the core reactor. But without the yellow keycard, the reactor will remain forever sealed and out of reach. Getting the yellow keycard will test the limits of your tenacity. It lies in a tunnel in the north side of the lunar courtyard. Get there, and you will have won only half the battle. The other half requires getting back to the main installation and facing off with the Battlelord, before you blow the reactor to bits.

## MAPS AND ROUTE

It's too bad there aren't guided tours of Lunar Reactor. As you can see in Figures 5.19 and 5.20, finding your way around this level can seem overwhelming.

## THE GOODS

This is a big level. It is only fair that the goods be just as substantial. See for yourself in Table 5.13.

### TABLE 5.13: THE GOODS IN LUNAR REACTOR

| WEAPONS | AMMO | POWER-UPS |
| --- | --- | --- |
| 2 shotguns | 5 cases | 1 portable medkit |
| 1 ripper chaingun | 4 cases | 5 atomic health units |
| 2 RPG launchers | 4 cases | 2 armors |
| 1 devastator | 8 cases | 1 NVG |
| 1 shrinker | 2 crystals | 2 jetpacks |
| 1 freezethrower | | 1 pair of boots |
| 4 laser trip bombs | | 1 holoduke |
| 2 pipe bomb cases | | |

## BLAZING THROUGH LUNAR REACTOR

Even if you want to blaze through this level, you're still in for a long and perilous haul. Don't worry too much, though, just stick with the plan and you might yet make it.

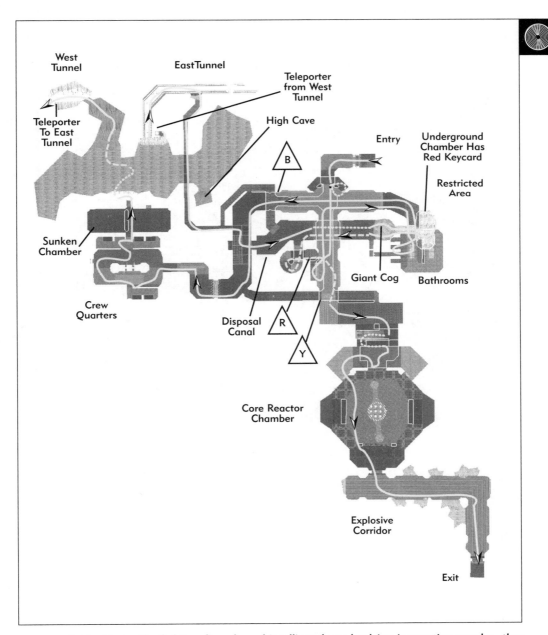

**FIGURE 5.19:** If you like fighting fiercely and intelligently and solving interesting puzzles, then you are in your element making your way through Lunar Reactor.

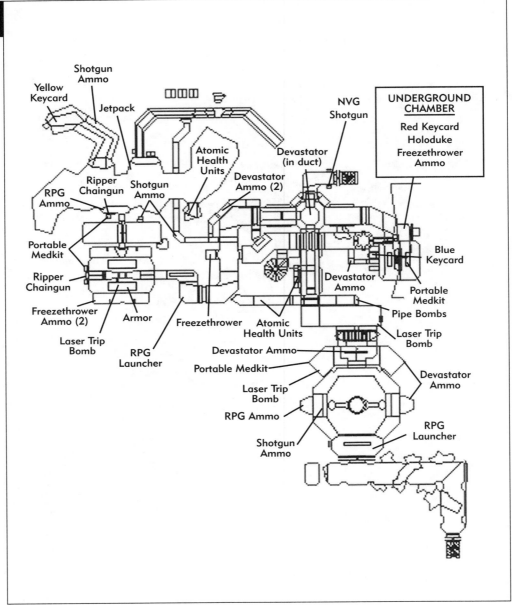

Yellow Keycard

Shotgun Ammo

Jetpack

Atomic Health Units

Devastator (in duct)

NVG Shotgun

UNDERGROUND CHAMBER

Red Keycard
Holoduke
Freezethrower Ammo

Devastator Ammo (2)

RPG Ammo

Ripper Chaingun

Shotgun Ammo

Portable Medkit

Blue Keycard

Ripper Chaingun

Devastator Ammo

Portable Medkit

Freezethrower Ammo (2)

Armor

Freezethrower

Atomic Health Units

Pipe Bombs

Laser Trip Bomb

Laser Trip Bomb

RPG Launcher

Devastator Ammo

Devastator Ammo

Portable Medkit

Laser Trip Bomb

RPG Ammo

RPG Launcher

Shotgun Ammo

**FIGURE 5.20:** Lunar Reactor boasts a bevy of booty.

## In the Entry and the Restricted Area

1. **Explore the ducts.** If you were to venture out immediately, you would find your access blocked by keycard gates in every direction except to the restricted area (to the east). Therefore, it behooves you to see how far you can go in the ducts. But even before that, take the shotgun and the NVG in the small compartment just outside the entry chamber. Then jump into either one of the ducts to the left or right as you come out to the spot where the corridors converge. You will have to clear the area of protozoid slimers, as they thrive in dark, moist places. Grab the shells and pipe bombs.

2. **Continue moving through the ducts.** Now stand in the middle of the ducts, face south, and jump forward to reach a higher space in the duct network. Reward your efforts with the devastator you just found. Continue north along the corridor and drop into a small space that branches off to the right. You will come upon an atomic health unit. Take the unit and kick the duct grill to emerge just outside the core reactor door.

3. **Fell an assault commander.** With your health properly boosted and you now holding a devastator, head toward the crew quarters. Open the door and be ready to take down the assault commander behind the door.

4. **Grab the blue keycard in the bathroom.** Storm the bathroom at the end of the restricted area. Clear the path of enforcers and their trooper underlings. Then explore the two stalls near to the entrance to collect a laser trip bomb, and most importantly, the blue keycard that grants you access to the crew quarters.

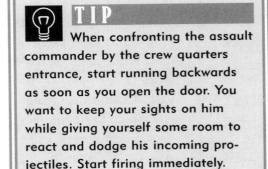

**TIP**

When confronting the assault commander by the crew quarters entrance, start running backwards as soon as you open the door. You want to keep your sights on him while giving yourself some room to react and dodge his incoming projectiles. Start firing immediately.

## In the Crew Quarters

1. **Penetrate deep.** Use the blue keycard in the crew quarters latch to the west. Follow the wide hallway and come upon a grilled section of the floor. If you have any, drop a pipe bomb or three down the grill to

fry a few protozoid slimers in their juice before they come bouncing after you. Also, fend off any sentry drones patrolling this area.

2. **Ransack the crew's sleeping and slumming quarters.** Open yet another gate labeled "Crew Quarters" and run for the RPG launcher in front of you. Enter the commons area, and battle your way to the north end where you can grab a ripper chaingun and other goodies from the adjacent cabinets. After grabbing the ripper chaingun, you will almost have to empty its contents on the encroaching aliens. Also, check out the closets for additional items.

3. **Reach the underground sandwich chamber.** Direct your attention to the sleeping chambers on the north side of the crew's quarters. Find the open chute between the cots, and drop into a small restricted space in a flooded and large underground chamber. Seemingly trapped, you must cross the chamber toward the duct directly north of your position.

4. **Reach the north courtyard.** Activate the switch in the small space, and run straight across as fast as possible while the giant metal slabs come apart temporarily. You have a matter of mere seconds to make it across. Avoid a wily coyote scene by stopping in your tracks as soon as you reach the grill. Otherwise, you could be plummeting to a precipitous fall and get to see the bottom of the north courtyard face first.

## In the North Courtyard

1. **Make it to the north side.** As soon as possible, take out the turret across the chasm. Then take the RPG ammo nearby and the portable medkit in the compartment by the console. If you have a jetpack, you're in good shape. If not, you will have to get the one at the bottom of the courtyard. This means taking a fall. Luckily, you have a portable medkit with you. So be brave and plunge into the open space below. Then collect the jetpack and elevate yourself to find a wide opening along the mountainside. Land in there and take the yellow keycard near the entrance.

2. **Teleport to the tunnel on the east side.** Now you are ready to get back to the main installation area and go in search of the reactor. However, there is the small matter of reaching the south side of the courtyard. Penetrate all the way to the end of the marble-like tunnel, and pick up

the shrinker crystals along the way. Don't be too discouraged by the sight of a mangled human body hanging upside down. At the very end of the tunnel, you will see a teleporter. Get on it and emerge on the eastern platform.

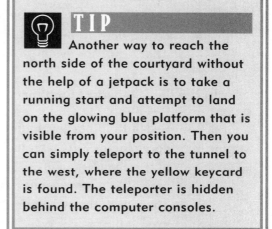

**TIP** Another way to reach the north side of the courtyard without the help of a jetpack is to take a running start and attempt to land on the glowing blue platform that is visible from your position. Then you can simply teleport to the tunnel to the west, where the yellow keycard is found. The teleporter is hidden behind the computer consoles.

3. **Collapse the tunnel.** Start into the tunnel, but be very cautious. Dispose of the small armada of troopers who will come barreling down the tunnel. When you feel the first set of tremors, you should stop on your feet. As you reach the middle section of the tunnel, entire sections will begin to crumble in succession. Get out of the way of crushing rocks by standing near the edges of the tunnel or, better yet, by running back near the entrance. The rock shifting will cause the south wall of the tunnel to blow open a hole where a duct is conveniently accessible.

4. **Get back via the duct network.** Enter through the duct and cross right over the courtyard back into the main installation. The duct will lead you directly to the area below the grill floor in the hallway outside the crew quarters.

5. **Get the red keycard.** Jump into the disposal canal and follow its downward slope. You will go past an opening on the right side leading to a spiral staircase and toward a giant turning cog. It will do you no good to run up the staircase without the red keycard. So keep going toward the cog. Stop when you are close to the turning cog. Synchronize your movement with the cog, and place yourself in one of its recesses. Then just let it turn you like a revolving door into the eastern end. You will happen upon an underground computer chamber containing the red keycard as well as a holoduke and freezethrower ammo.

6. **Ascend the spiral staircase.** Go back through the cog in the same way you came in. Trudge up the canal to find the opening along the left wall leading to the staircase. Enter and climb. Use the red keycard when you reach the top to emerge right outside the core reactor quarters. Use the yellow keycard to enter the core reactor chamber.

7. **Cream the Battlelord.** The entrance to the reactor chamber is guarded by a Battlelord. Leave yourself plenty of room to retreat. Because the area is dark, you might also want to break out your NVG. Jump over the dead heap, and enter the core reactor chamber.

## In the Core Reactor Chamber

1. **Reach the floor level and blow up the core reactor.** Go down the flight of stairs in the chamber's entry. Clear the floor area of as many enemies as possible. Then press the switch on the right side to expose the reactor core. A single rocket at the power source should cause it to blow up and take the southern door with it.

2. **Get out quickly.** Go through the hole in the door into a steel gray corridor. Without a moment's hesitation, hoist the RPG, and run eastward to catch a couple of hovering assault commanders in midair as the entire hallway begins to explode behind you.

If you move fast enough, you will see the hallway exploding behind you in the mirror at the far end of the hallway. If you have survived all of this, all that remains to do is to punch the exit switch.

## ADDED ATTRACTIONS IN LUNAR REACTOR

There are plenty of moments during your mission in Lunar Reactor that bear a closer look. One such scenario unfolds when you reach the north courtyard.

### Strolling in the Lunar Courtyard

Besides the compelling reasons to visit the courtyard (fun, challenge, and adventure), you really have no choice. The yellow keycard, which unlocks the core reactor chamber, is found in a remote cave along the courtyard's north mountainside. You need this keycard so you can destroy the reactor and find the exit.

There is only one way to reach the north courtyard. That involves reaching the underground chamber just north of the crew's sleeping quarters. The chute between the cots lets you drop inside the chamber. Once there, timing and execution are essential. You must cross the chamber to reach a narrow platform overlooking the courtyard from its south side. If you don't feel particularly perky, ingest some steroids before punching the switch in front of you. As the metal slabs part momentarily, you have seconds to cross the chamber and reach the grill at the north end.

Apply the breaks as soon as you reach the grill. By now, the metal slabs will have joined again in the middle of the chamber. Kick the grill and come out into the narrow platform. Take out the few troopers gathered there, and destroy the turret mounted on the mountainside across the courtyard. Collect the RPG ammo and the ripper chain-gun inside the compartment. Now it's time to make some tough decisions. Your decisions will be narrowed down by one factor: Do you have a jetpack? If not, you should try to jump the chasm to land on the blue platform visible below and to the right from your position. If you have a jetpack, you can hover directly across to the cavernous opening due northwest to reach the western tunnel where the yellow keycard can be found. Going directly is no problem. Start the jetpack and hover up a few dozen feet and head northwest.

To get the keycard the hard way, give yourself every inch to take a running jump onto the platform. Should you miss the platform entirely, be ready to activate your portable medkit as you start to plummet. With any luck, you will survive the fall and be able to collect a jetpack at the bottom of the canyon. Assuming you make it to the platform, resist entering the tunnel. Instead, access the hidden teleporter behind the computer console, and emerge inside the other tunnel on the west side. You will come out facing the gruesome sight of a slightly dismembered human hanging upside down from a rope. Go toward the entrance of the tunnel and take the keycard. Then return to the teleporter.

Back on the east side platform, proceed inside the tunnel, but move with utmost care. First, resist any temptation to run. You will only cause the tunnel to collapse and crush you like a bug. Instead, as you reach the mid point along the tunnel's length, stop to riddle with bullets the thick crowds of troopers rushing you from the tunnel's far side. As you reach an area where a rock juts out from the tunnel's top side, and as you begin to hear deep rumblings, start running back.

Entire sections of the tunnel will collapse in a matter of seconds. If you cannot get back fast enough, try standing near the wall to avoid the falling slabs. When the rumblings and aftershocks subside, find the new opening along the south wall of the tunnel. It is an access point to a duct that crosses over to the south side of the canyon. Hop in and pray for a better tomorrow.

**DISC DEMO**
Take in the walk-through file for this level and see what timing is all about. Load E2L7.BLZ from the CD-ROM.

## COVERT DETAILS

Table 5.14 bares every secret in Lunar Reactor.

| TABLE 5.14: THE SECRETS IN THE LUNAR REACTOR | | |
| --- | --- | --- |
| **AREA IN LEVEL** | **SECRET ITEM** | **HOW TO GET IT** |
| Underground chamber at the end of the disposal canal | freezer charges (2) holoduke | These are behind the secret partition in the east wall of the chamber. The only way to reach the disposal canal is via a long duct, starting at the eastern tunnel in the canyon. |
| West side and around the canyon | teleporter | It's behind the rock enclosure at the very end of the canyon's western tunnel. The teleporter places you east at the platform entrance to the collapsing tunnel. |
| | armor RPG ammo atomic health unit | These are in a high location, which you can only hover to, if you posses the jetpack. |
| | ripper chaingun portable medkit | These are behind the computer panel on the elevated platform, just north of the sunken chamber. |
| Sunken chamber | atomic health units | These are behind the secret compartment in the southeast pillar in the corner. |
| | RPG ammo | You can find this on a similar platform on the west side of the chamber. |

# THE DARK SIDE

The Alpha, Beta, and Gamma transports—subway-like boxcars—converge in a central hub. But The Dark Side is a crossroads in more ways than a literal one. It is also your link to Spin Cycle, one of the two secret levels in the Lunar Apocalypse episode— if you're clever enough to find the secret exit. The Dark Side is also a place where you might become closer to your own soul as you ponder some very deep questions. For instance, where did the buried monolith come from? What sort of intelligence created it and planted it? For what purpose was it planted, and how long ago? And why are so many women hanging upside down or found in otherwise compromising positions? Oh, the horror and the wonder of it all, baby.

Besides exploring a morgue, blowing up a reactor chamber, visiting a collapsing cave, and taking many free subway rides, you also get to go for a moon walk in The Dark

Side. An immense lunar crater is the backdrop for a battle scene involving flocks of darting drones.

You can approach The Dark Side from two angles. You can either set out to find the secret exit and make the rounds in Spin Cycle, or you can go on a longer ride, filled with more danger and possibilities, to reach the regular exit and move on to the next level. To reach the secret exit, you have to gain access to the Gamma transport. That requires you to reach the top level of the central hub. But without the blue keycard, you won't be able to reach the second floor (unless you have a jetpack).

For most people, getting to the top involves visiting the morgue at the end of the Alpha route to get the blue keycard. The story to reach the normal exit follows the same script. However, you must also obtain the yellow keycard from the reactor chamber. This entails a subway ride in the Gamma transport. After that, you're free to board the Beta station and meet your fate in the lunar crater to the north.

## MAPS AND ROUTE

If you enjoy traveling, come along for a trip on The Dark Side. Figures 5.21 and 5.22 show you the routes and connections. But *you* are responsible for your own itinerary.

## THE GOODS

You will find, as you might have already suspected, that The Dark Side has its goods too. There are plenty to tempt the most righteous among us. Check out Table 5.15.

### TABLE 5.15: THE GOODS IN THE DARK SIDE

| WEAPONS | AMMO | POWER-UPS |
| --- | --- | --- |
| 1 shotgun | 9 cases | 2 portable medkits |
| 2 ripper chainguns | 2 cases | 7 atomic health units |
| 2 RPG launchers | 5 cases | 5 armors |
| 3 devastators | 6 cases | 1 steroid flask |
| 3 shrinkers | 3 crystals | 1 NVG |
| 1 freezethrower | | 1 jetpack |
| 1 laser trip bomb | | 1 holoduke |
| 7 pipe bomb cases | | 1 pair of boots |

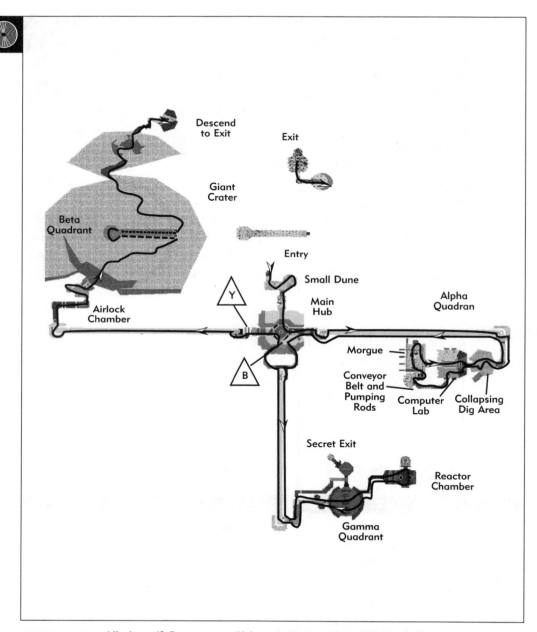

FIGURE 5.21: All aboard? Brace yourself for a hell of a ride in The Dark Side.

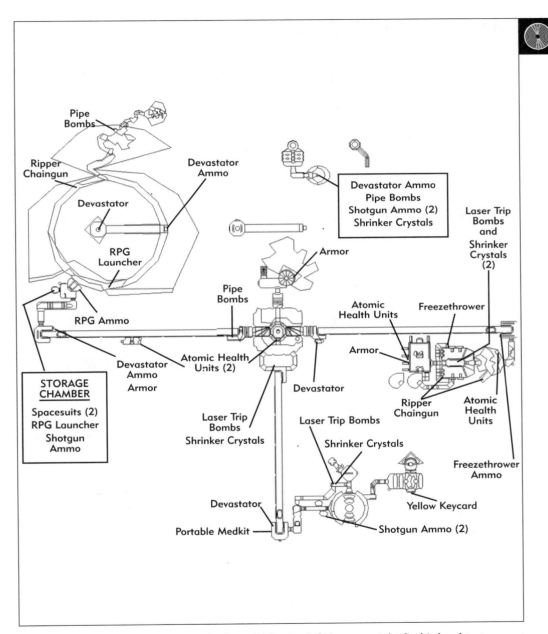

**FIGURE 5.22:** After experiencing the lure of The Dark Side, you might find it hard to tear away and go back to normal life.

# BLAZING THROUGH THE DARK SIDE

Whether you want to get to the secret level or complete the Lunar Reactor in its entirety, you must still complete the first leg of the trip. And speaking of extremities, you are about to cover what will seem like miles of territory. See you on the other side, wherever that turns out to be.

## In the Small Dome

1. **Get armored.** Losing no time as you come out the entry door, take out the eggs in the domed room before their slimy hatchling crawl out. Dispense with the enforcer too. Then take the armor, and ride the small platform up to the hub level.

2. **Shoot it out at the hub.** Emerging from the platform, grab the nearby shotgun, and tear through a duo of troopers. Then head for the door to the south and open it. Accommodate the sentry drones and enforcers as best you can. Notice there is also the freezethrower directly ahead. Run straight for it and then use it to freeze the enforcers in their tracks. Check the secret compartment behind the panel to get an atomic health unit.

## In the Alpha Quadrant

1. **Take the Alpha route.** You really have no choice but to take this route, as it is the only way you can possibly go without any of the keycards. Before boarding, pick up the case of pipe bombs. Then push the large switch by the dock to beckon the transporter. At the end of the route, collect two shrinker crystals before proceeding into the collapsible dig at the end of the hallway.

2. **Deal with the pressure.** As you come upon the seemingly tranquil dig, notice the lasers crisscrossing the room. You don't have to violate the lasers to cause a shake-up. Step in a few feet and back out immediately as the dig in front of you collapses and shifts shape. Drop a few pipe bombs to dispose of the enforcers hiding in the crevices. Then explore the dig to collect all manner of goods, including devastator ammo, atomic

health, and even a ripper chaingun. Then go into the computer lab behind the blue door.

3.  **Take over the lab, and ride the waste conveyor belt .** Sorry. There's just no other way to get to the morgue. (How's that for an ultimate destination?) Storm in pouring lead on all present at the lab, which is divided into left and right chambers with a central corridor. In the left chamber, jump and then squat to get inside the conveyor belt. You will come upon a series of heavy pistons whose function seems all too clear. Clear the pillars by stopping in your tracks and dashing forward just as the piston begins to ascend. You'll wind up plunging into a disgusting tank of assorted refuse.

4.  **Get to the morgue on time.** Don't hang down there for too long. Besides a few ferocious octabrains, there really isn't much else to see. Jump out as soon as you can, and take the small platform up to the morgue.

5.  **Bounce some bodies and score the blue keycard.** As you reach for the blue keycard, a sensor triggers open the body chambers lining the walls of the room. Within seconds, the morgue will be crawling with protozoid slimers. Hose the place down with your ripper chaingun. Then collect the goods inside the body chambers. (See Figure 5.23.)

**DISC DEMO**

Do you want to see what it's like to jump on a waste conveyor belt that moves whatever is on it through a series of crushing pistons? You just might because, sooner or later, you will find yourself in the same position, and hopefully not flattened. The file you need to load from the CD-ROM is E2L8.BLZ.

6.  **Head back to the hub.** Pound your way through the crowd of enforcers. The devastator is your best bet.

FIGURE 5.23: Squish, squeal, and squirm. Clear the morgue of protozoid slimers, once you grab the blue keycard.

## In the Gamma Quadrant

1. **Get upstairs.** Use your newly acquired blue keycard in the wall switch, and ride the elevator to the second floor. Collect the NVG and armor, and proceed to the door on the west side.

2. **Get loaded.** Enter the Gamma transport station and look behind the route map on the wall to collect a shrinker and some laser trip bombs. Summon the transport, and, at the end of the route, be sure to claim the devastator ammo and the portable medkit.

3. **Make a momentous decision.** Do you want to get to the secret exit or hang out and continue searching for the main exit? To go on ahead, go on to the next step.

4. **Venture in the tunnel.** But only go in a few feet to avoid the ensuing explosion. The place is rigged. Back up and pummel the enforcers. Then proceed into the large pit chamber.

5. **Build a bridge and cross the pit.** Take out as many octabrains before hitting the switch that moves the metal blocks in the pit to align down its center. Cross over to the other side, and head toward the reactor chamber.

6. **Destroy the reactor to claim the yellow keycard.** Upon entering the chamber, take out the snipers across the room on the elevated computer panel that also holds the yellow keycard. Don't go in too far, for you might run into not one but two assault commanders. Should they come after you, don't be too concerned about saving devastator ammo. Standing at a safe distance from the reactor room, aim the RPG at its crown. Pull the trigger, jump out of the way of the crashing ceiling, and then climb over the rubble to get the yellow keycard.

7. **Trace your steps back.** Collect yourself and find your way back to the transport, and ride it back to the main hub. You are ready to enter the Beta quadrant.

## In the Beta Quadrant

1. **Enter the Beta transport.** Slap the keycard on the entrance, and cash your ticket to enter the Beta

**TIP**

However, if you want to make short work of it and visit the Spin Cycle, as quickly as possible, here is what you can do. Avoid the door and go through the duct. Follow its steep ascent until you come to a sudden drop off into a gruesome pit, where many of Earth's females have been desecrated. Contend with the contemptuous heard of octabrains and then blow a hole into the crack of the wall at the northeast corner. Run up into the tunnel you dug, where you will come upon the secret exit. Spin Cycle, here you go!

**WARNING**

The radiation levels in the reactor room are very harmful, and you will feel instantly debilitated if you stand too close. After you destroy the reactor, the ceiling of the control chamber comes crushing down. This means that after making impact with the reactor, you should do your best to get out of the way of the crashing ceiling by running toward the entrance.

quadrant. At the end of the ride, pick up the devastator ammo and watch out for the sentry drone.

2. **Bust into the airlock chambers.** Rip through the aliens standing guard, and look behind the desk for freezethrower ammo. Look in the storage chamber on the east side, and take a space suit, the freezer ammo, and the RPG launcher. Then take your stuff with you to the airlock cage, and step out into an impressive vista of a huge lunar crater with a man-made, crane-like structure rising high above the crater's center, which is very much like a parabolic antenna.

3. **Pick off sentry drones like clay discs.** The dots growing suddenly larger across the lunar sky are sentry drones homing in on you. Douse them with an assortment of devastator charges, rockets and even shotgun blasts. When the coast is clear, cut a path straight for the bottom of the giant crane.

4. **Deactivate the force field.** Ride the lift to the top of the crane structure. Inside the circular chamber at the very top, you will find a devastator and the switch that turns off the field barring access to the level's exit.

5. **Go through the crack and dig up your own tunnel.** Get back to the crater's ground level, and dash toward the crack directly due north. Proceed cautiously and don't let the assault commander at the end keep you from your goal. Drop a pipe bomb inside the small cave-like aperture, and detonate a hole through the rock.

6. **Confront the object of someone's desire.** Follow the newly dug tunnel into a dark chamber holding a half-buried rectangular structure. Don't succumb to the eerie, alien atmosphere and fight the real alien presence all around you. Postpone your awe for a second, and jump right into the monolith. Doesn't it seem like the only sane thing to do?

## On the Other Side

1. **Just be glad you're alive.** But you're still not out of The Dark Side. Take the shrinker and any other useful stuff around the strangely organic

emerald chamber. Obviously, the upside down human females suspended by the walls aren't simply decoration. Follow the short hallway into a circular chamber with a water tank at its center.

2. **Freeze-dry your way out.** As you cross the path of the small chamber, a swarm of octabrains descends from the chamber's top. Back off and freeze the house down. Then break everyone's heart, and jump in the pool. Look for the exit switch, and don't look back.

## ADDED ATTRACTIONS IN THE DARK SIDE

It's hard to pick a single feature of The Dark Side to elaborate upon further or examine closer. But there is a technique that you can master now, and who knows, maybe you will put it to use later in similarly tight situations.

### Getting Off of a Moving Train

Why would anyone in their right mind ever want to jump off a fast moving train? Stupidity? Thrill-seeking? Suicidal tendencies? Overdue car payments? Receding hairline? Go figure. One good reason to do it in the Beta quadrant is if you're in desperate need of a health boost. Another might be that the enemies waiting for you at the end of the route are overwhelming and you want to postpone the meeting a little longer. For whatever reason you might want to jump off, if you can jump directly into a small wall recess, you will have two atomic heath units for your troubles and near-death experience.

If you see yourself in the dire need to jump off the train, there is something you can do to cushion the fall. It involves using your cushion. That is to say, your butt. As the train picks up speed, position yourself so that your back is towards the door and you are facing the transporter's switch. Maintain a firm pressure against your back. The ride may be bumpy, especially on your back side. But if you keep trying to push off and back out, as it were, when the crevice on the south wall and the transporter intersect, bingo. You will more than likely pop out of the train like a cork off a bottle of foaming champagne. Okay, maybe more like the bottle cap off a cheap beer. But you get the picture. You will be inside a dark little cove with two glowing atomic heath units and a teleporter booth.

## COVERT DETAILS

For its impressive dimensions, there's only a handful of secrets in the Dark Side, but they are juicy ones at that, as Table 5.16 indicates.

### TABLE 5.16: THE SECRETS IN THE DARK SIDE

| AREA IN LEVEL | SECRET ITEM | HOW TO GET IT |
|---|---|---|
| The Gamma quadrant | secret exit to the Spin Cycle (one of two secret levels in this episode) | You literally have to blow a hole in the northwest wall of the crims on pit that contains the females impaled on giant stakes. |
| The Alpha quadrant | devastator | Blow a hole in the wall by the boarding area to reach it. |
| | ripper chaingun and freezethrower | You will find these inside water holders in the computer lab. The steel panel right by the table near the canisters is a secret door that takes you inside the wall so you can claim the goods. |
| The main hub | atomic health unit | You will find this behind the map, inside the covered area in the main hub. You must push it open and then crouch below to gain access. |
| The Beta quadrant | teleporter cubbyhole | This teleporter is halfway down the path from the main hub to the end of the Beta station. You must jump off the transport to get there. |

# OVERLORD

There had to be moments when you doubted if you would make it this far. Overlord closes down the Lunar Apocalypse episode with a giant exclamation mark. Of course, there are two secret levels that you can venture into if you haven't already.

What manner of beast is this Overlord? If its shape and organic quality seem somewhat familiar, you might recall the gem you found encrusted in the rocks of The Abyss, at the memorable conclusion of the L.A. Meltdown episode. It seems as though you're aboard one such alien ship. Your fears will be confirmed when you reach the egg-laden, octagonal chamber and witness a massive cannon aiming a concentrated energy beam at California's San Andreas Fault. The eggs and their slimy hosts will seem like a minor distraction, when you consider you're actually sharing the floor with the boss for this episode, the sanguine and completely charmless Moon Assault Leader. Also, early in this level, the Battlelord makes a cameo appearance.

## MAPS AND ROUTE

Hop aboard the decisively alien construction of spaceship Overlord. Figures 5.24 and 5.25 help you make sense of the structure's layout.

## THE GOODS

There is much to see and much to lay your hands on in this level, and you will need every bit of it. Table 5.17 lays out the goods in Overlord.

### TABLE 5.17 THE GOODS IN OVERLORD

| WEAPONS | AMMO | POWER-UPS |
|---|---|---|
| 1 shotgun | 5 cases | 1 portable medkit |
| 1 ripper chaingun | 1 case | 4 atomic health units |
| 1 RPG launcher | 5 cases | 1 armor |
| 3 devastators | 3 cases | 2 scuba gear sets |
| 1 shrinker | 2 crystals | 1 jetpack |
| 1 freezethrower | | 1 NVG |
| 1 laser trip bomb | | 1 holoduke |
| 1 pipe bomb case | | |

## BLAZING THROUGH OVERLORD

There are both lightening fast and more involved ways of reaching your final destination in Overlord. But either way, you must eventually arrive at the same place, inside the large octagonal saucer section. After that you and the histrionic Moon Assault Leader get to exchange bows in a dance of life and death.

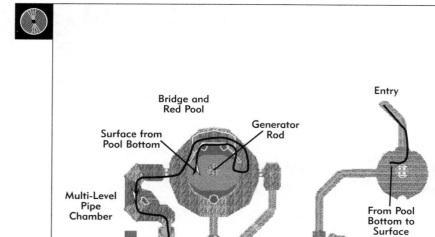
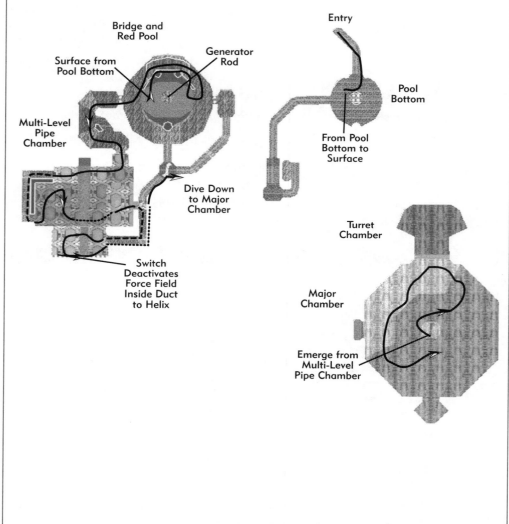

**FIGURE 5.24:** You're a virtual stowaway in Overlord. Try not to get discovered too quickly.

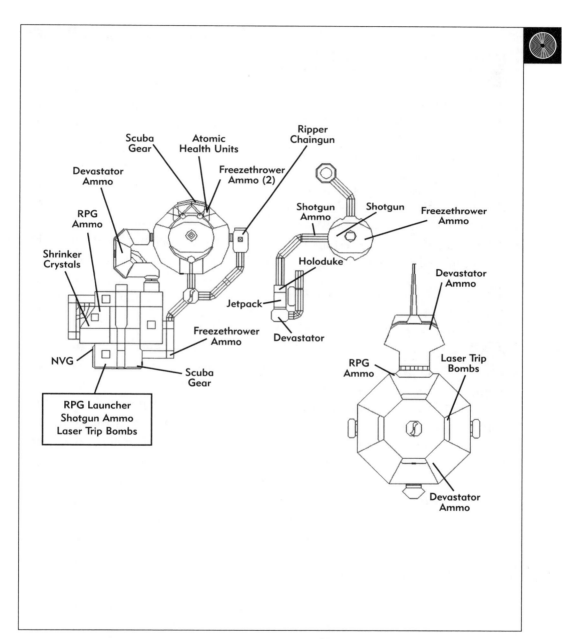

**FIGURE 5.25:** Overlord marks the end of a cycle and the start of something huge. Hopefully, your own cycle will continue to make the rounds.

**NOTE**

If you have a jetpack and want to make short work of this level, find the circular duct at the south end of the bridge, blow a hole in it, and enter it with the aid of a jetpack. You'll come upon a rotating helix in the middle of large silo-like space. If this is indeed the case for you, skip the remaining steps and refer to the section headed *In the Major Chamber*.

**TIP**

Although your first impulse might be to face off against the Battlelord, it might be more prudent to save your strength for the real boss in this level. One useful technique involves drawing the Battlelord out onto the bridge and then simply locking him there. Blow up the C-9 canister next to him and run back to the bridge. (The explosion also blows a tunnel right through the wall.) Encourage the Battlelord to give chase. The lack of room to move will force him to go into the pool. This is what you want. Run into the eastern chamber, and close the door behind you.

## On the Bridge and in the Pool Area

1. **Build your arsenal.** Before emerging onto the bridge, look for two cylindrical pillars at the north end of the pool. Stick your upper body out of the water so you can breath normally, and run straight for the secret horseshoe-shaped crawl space. You can enter through what looks like solid wall right next to each pillar. (The wall between the pillars is solid.) Take the healing atom and the two freezethrower charges.

2. **Take the goods from the bridge.** Storm the bridge and collect all manner of goods, including the scuba gear by the control panels. Activate the combination switches to lower the generator rod. From left to right, the four switches should be set as follows: on, off, on, and on. When the rod lowers to the right height, jump on top of its small surface and capture the freezethrower.

3. **Head for the multilevel pipe chamber.** Upon entering through the door on the west side and turning the second corner, you will have to contend

with the Battlelord. If you are not well armed for the occasion, you can try to get past him.

## In the Multilevel Pipe Chamber

1. **Hose the place down.** Before you can venture too far into the multilevel pipe chamber, you will come under fire from troopers, assault captains, and enforcers in every direction. Rely heavily on the ripper chaingun for long-distance engagements. Then whip out the shotgun in closer struggles.

2. **Get on top.** Cross the narrow water canal, and work your way toward the stairs on the west side. Climb to a floor area where you can get a shrinker. Turn eastward and drop onto a lower floor area to reach the eastern stairs. Take these stairs to reach the highest floor level in the chamber. Collect the RPG launcher, and most importantly, throw the switch at the very southwest corner, behind the unfortunate young maiden.

3. **Find the helix silo.** Get back down the first flight of stairs, and bash the duct grill to access it. You will come upon the breathtaking view of an imposing cylindrical opening with a floating helix spinning below you.

4. **Take a plunge for humanity.** This is the only way into the major chamber. Dive below and do your best to avoid the massive turning blades of the helix.

## In the Major Chamber

1. **Blow up the eggs.** Without moving from your landing position, aim at one of the explosive canisters by the large circle of alien eggs around you. The ensuing chain reaction will scramble the eggs beyond recognition. Avoid stepping over gooey egg remains as you collect every possible weapon, before facing the dreaded Moon Assault Leader.

2.  **Unleash the Moon Assault Leader, and put an end to Lunar Apocalypse.** Flip the hand print switch to the turret chamber, and pummel the Moon Assault Leader with every rocket you can release before he has a chance to react.

After that, it's open warfare. Your wit and speed can see you through.

## ADDED ATTRACTIONS IN OVERLORD

By far the most shocking, dangerous, and inevitable encounter in Overlord is the tête-à-tête with the notoriously vicious Moon Assault Leader, the big, bad boss of Overlord.

### Downing the Overlord Boss

The gargantuan rocket-launching Moon Assault Leader is not your average adversary. You have to hit him with everything but the flower pot to bring him down. Therefore, it makes sense to avail yourself of every chance to inflict pain upon him. As for your saving your own skin, you really haven't got many defenses in the way of hardware. However, your mind can churn out enough cycles per second to outdo the reptilian brain in the hulking body of the Moon Assault Leader.

If up to this point you haven't used up all your laser trip bombs, deploy them all where they can harm the Moon Assault Leader but not you. This means you should place them high along the threshold of the chamber where the untamed alien beast is kept. You want to be able to run or crouch under the laser projections and give the Moon Assault Leader a massive headache. This sounds great, you say, but without a jetpack you're as good as minced meat. Don't fret too much. Luckily, a jetpack and a devastator are within reach.

To get the jetpack and the devastator, find the crack along the west side of the major chamber and jump into the water enclosure. Emerge into a J-shaped tunnel that turns into a very large tank, at the bottom of which is the sought-after jetpack. Venture further north into an even larger water tank, and claim the devastator from the clutches of the octabrains. Then head back to the major chamber.

Use your jetpack to deploy vertical rows of tightly packed laser trip bombs. This maneuver is delicate and requires precision moves. Put off the double lattes for awhile. Once you've deployed your laser trip bombs along both sides of the threshold in the major chamber, deploy the holoduke at the south end, if you have it. Then carpet the area just outside the door with as many pipe bombs as you have. Now comes the moment of truth: Open the turret door at the north end, and run backwards immediately. As the Moon Assault Leader comes into view, wait a second for him to set off the laser trip bombs, and, at the same time, detonate the pipe bombs with one big bang.

Pull out the RPG launcher and feed a steady pounding to the Moon Assault Leader before he has a chance to fire off a rocket or stomp you like a bug. If you have any steroids left, swallow them. Play a lethal game of keep-away and take every opportunity to unload your weaponry. There is no sense in holding back; you won't have another chance. With

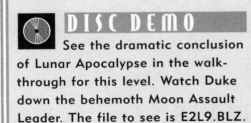

**DISC DEMO**
See the dramatic conclusion of Lunar Apocalypse in the walk-through for this level. Watch Duke down the behemoth Moon Assault Leader. The file to see is E2L9.BLZ. Get it from the CD-ROM.

any luck, the Moon Assault Leader will be confused by the holoduke at the south end. You can take this opportunity to get inside the turret chamber, where you can continue pounding the Moon Assault Leader from the rear. If it becomes necessary, you can close the heavy gate to take refuge from the oncoming rain of rockets. Hopefully, by this point, you will have inflicted enough damage on the heinous beast to be able to knock him completely with a few more RPGs. The freezethrower can also be instrumental in delivering the final blow.

No one can blame or judge you too harshly for what you will do to the Moon Assault Leader after his limp, but still warm body bounces to the floor. After all, what the aliens are doing to human females does not exactly speak of gentility. Meanwhile, back on Earth . . .

## COVERT DETAILS

Not exactly overflowing in the secrets department, the Overlord level still offers some nifty finds, as shown in Table 5.18.

### TABLE 5.18: THE SECRETS IN OVERLORD

| AREA IN LEVEL | SECRET ITEMS | HOW TO GET IT |
|---|---|---|
| Bridge and pool | atomic health unit freezethrower ammo | Go through the secret wall openings beside the pillars at the north end of the red pool. |
| | atomic health unit | Inside the pool, find the hand print switch along the south pillar. Activate it to cause the entire pillar to lift and reveal an opening that you can actually swim through as you collect the atomic health unit. |

*(Continued on next page)*

*(Continued from previous page)*

| AREA IN LEVEL | SECRET ITEMS | HOW TO GET IT |
|---|---|---|
| Major chamber | RPG ammo<br>atomic health unit | Activate the hand print switch on the map panel in the turret chamber. Then rush back to the south end to climb into a secret chamber in the wall. |

# SPIN CYCLE

A strong stomach and a robust constitution are vital if you want to complete Spin Cycle on your feet. This, the first secret level in Lunar Apocalypse, could be fanciful and reminiscent of cotton-candy and childhood days riding the merry-go-round at the carnival. Spin Cycle, however, is far from such innocence; it is more of a romp for spirited multiplayer battles than the type of level you would normally encounter in solo matches. But even if you are playing it alone, Spin Cycle still delivers plenty of fun and thrills.

Spin Cycle's design is simplicity itself—it offers a central, circular dome surrounded by a wide, rotating band that spins incessantly counterclockwise. That is it! Around the periphery, there are four narrow walkways that follow the great circle's contour. These walkways appear incidental, as though they were put there as an afterthought. But in reality, you can cling to life and find refuge in these areas from the onslaught you will most definitely experience near the center of the structure.

The centrifugal force of the spinning band in Spin Cycle is real enough. Any time you set foot on it, you will feel its effects. Simple movement will seem hard, almost as though you were twice as heavy. This same undeniable physical force also affects your weapons and their projectiles. This means that you will have to compensate for your acceleration as you aim and fire at your opponents, whose weapons are also affected in the same way. But hovering opponents like the assault commander, assault troopers and captains, and sentry drones are all capable of canceling the centrifugal force by their ability to hover and fly.

## MAPS AND ROUTE

If you were to slice Spin Cycle into four equal pieces, you would see that each one is identical to all the others. But in spite of its very basic architecture, as you can see in Figures 5.26 and 5.27, and its void of secret passageways or hidden chambers, Spin

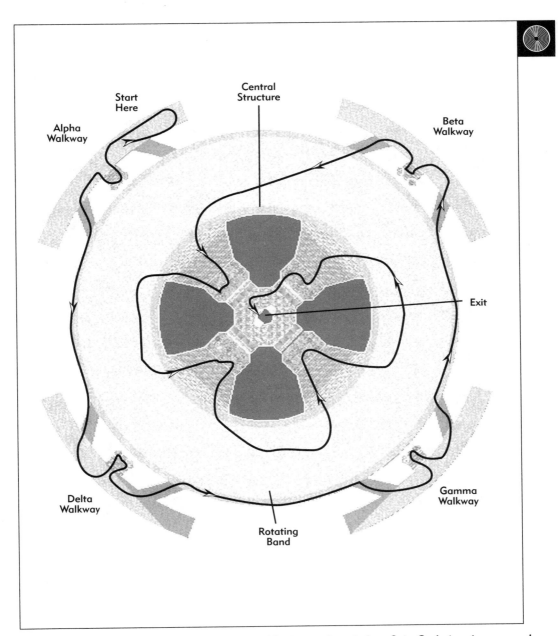

**FIGURE 5.26**: Throw deductive reasoning and logic out the window. Spin Cycle is prime ground for unabashed skull bashing.

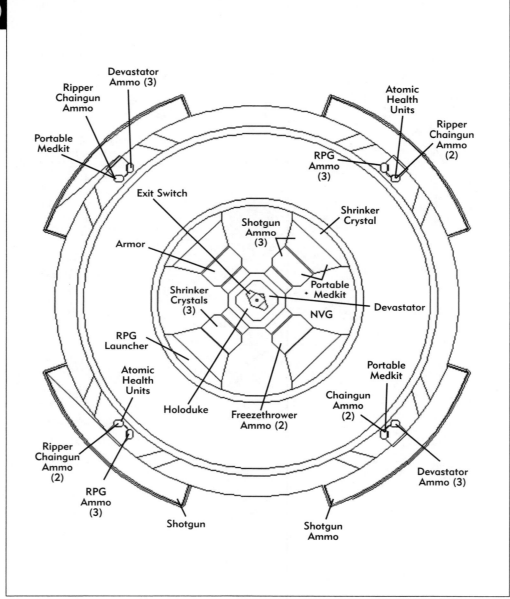

**FIGURE 5.27:** Do yourself a favor and explore the peripheral walkways for their weapons and power-ups before you step on the spinning band.

Cycle, by virtue of its cruel inhabitants, can make a person look for a new circle of friends.

## THE GOODS

Spin Cycle brims over with weapons and more than a stockpile of ammo. The amount of power-ups in this level is also respectable. Table 5.19 catalogs the goods you can get in this level.

| TABLE 5.19: THE GOODS IN SPIN CYCLE | | |
|---|---|---|
| **WEAPONS** | **AMMO** | **POWER-UPS** |
| 2 shotguns | 5 cases | 3 portable medkits |
| 1 ripper chaingun | 8 cases | 2 atomic health units |
| 1 RPG launcher | 6 cases | 1 armor |
| 1 devastator | 6 cases | 1 NVG |
| 2 shrinkers | 3 crystals | 1 holoduke |
| 1 freezethrower | | |

## BLAZING THROUGH SPIN CYCLE

There really is not one particular way of solving Spin Cycle. In fact, there really aren't any puzzles to solve. The exit is in the central structure. All you have to do is unlock all of the gates. Then waltz inside and push the exit switch. "Waltz," however is only a figure of speech. Actually, most of the dancing in this level occurs around the ever-spinning band. There are four external gates, which are plainly visible from the periphery. There are also four internal gates. The spaces between the gates serve to contain pockets of your loathsome alien foes.

Switches in the peripheral chambers open the external gates. The internal gates, however, work in tandem and open only when you activate each of the four switches, one outside each gate. By the same token, the same four inside gates can be closed together by pushing any of their switches. Use this level to sharpen your fighting, shooting, and defensive techniques. But if you want a semblance of a plan, consider the steps that follow.

### In the Perimeter and on the Spinning Band

1. **Score everything you can.** Starting with the Alpha walkway, near where you first materialize, explore the curving corridor to get everything from

shotguns and shrinkers to shotgun shells, RPG ammo, and atomic health units. Each of the four walkways (labeled Alpha, Beta, Gamma, and Delta) has a small chamber near its center. Enter each chamber, press the central switch, and take the goods from the cylindrical containers.

2. **Ride the spinning band.** Armed to the teeth, get on top of the band and fight off the sentry drones before they get too close. If you are being pummeled too hard, jump off the band and find shelter in any of the four perimeter walkways.

3. **Face the central structure.** Once you have decreased the drone, trooper, and captain population to a more manageable level, focus your attention on the assault commanders who like to hang out near the central structure's entrances. Get off as many RPGs as possible as you circle past the assault commanders.

## Around the Central Structure's Entrances

1. **Grab more weapons near the entrances and throw every switch.** Every one of the four entrances in the central structure has something useful to offer. However, your foray to the center may be stopped short by droves of floating troopers and other hovering enemies. Once you take possession of the shrinker, you will have a better time of cutting the opposition down to size. Also, take a second to push each of the four buttons in the entrances.

2. **Make a dash for the final exit.** Once you push the last of the switches, all four doors will open simultaneously. You can then step in and rush toward the exit switch in the central pole in the middle of the chamber. Or, you could be rendered into a lifeless mass of tissue and bone by, not one, but two Battlelords who will materialize the second you set foot inside the chamber.

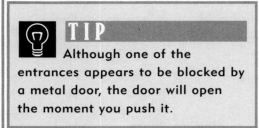

**TIP**

Although one of the entrances appears to be blocked by a metal door, the door will open the moment you push it.

## ADDED ATTRACTIONS IN SPIN CYCLE

If you aren't able to reach the exit switch before the Battlelords converge on you, you will definitely have a fine mess in your hands. However, your cunning and resourcefulness can help you through this dire situation. The first thing to do is to get out of the line of fire. It's useless to confront one Battlelord, let alone two, if your health is lower than one hundred percent and you don't have a powerful weapon like the devastator or the RPG launcher. But even if your health isn't what it once was and your weaponry is starting to dwindle, you can still triumph over the Battlelords.

As the Battlelords give chase, one is bound to get in front of the other and be subject to friendly fire from behind. If this happens, avail yourself of the chance to pound the Battlelord

 **TIP**

An effective technique for dispensing with assault commanders when they are near the central structure, is to aim your weapon to the left of your intended victim, and shoot after the spinning band has carried you past the target. Let the laws of physics work for you and drive the projectile home. Similarly, when you are aiming at targets moving ahead of you over the band, aim to the left of the target. You want to time your projectile for the moment when the target intersects it curving path. (See Figure 5.28 for an illustration of the technique.)

**FIGURE 5.28:** Shoot to the left of your intended target to connect just at the right time.

from the front and double the damage he sustains. You can also always buy breathing room by confining the Battlelords in the central chamber. Pushing any of the switches in the chamber's entrances causes all of the doors to close at once. Knowing this, you can also draw one of the Battlelords outside of the chamber and keep his compadre captive inside. With only one Battlelord to worry about, you should be able to out-maneuver him and hit him with your best shots, as you are both spun in the incessant cycle of life and death.

Having taken care of the first Battlelord, employ a similar technique to deal with the second menace. When the Battlelord's heavy armor hits the deck, run past his smoldering remains and punch the exit switch inside the central chamber.

# LUNATIC FRINGE

Are you here by design or because you stumbled upon the secret exit in The Dark Side? No matter. Lunatic Fringe is a wild romp over the edge that will have you questioning just how reliable your senses are. But take heart—you are not seeing things. The reality of this level, as in real life, is that reality is fundamentally relative. If this sounds like circumlocution, you better get used to going around in circles, quite literally. Solving the puzzle of Lunatic Fringe will have you doing what amounts to chasing your own tail. The careful observer, however, will begin to see a pattern and act accordingly.

If you are not entirely sure of where you are, how are you ever going to find the exit? And it's not just that. You'll never get to wander about your whereabouts if you don't survive the first few instants in Lunatic Fringe. You have to be ready to fight from the word go. The central chamber, where the exit switch is heavily guarded by two Battlelord Juniors, will remain a question mark until you throw the proper switches, all four of them.

## MAPS AND ROUTE

"Simple enough," you might think after giving Figures 5.29 and 5.30 the once over. However, wait until you make the rounds in Lunatic Fringe before you render a more qualified opinion.

## THE GOODS

You don't get just one, but two chances to score goods in Lunatic Fringe. The two realities of this level let you double-dip into the bag of goodies as Table 5.20 shows.

| TABLE 5.20 THE GOODS IN LUNATIC FRINGE | | |
|---|---|---|
| **WEAPONS** | **AMMO** | **POWER-UPS** |
| 3 shotguns | 2 cases | 1 portable medkit |
| 1 ripper chaingun | 2 cases | 3 atomic health units |
| 1 RPG launcher | 5 cases | 1 armor |
| 1 devastator | 2 cases | 1 steroid flask |
| 1 laser trip bomb | | 1 holoduke |
| | 2 shrinker crystals | |

## BLAZING THROUGH LUNATIC FRINGE

Stick to the path outlined below, and find out why sometimes the closest distance between two points isn't always a straight line. (Keep in mind, you might be oscillating between two visions of reality with different physical laws.)

### In the Entry Spot

1. **Emerge into the daylight.** Push the small switch behind you to open a screen panel and come out into a small platform overlooking the large central chamber and a narrow walkway extending to both sides around the chamber.

2. **Activate the switches.** Notice the switch on either side of the screen with the map of the United States. Use your handgun to activate each of these switches.

3. **Cash in while you can.** Walk along the ledge to the right and collect every weapon and power-up along the way. Protect yourself as you go, and be ready to fend off hovering assault captains and their insubordinate troopers.

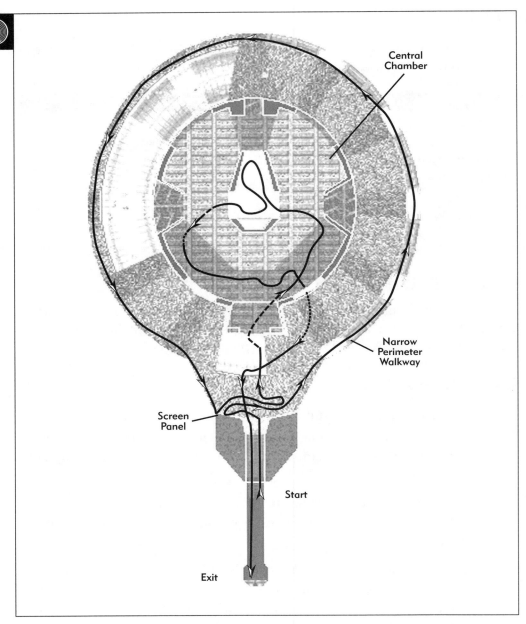

Central Chamber

Narrow Perimeter Walkway

Screen Panel

Start

Exit

FIGURE 5.29: Once inside, sane or not, there is no easy escape from Lunatic Fringe.

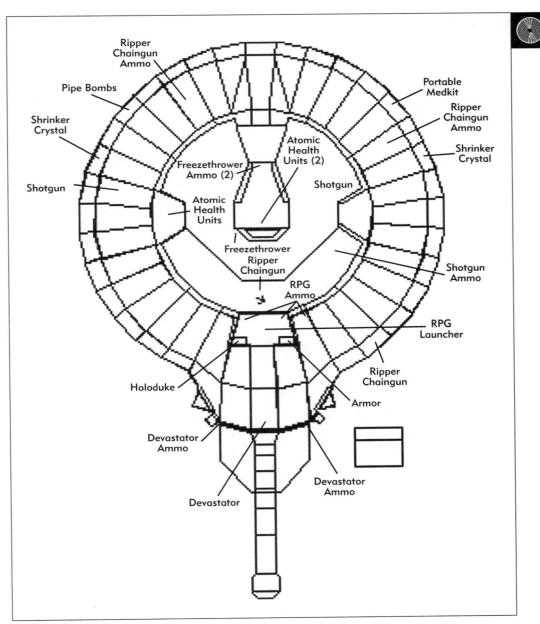

**FIGURE 5.30**: No, you're not quite ready for a straitjacket and a padded cell. Lunatic Fringe just makes you think you might be missing a screw.

## In the Same Entry Spot

1. **Contain your astonishment.** When you complete the round and come upon the same entry spot, you will see what appears to be a different panel. In fact, even the central structure will seem to have changed. It is and it has. The panel now shows what appears to be a picture of a distant alien planet.

2. **Activate the last two switches.** After you activate the last two switches, listen for the hissing sounds of several openings forming at various heights along the central structure.

3. **Get inside.** The current view in the large screen determines the route you should follow to get in. If it's North America, you can enter either through the small opening right across from the actual screen or by jumping from the ledge along the east side into an elevated opening in the structure. But if the view is of the alien planet, then you can enter either by jumping from the south tip on the ledge or by walking down the stairs through a side door on the west side.

## Inside the Central Structure

1. **Hop around a bit, if you feel lucky.** Collect any useful stuff you can grab. It is possible to jump into the small apertures housing atomic health units. You take a chance in falling down and sharing the floor with the Battlelords, but any reward usually involves an element of risk.

2. **Get to the central platform.** Get a good angle from one of the many elevated openings, and jump into the green glowing enclosure in the center. Pay no mind to the incessant growls of the Battlelord s below, and take the atomic health units and the freezethrower ammo.

## Back to the Front

1. **Throw the hand print switch.** Get back on the platform on the south side, inside the chamber. Look for the hand print switch along the left

side of the opening into the outside. Throw it and jump out of the window through the side window on the left side, where you can see a panel lowering in the middle of the screen with the alien world. If you try to get out of the front opening after throwing the hand print switch, you will see only the North American continent on the panel, and the opening you saw earlier will seem like it was only a hallucination. But it wasn't.

> **TIP**
>
> Unless you are eager for a show-down with the two Battlelords patrolling the area, you should enter through either the back door at the south end or through the front. Both of those locations are on higher ground from the Battlelords, where it is very difficult for them to spot you in their lethal sights.

2. **Get small and get out.** As you come upon the opening in the panel, you will notice that it's way too small to crawl in. But almost at the same time, you will be hit by a shrinker emanation that will allow you to filter through the small opening and reach a larger area as you start to regain your normal size. Then just hit the exit switch.

## ADDED ATTRACTIONS IN LUNATIC FRINGE

If you're not entirely happy unless you have a major confrontation at least once a day, then proceed to the account of how you might work out some natural aggression with the Battlelords in Lunatic Fringe.

### A Memorable Encounter

After you have determined that you are not crazy and have activated all four switches around the screen with the alternating views, try a little deception to confound the Battlelords in the central chamber. Enter the central chamber through either of the elevated areas, and drop a good dosage of pipe bombs into the space below. Detonate them in bunches to cause major damage.

Run out to the periphery and deploy the holoduke in front of one of the side entrances. Back off and quickly plant some laser trip bombs like spokes of a wheel with the main structure at the hub. As either or both of the Battlelords give pursuit, entice them to cross over the laser trip bombs. Switch to the RPG launcher, and proceed to dish out as many projectiles as you possibly can.

If, by good fortune, both Battlelord Juniors are after you, usually the one in front will receive friendly fire from his pal behind him. By backing off continually, and releasing projectiles as the surviving Battlelord Junior gives chase, you should be able to finish him in less than one full circle around Lunatic Fringe.

# CHAPTER 6

# Shrapnel City

Alas, welcome home at last, Duke Nukem. But once again, so sorry the reception is not exactly befitting of one whose legendary deeds could fill volumes. You fought bravely and sometimes savagely in Lunar Apocalypse. You saw action in what now seems like countless orbiting stations and surface installations. And never once did you question your role as humanity's savior. It's just something you seem to do so well.

In Overlord, the last mission of Lunar Apocalypse, you penetrated an alien ship to discover a massive turret pointed at California's San Andreas Fault. With providence on your side, you also battled the boss of the episode, the Moon Assault Leader, and put him out of commission permanently. To say it wasn't easy would be a major understatement; but you were never big on words, Duke, and complaining just isn't your nature. That's all history now, anyway. Now you're back on Earth. Unfortunately, things haven't really changed for the better since you left. In fact, they are positively out of hand. Thank God you're back.

## RAW MEAT

Its hard to think of a better place to cut your teeth in Shrapnel City than Raw Meat's sushi bar. Culinary delicacies aside, Raw Meat serves up an intricate complex of chambers, tunnels, and interconnected underwater passages. Speaking of liquids, wait until you check out the wet bar. The dance floor also offers a relief for sore eyes; and speaking of eyes, no matter how you slice it, the main dish in Raw Meat is the food. There are obviously two types of clientele who frequent Raw Meat. The dining areas on the first floor will seem ordinary enough, but wait until you find the underground eatery. By the looks of the table scraps, you might guess the diners down there like their meat, well, very rare.

Making the cut in Raw Meat is much like a three-course meal. First, tease your taste buds for the ensuing action while you are still in the outside area. Next, partake of the main dish as you devour your opponents in the dining chambers, where you must also score the blue keycard. Finally, top off the evening's meal with a few libations at the bar and some live entertainment. Of course, your culinary experience won't be complete until you visit the kitchen, where you can score additional power-ups and weaponry. And, finally, find the passage to the main pool, where you can nab the red keycard. This keycard opens the door that grants you access to the back door—perhaps the best way to leave Raw Meat after your violent binge.

## MAPS AND ROUTE

Raw Meat features a totally different sushi bar. If the food doesn't kill you, the diners will. Check out Figures 6.1 and 6.2 to whet your appetite.

## THE GOODS

Raw Meat gives you plenty of reasons why you might want to stop in, even if you are not particularly hungry or don't care for Japanese food. Table 6.1 shows you everything you can collect in this level.

### TABLE 6.1: THE GOODS IN RAW MEAT

| WEAPONS | AMMO | POWER-UPS |
|---|---|---|
| 1 handgun | | 1 portable medkit |
| 1 shotgun | 3 cases | 4 atomic health units |
| 1 ripper chaingun | 1 case | 1 armor |
| 1 RPG launcher | 1 case | 2 steroid flasks |
| 1 devastator | 6 cases | 2 jetpacks |
| 1 shrinker | 2 shrinker crystals | 1 NVG |
| 1 freezethrower | 2 charges | 1 holoduke |
| 1 laser trip bomb | | |
| 2 pipe bomb cases | | |

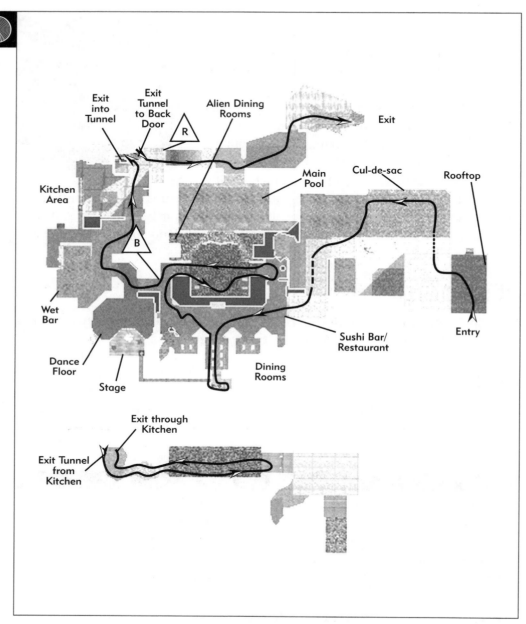

**FIGURE 6.1:** However experimental your culinary leanings, abstain from ordering the sliced eyeball in Raw Meat.

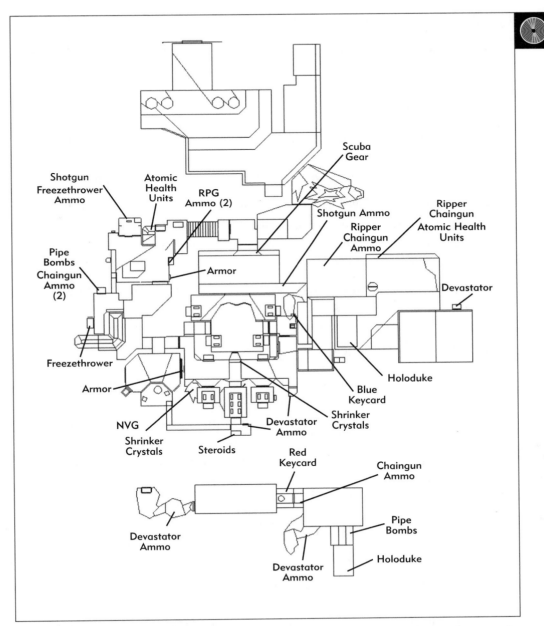

**FIGURE 6.2:** Even if you decide to stay away from the culinary delights, don't neglect to collect all you can in Raw Meat.

# BLAZING THROUGH RAW MEAT

Despite its voracious appetite for human flesh and suffering, you can really make a short meal of Raw Meat, if you follow the main course outlined below.

## In the Cul-de-Sac

1. **Load up on weaponry.** Dash to the wall compartment north of your location on the rooftop and grab the devastator. Get near the rooftop's ledge to entice a sentry drone and an enforcer or two to come after you.

2. **Take a plunge.** Get a running start and jump along the side of the building, from where you got the devastator. You want to land on the ledge that skirts the building on the north side of the cul-de-sac. At the end of the ledge, you can claim an atomic health unit and a ripper chaingun.

3. **Eat sushi and don't pay.** Work your way toward the ramp entrance to the sushi bar and proceed cautiously.

## In the Sushi Bar's Entrance

1. **Forget the reservations.** Stepping onto the restaurant's ramp, you will become fodder for a group of enforcers. You are also in the sights of a turret mounted high up on the wall. If necessary, back out into the cul-de-sac to avoid being mobbed and so you can work your devastator with some elbow room. When the moment is opportune, rush back onto the ramp, aim your weapon upward, and destroy the turret as you make it to the door.

> **TIP**
> You want to thin out the alien marauders, even by one or two, before you take a plunge to face additional enemies in the cul-de-sac below.

2. **Dine and dash.** Walking into the restaurant's foyer, take out the turret in the small space due directly south. Then rush to that same spot to collect some crucial devastator ammo. Proceed into each of the dining rooms along the left wall, and collect all the goods you can. The large dining room in the center hides a secret area behind the table. When the

table sinks under your weight, crouch to enter the small chamber. Then collect more ammo for your devastator and the steroids on top of the metal box with the fans.

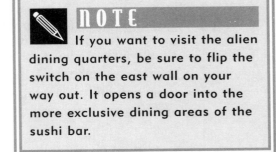

**NOTE**
If you want to visit the alien dining quarters, be sure to flip the switch on the east wall on your way out. It opens a door into the more exclusive dining areas of the sushi bar.

3. **Take a major shortcut and cash in your chips.** With a three- or four-step running start, jump right into what might seem like a solid wall to the left of the greeting geisha near the restaurant's main entrance. You will reach a dark rectangular area that leads directly to the cash register. Open the small compartment behind the register to get the blue keycard. It grants you entry to the bar. Then get out into the restaurant's main hallway, using the same way you got in.

## In the Bar

1. **Mingle with some reserve.** The bar crawls with pig cops and other unsavory characters, and assault commanders play the role of bouncers. So keep a low profile by ducking, creeping around corners, and otherwise disposing of your opponents by picking your shots carefully.

2. **Enjoy a few libations and a floor show.** At your earliest convenience, get to the wet bar at the south end, make the rounds to consume every power-up and ammo. You also might want to grab the RPG launcher behind the speaker on the right side of the stage. Just beware of the rushing waves of pig cops. When you have had enough of the bar scene, move to the kitchen, on the north end of the bar, and don't be too alarmed at the food-preparation techniques you will see displayed. They're not exactly in accord with the fundamentals of hygiene and sanitation.

## In the Kitchen

1. **Face the heat.** Take the chefs by surprise, and douse the place with lead. A couple of pipe bombs will also help clear the air before you raid the

kitchen. Take all the weapons, ammo, and power-ups you can find. Look in the cold room for a freezethrower and shotgun ammo. The wine rack also hides two cases of RPG ammo.

2. **Do the dishes.** Find a water tank next to the oven grill (to the right of the walk-in cold room) and, taking a deep breath, jump in. Follow the tunnel leading south and then east. You will come into the main pool area where an octabrain or two might live.

## In the Main Pool Area

1. **Get the scuba gear.** Emerge from the pool to take the scuba gear along the north side. Then dive right back in.

2. **Get the red keycard.** Head east toward the end of the pool, where you will find the red keycard. This key will let you get out of the sushi restaurant through the back door.

3. **Get back to the kitchen.** Now that you have the red keycard, retrace your route back to the kitchen sink. Jump out dripping wet and head for the back door.

## Into the Back Alley

1. **Endure another battle.** Use the red keycard on the latch and venture out, but expect another enforcer ambush. Your devastator weapon will help you cut a path through the wall of alien flesh.

2. **Avoid a serious concussion.** The instant you reach the top of the ramp out of the back alley, you will sense a deep rumbling. This is a sign to run back inside as fast as possible. In a matter of instants, a huge explosion causes an entire wall to crumble in the adjacent building. The explosion also unearths the tunnel to the exit.

3. **Reach the tunnel and find the exit.** When the aftershocks subside, get back outside, and crawl through the demolished side of the building. Make your way among the rubble to the glowing red exit switch at the very end of the tunnel.

## ADDED ATTRACTIONS IN RAW MEAT

This level is really large, and there are plenty of things to discover on your own. Regardless of where your meandering takes you, the alien dining hall is a must-see for anyone with even a mild interest in intergalactic culinary experiences.

### Power Lunch with the Big Boys

There are obviously two types of clientele who frequent Raw Meat's sushi establishment. Those who like to eat the standard sushi fare, and those who like their meat, well, even more raw. The dining areas along the restaurant's main hallway seem ordinary enough. However, there is a large dining hall reserved for the alien elite. And judging by the look of the remains on the tables, it is obvious the aliens' appetite is quite insatiable.

You might want to visit the alien dining hall for a couple of reasons. Maybe you are just interested in alien nutritional habits. Or perhaps morbid curiosity drives you to see the spoils. But maybe a more sensible reason would be that you missed the shortcut to the cash register area and wish to collect the blue keycard the hard way.

If the alien dining room is open, step right on in. However, if the entry way is blocked, you have to throw a key switch in the large dining room along the hallway. (The switch is inside the small chamber behind the table.) Stepping inside the alien dining hall, you will run into what appears to be the aliens' dessert, a group of surrounded, bound human females. There are also a good number of explosive tanks lying about the place and especially around the bound women. Bite your lip and press the trigger to blow up a tank. Run out of the hall to avoid suffering any damage from the big explosion.

When things cool down a bit, step inside and proceed to sweep up the remains. Collect all the weaponry and armor you can carry. Then move eastward to find the cash register area. Don't expect to find a helpful cashier. Instead, get behind the counter, and take the blue keycard from the compartment. Now that you have the blue keycard, you can proceed to the bar where you are sure to pick up a good fight.

## COVERT DETAILS

You would expect there to be scores of secrets in Raw Meat, but there are only two, as you can see in Table 6.2.

| TABLE 6.2: THE SECRETS IN RAW MEAT | | |
|---|---|---|
| **AREA IN LEVEL** | **SECRET ITEMS** | **HOW TO GET IT** |
| Sushi bar entrance | blue keycard | Jump into what looks like a solid wall to the left side of the geisha near the entrance. The secret passage leads you to the cash register room, where you will ultimately score the blue keycard. |
| Wall behind the wet bar | freezethrower | Find the hand print switch on the menu to the left of the wet bar and activate it. Then rush into the secret enclosure behind the wet bar. |

# BANK ROLL

Legal tender, it's what it's all about. Isn't it? By day, you sell your soul to the man for the privilege of keeping up with others who are also sweating to keep up with others. Occasionally, you enjoy the fruits of your labor, but more often than not, you're being squeezed into pulp by the cogs of our run-away economic machinery, which seems more intent on feeding itself than clothing the masses.

Bank Roll, like the institution it represents, seems unfeeling, uncaring, and ultimately self-serving. In spite of its smug exterior, Bank Roll is really a fun level to play. Perhaps it's the emphasis on action and clever puzzles. Or maybe it's the very convincing bank, complete with its foyer, main office, and giant safe box. You are sure to discover other reasons on your own.

Although it might be tough to get into the bank, let alone speak to a loan officer, your ambitions run much higher. You want nothing less than to get to the bank's safe box and crack it wide open. The bank's entry requires you to have the blue keycard. Once inside the bank, you will need to obtain the red keycard for clearance into the safe box.

## MAPS AND ROUTE

You can almost see the cogs of the business machinery at work in the design of Bank Roll, as portrayed in Figures 6.3 and 6.4.

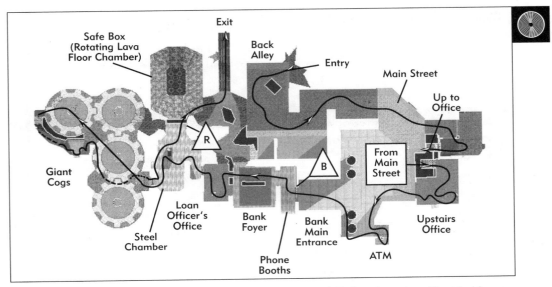

**FIGURE 6.3:** One thing you can bank on after visiting Bank Roll is that you will probably want to do your own banking.

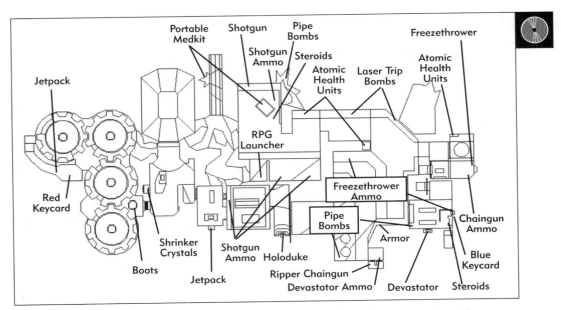

**FIGURE 6.4:** Don't let Bank Roll take you to the cleaners; grab what you can from the comprehensive cache available.

## THE GOODS

However stingy and tight lending institutions tend to be, Bank Roll is exceptionally generous when it comes to the goods at your disposal. Table 6.3 shows you the bottom line.

### TABLE 6.3: THE GOODS IN BANK ROLL

| WEAPONS | AMMO | POWER-UPS |
|---|---|---|
| 1 handgun | | 1 portable medkit |
| 1 shotgun | 3 cases | 4 atomic health units |
| 1 ripper chaingun | 1 case | 1 armor |
| 1 RPG launcher | 1 case | 2 steroid flasks |
| 1 devastator | 6 cases | 2 jetpacks |
| 1 shrinker | 2 shrinker crystals | 1 NVG |
| 1 freezethrower | 2 charges | 1 holoduke |
| 1 laser trip bomb | | |
| 2 pipe bomb cases | | |

## BLAZING THROUGH BANK ROLL

Why wait in line for your turn when you can blaze through and make out like a bandit? Stick to your guns and the plan below, and you just might make it out alive on the edge of town.

### En Route to Main Street

1. **Take down some pig cops.** Coming out from the crack on the wall, grab the pipe bomb case, dash for the shotgun on the ledge, and jump down onto the street level—all the while dodging blasts from a couple of pig cops perched on a ledge across the alley. Get the portable medkit inside the trash Dumpster.

2. **Claw your way to Main Street.** Advance toward Main Street, but be careful of pig cops and enforcers jumping out of nowhere. The place where the alley narrows is particularly perilous because you can be easily ambushed by no less than a pig cop, an enforcer, and another RPV-mounted pig cop. (Deft footwork and a devastator would be most appropriate in this situation.)

## On Main Street

1. **Visit the offices across the street from the bank.** The blue keycard is in an upstairs office, and without it, you are forever locked out of the bank. Look for the first entrance along the north side of the street. As you walk up to it, a sensor opens it and a window to your right.

2. **Get some goods before you go up to the office.** Grab the atomic health unit atop the soda machine and the ripper chaingun from on top of the other vending machines; then it's impossible to overlook the freezethrower. Now head for the elevator.

3. **Storm the office and take the blue keycard.** As you step inside, be ready to deal with a couple of belligerent enforcers who materialize out of thin air. Behind the partition, take care of the pig cop, and push the button on the desk as you reach for the steroids. Then take the blue keycard from the lowering bookshelves. As you exit, grab the devastator that was hidden behind a wall picture.

**TIP**

Get ready to back out as soon as the door and window open. Waiting to run you down behind the door is an RPV. The window on the right also makes you an easy target for the pig cops inside. If you can release a shot from your RPG launcher and do away with the RPV, then you only have to worry about the pig cops. And once you know they're there, the pig cops are sitting ducks. Dump a bomb or two in their enclosure, and detonate it from a safe distance.

## In the Bank

1. **Hold up the place.** Take out the turret mounted high outside the bank's entrance, and then use the blue keycard to get in. Deal with the first of several pig cops, and step just outside the foyer, hiding partially behind the plant. From this position, fire upon the pig cops congregated in the main office. Also, hit the turret by the right side of the foyer so you can move more freely.

2. **Get to the main office.** Be sure to jump in through the small side window because the regular entry is lined with laser trip bombs. Press the desk button to unlock the door to the safe and to reveal a hiding place above the desk (behind the painting, naturally), which stores a jetpack. Proceed to the area in the back that houses the safe box.

## In the Safe Box Zone

1. **Throw three switches in a row.** The safe box will remain bolted shut until you find the red keycard. For that reason, dispose of the few enforcers and troopers standing guard in the steel chamber of the safe. Walk behind the desk and throw all three switches. This opens up the three-stage door on the south wall.

2. **Get through the cogs.** Hop onto the circular platform to get the protective boots. Notice how the giant cogs turn, sensing your move on the platform. Get off and walk toward the Beta platform. (Each platform is conveniently labeled.) Again, hop on and then walk into the space leading to the Delta platform. Get on the last platform and face west directly. As the cog turns, its opening reveals a small recess on the wall behind it. Using this small window of opportunity, jump off the platform and rush toward the wall recess. Ride the platform up into a dark corridor.

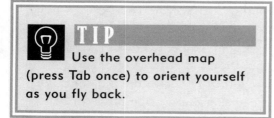

**TIP**

Use the overhead map (press Tab once) to orient yourself as you fly back.

3. **Score the red keycard.** If you have your devastator handy, destroy the pig cops in the corridor as you reach for the plainly visible keycard. Also take the jetpack and the other goods behind the wall compartment. Fly back to safety and the safe box. Use your newly acquired jetpack to get back to the safe box area.

4. **Crack the safe.** Use the red keycard and then walk up to the safe and push it open. The door swings outward to reveal a very nasty scene indeed. Throw a pipe bomb inside and immediately close the safe box door. Detonate the pipe bomb and grab a hold of something, for the place is about to shake.

5.  **Reopen the safe and fight to the end.** Although mostly everyone and everything inside the safe is either dead or dying, don't count on it completely. In fact, the explosion blew up a large tunnel and a Battlelord has crept up from underground. You can choose to confront the Battlelord, or simply dash for the exit at the north end of the tunnel. The choice, as always, is yours.

## ADDED ATTRACTIONS IN BANK ROLL

Although the pace in Bank Roll moves quite steadily, it really crescendos when you are finally ready to deal with the safe box. For this reason, this particular scenario is worth examining more closely.

### Cracking the Safe and its Contents

Stand outside the safe box with the red keycard in hand, check yourself to be sure you have a good dose of health. If it is anywhere below 90 percent, give yourself a boost with the portable medkit. Then, reach for a pipe bomb. Stick the red keycard in the slot, and walk up to the heavy safe box door. Press on it and the massive door will swing open toward you. Don't gawk at the horror in there longer than you need to. (Although the place is buzzing with octabrains and there are dozens of alien eggs everywhere you look, perhaps what is most disturbing is the image of human females hanging upside down from the ceiling.) Throw the pipe bomb near the eggs and the ever-present explosive tanks. Then rush back out and close the safe box door behind you.

The entire building will rumble as the explosive charges go off inside the safe box. You will hear a mixture of explosions and alien flesh splashing the walls red. It is possible and likely that an octabrain or two might make it out of the safe box. If this is the case, use the ripper chaingun to put any survivor down. You want to save your devastator and RPG ammo for one last opponent, should he get in your way. The last hurdle to overcome is none other than the Battlelord. Formidable though he is, he can fall under the force of your devastator, especially if you manage to catch him while he is facing the other way.

Open the safe a second time. Step in looking left and right for any signs of alien life. You might have to quell another octabrain, but you are really mostly concerned now with the Battlelord. He likes to hang near the right corner. So waste not a moment in pouring whatever you have left in him. If he reacts quickly and gives chase, you can either run back out to the steel chamber or find refuge along the cracks in the newly dug tunnel on the northeast side of the safe box. From either of these places, you can

> **NOTE**
>
> Before you move on to the next level, you can also choose to explore the ledges around the buildings on Main Street. You can either use the jetpack or climb along a portion of the tunnel along the southeast side. It leads to the ledge of the building overlooking the alley on the south side.

manage to keep the Battlelord in your sights. However, it is easier to avoid his ripper chaingun and explosive pellets if you are not confined to the small spaces, as you are in the tunnel. When the Battlelord crumbles under the weight of your attack, just head for the exit switch.

## COVERT DETAILS

There are only a handful of secrets in Bank Roll, and Table 6.4 summarizes them for you.

| **TABLE 6.4: THE SECRETS IN BANK ROLL** | | |
| --- | --- | --- |
| **AREA IN LEVEL** | **SECRET ITEMS** | **HOW TO GET IT** |
| ATMs across from the bank building | ripper chaingun | Push either of the ATMs and jump through the small opening. |
| In the bank's lobby | holoduke | Use the handgun to hit the switch high on the angular wall on the north side of the narrow lobby. The phone booths at the opposite end will lower to reveal the holoduke. |
| Main office in the bank building | jetpack | Throw the desk switch to expose the jetpack behind the painting on the south wall. |

# FLOOD ZONE

If you like it wet and wild, you will love it in Flood Zone. Get ready to spend half the time underwater and the other half climbing along precipitous paths on rocky mountainsides. Flood Zone is basically a piece of downtown Los Angeles that went under during the last big earthquake. Of course, the alien's power beam targeting the San Andreas Fault from space didn't help matters.

To find the elusive exit in Flood Zone, you must travel high and low in search of all three keycards. Start out with the blue keycard. It sits atop a set of rock stairs at the west end. With the blue keycard you can get inside the underwater alien egg nest, which is also at the west end. Not only do you need to go in there for the yellow keycard, but you must also destroy every egg. With the yellow keycard you can finally gain access to the square, half-sunk building. Inside this building you must access the bottom floor to activate the switch that reveals the hiding place for the last and final red keycard.

This level is highly populated with octabrains, assault commanders, sharks, and even a Battlelord. To make a tense situation even more so, you have a limited oxygen supply so your underwater excursions must be rather methodical.

## MAPS AND ROUTE

Figures 6.5 and 6.6 let you see surface and submerged views for Flood Zone.

## THE GOODS

You will not be diving for pearls in Flood Zone, but pearls are the last thing you could wish for when your life could be snuffed out at any moment. The top side also holds many weapons and other useful finds, which will seem more precious than any treasure anyone could hope for. Table 6.5 tallies the goods in the Flood Zone.

### TABLE 6.5: THE GOODS IN FLOOD ZONE

| WEAPONS | AMMO | POWER-UPS |
| --- | --- | --- |
| 1 shotgun | 5 cases | 2 portable medkits |
| 2 ripper chainguns | 6 cases | 5 atomic health units |
| 1 RPG launcher | 7 cases | 1 armor |
| 1 devastator | 9 cases | 1 steroid flask |
| 1 shrinker | 1 shrinker crystal | 1 jetpack |
| 1 freezethrower | | 2 NVG |
| 2 laser trip bombs | | 1 holoduke |
| 2 pipe bomb cases | | |

## BLAZING THROUGH FLOOD ZONE

It's easy to feel overwhelmed in this level. The place teems with alien life, which means yours could end anytime. Also, solving the puzzle of Flood Zone could have you guessing indefinitely. That's why this section is here, to keep you from second guessing yourself.

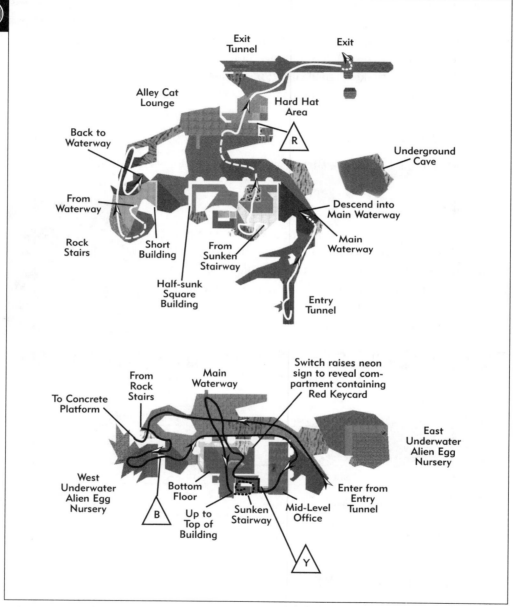

**FIGURE 6.5:** Don't hold your breath for too long. You're about to make a splash in Flood Zone. These maps show the top and the submerged areas.

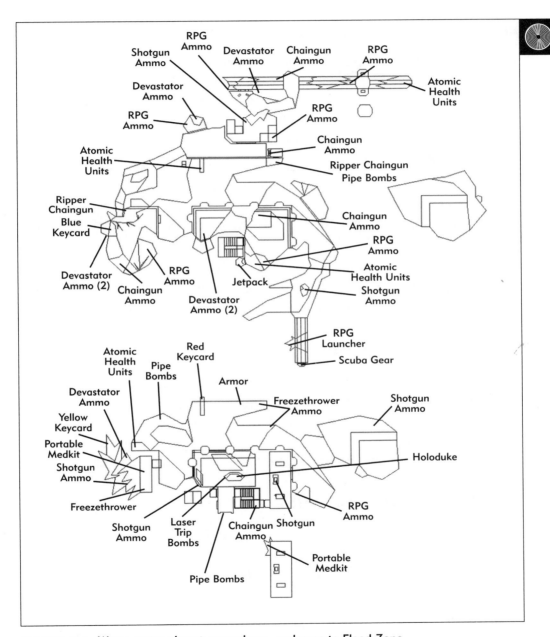

**FIGURE 6.6:** Water, water almost everywhere—welcome to Flood Zone.

## In the Elevated Entry Tunnel and Main Waterway

1.  **Get ready for a dive.** Look behind you and take the scuba gear in the compartment. A few steps on the left you will find the RPG launcher. As you come out of the tunnel where a water stream comes out of the rocks, you will be confronted by an octabrain. Use your RPG launcher for the first time. Then plunge into the depths.

2.  **Travel westward.** Move either over or under the water's surface; but either way, open yourself a path through the herds of octabrains and rogue sharks, and continue moving east. As you get near the end of the water way, look for an underwater tunnel that leads to a small concrete platform.

3.  **Climb after the blue keycard.** Find the rock path along the curving south wall, and climb a few large rocks to reach the blue keycard. Then, get back into the water. It's time to visit the west side egg nursery.

## In the West Side Egg Nursery

1.  **Blow up the nursery and take the yellow keycard.** Use the blue keycard on the latch for the alien egg nursery. Drop a pipe bomb or use your favorite method for hitting one of the incubator accelerator tanks. Close the door and bide your time for a few seconds. Then go back inside and collect the yellow keycard. Get to the east side of the waterway.

## Inside the Submerged Square Office

1.  **Get to the bottom of things.** Enter the submerged office in the east side of the building. Use the keycard on the latch, and go all the way down to the bottom floor, using the sunken stairway.

2.  **Push the right switch.** Go inside the large reception area, and push the switch along the front wall. It raises the metal window covers, and it also causes the neon Alley Cat Lounge sign to lift a few meters. Swim

out toward the Alley Cat Lounge, and open the door behind the sign to uncover the red keycard.

3. **Hover over to the other side.** Get back into the submerged office, and take the flight of stairs all the way to the top of the building, which is well above the water level. After surviving one of the most intense battles you are likely to face anywhere, anytime, climb along the rocks on the south side to pick up an atomic health unit. Also, push the solid rock wall at the end to pick up a jetpack. Activate it and hover to the Alley Cat Lounge's rooftop.

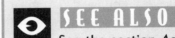
**SEE ALSO**
See the section *Added Attractions in Flood Zone* for a full account of what to expect and how to survive on top of the square building.

## On the Alley Cat Lounge's Rooftop

1. **Wear a hard hat.** Use the red keycard to enter the hard-hat area. Fight off the leaping enforcers, and move north toward a water brook. Continue ascending into a straight long tunnel that might have been a subway route or a tunnel for a train.

2. **Dive into the hole.** Move east along the tunnel, watching your back for octabrains creeping up behind you. When you come upon a small opening in the tunnel, just let yourself go and drop all the way to the bottom, where water will soften your fall.

3. **Face the switch and take your leave.** Jump out of the water facing north to reach a small platform right in front of the exit switch.

## ADDED ATTRACTIONS IN FLOOD ZONE

One of the many tenuous moments in Flood Zone occurs when you reach the rooftop of the square building. If you can survive the onslaught in this heavily contested area, the human race might still have reason for optimism.

**WARNING**
You don't want to stick your head out of the water and sit there for very long. A strategically placed turret is perched at eye level and can fry your head in no time at all.

## Showdown on the Square Building's Rooftop

When you finally reach the rooftop of the half-submerged building, don't expect any fanfare. First of all, you should know that there are several hidden areas nestled in the rock tops, and all of them overlook the very exposed rooftop where you stand. As soon as you open the door leading to the rooftop, get ready to pummel several assault commanders making their way over the waterway from an area above and to the right of the Alley Cat Lounge. Don't make the fatal mistake of rushing to the west side of the rooftop. You would only increase the number of enemies that are free to roam. Instead, retreat to the stairs if you are overwhelmed by the commanders. The weapon of choice to deal with matters on the rooftop is the devastator. You need the most effective means of tearing down opponents with the least effort. See Figure 6.7 for a snapshot of the action you can expect on the rooftop.

When the action on the east side of the rooftop subsides somewhat, climb over the small rock outcropping to get an atomic health unit. Then, press against the smooth, flat rock to uncover a jetpack. Strap it on and get ready for your next daredevil, yet coldly calculated, maneuver.

Move over to the west side of the rooftop, and anticipate another commander onslaught. This time, however, the commanders will come rushing at you from an

**FIGURE 6.7:** When you reach the rooftop, don't expect fanfare.

opening in the rocks above and to the left of the once legendary Alley Cat Lounge. If you keep your back pressed against the wall as the commanders slice their way through the air, you will keep a nearby Battlelord from joining the party. "How nearby is the Battlelord?" you ask. So nearby he could almost jump right on top of you. In fact he is perched in a large recess on the rocks above your head.

When you have taken out most or all of the commanders. Fire up your jetpack and fly as fast as you can across the waterway. When you have gone far enough, turn 180 degrees to face the Battlelord from your elevated position in mid air. Then use your complete freedom of movement to avoid the Battlelord's projectiles, while you shower him with a few rockets of your own. When he succumbs under the pounding of your RPGs and devastator combination, continue toward the exit.

## COVERT DETAILS

The secrets abound in Flood Zone, as Table 6.6 makes plainly obvious.

### TABLE 6.6: THE SECRETS IN FLOOD ZONE

| AREA IN LEVEL | SECRET ITEMS | HOW TO GET IT |
|---|---|---|
| Large cave serving as an egg nursery on the northeast side of the main waterway | devastator and shrinker crystals | Drop a pipe bomb or use the RPG launcher on the bottom section of the wall. Penetrate the tunnel, and battle a good number of octabrains. Rise to the air bubble in the nursery, and collect the goods. |
| On the rooftop of the square building | jetpack | Climb over the rock boulder on the south side of the rooftop. Grab the atomic health unit, and then push the flat rock at the end. Watch it lift, and grab the jetpack before the rock comes down. |
| Rock stairs at the west end | blue keycard | Climb over the large rock stairs starting at the south side of the short building at the far west. |
| Small chamber at the east end of the Alley Cat Lounge | ripper chaingun ammo | Use either the jetpack to rise to the small rock platform halfway up from the water level to the top of the Alley Cat Lounge, or simply jump there if you are at the top of the lounge. Push against the second window from the end, and enter into the small chamber with the ammo. |

# L.A. RUMBLE

Far away from the country side or anything remotely close to nature, L.A. Rumble is a big pile of concrete, steel, glass, and other materials forged by the hands of humans. But for all the trappings of culture and sophistication, the action about to unfold will be anything but civilized. Hollywood Boulevard and the East Town Towers provide a suitably cosmopolitan backdrop. To make sense of L.A. Rumble, you will have to take care of business inside both towers. But getting from one tower to the other without a jetpack might present a bit of problem. Don't forget you are in Los Angeles, and the landscape could change quite unexpectedly, for this is tremor country.

## MAPS AND ROUTE

Figures 6.8 and 6.9 show you the layout of L.A. Rumble, once a place of fame and glamour.

## THE GOODS

Known for its lavish ways, L.A. Rumble includes a plethora of weapons, ammo, and power-ups. Check out the pickings in Table 6.7.

### TABLE 6.7: THE GOODS IN L.A. RUMBLE

| WEAPONS | AMMO | POWER-UPS |
| --- | --- | --- |
| 1 shotgun | 5 cases | 3 portable medkits |
| 1 ripper chainguns | 3 cases | 3 atomic health units |
| 2 RPG launchers | 5 cases | 1 armor |
| 1 devastator | 5 cases | 1 steroid flask |
| 1 shrinker | 1 shrinker crystal | 1 jetpack |
| 2 freezethrowers | | 1 NVG |
| 2 laser trip bombs | | 1 holoduke |
| 2 pipe bomb cases | | |

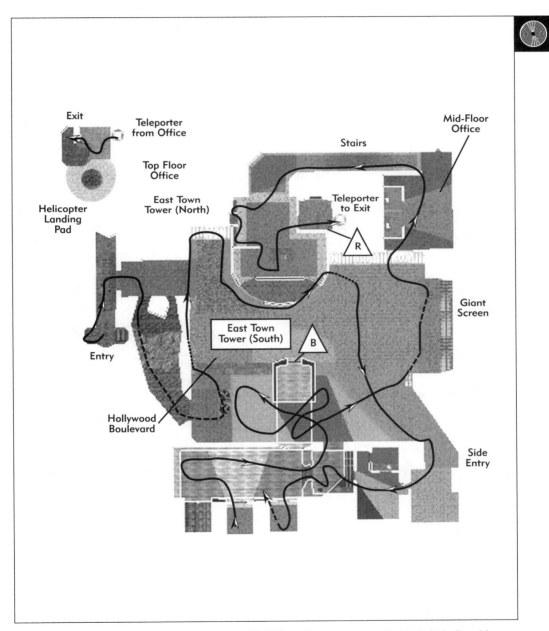

**FIGURE 6.8:** Are you ready for quite a tumble? If you're not, too bad, this is L.A. Rumble.

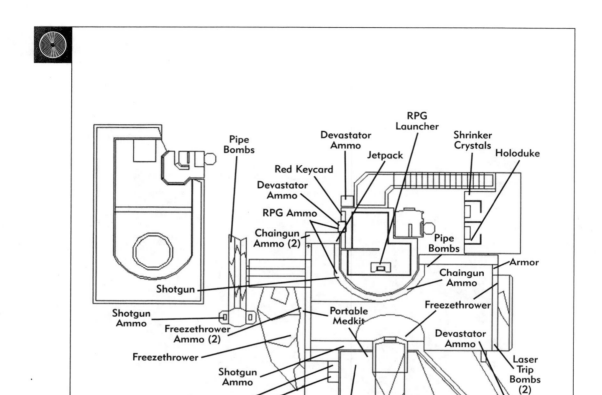

**FIGURE 6.9:** Pray that some day you forgive what you're about to do in L.A. Rumble.

# BLAZING THROUGH L.A. RUMBLE

Get ready for urban assault tactics and guerrilla-type warfare in the streets and buildings of L.A. Rumble. Although blue and red keycards are available in this level, you only really need to score the red one. It opens a teleporter that beams you directly to a landing pad on top of the north of the East Town Towers. Waiting nearby is your getaway helicopter. But first, you must make it inside the north tower. Without a jetpack, it takes a few neurons to figure out how.

## On the East Side

1. **Dig a tunnel.** Crawl out of the manhole, grab the shotgun shells nearby, and walk down the tunnel. Step through a cross-shaped hole along the tunnel's wall, and emerge into a dark passage leading out to Hollywood Boulevard. Halfway up the dark passage, drop a pipe bomb or use your RPG launcher on the south side wall to open up a big, gaping tunnel.

2. **Take a walk around the perimeter.** Climb along the rubble and cross the length of the tunnel to reach the lower side of the south tower. Hop on the air ventilators to collect an RPG launcher and some ammo. Look towards your left, and hop onto a lower ledge that lines the building front on the east side. Follow the narrow ledge north first, then east, and then around the half-circle of the north tower. Among the items you can collect in this short jaunt are ripper chaingun ammo and more RPG ammo. Drop off the ledge when you've collected everything you possibly can. Start heading down the hill toward the side entry to the south tower.

## In the South Tower

1. **Take over the first floor.** Step in cautiously and deal with the obstinate pig cops in the only language they understand, the language of hot lead. Access a laboratory-like chamber with embryo flasks, dispense with a few more pig cops, and then blow a big hole in the lab's west side wall.

2. **Going up?** Proceed into the next large rectangular chamber, and drop into the empty shaft of the elevator on the far end to pick up a devastator. Then hop aboard the functioning elevator. It takes you to a similar

rectangular chamber filled with undesirables. Count on a few more encounters with alien enforcers in this part of the building. Eventually, work your way to the front side of the building, where you will find yourself overlooking Hollywood Boulevard from the building's roof.

3.  **Cause a major stir.** Stepping out onto the building's rooftop, walk up to the earthquake warning sign. A bone-jarring rumble will shake the place up. Notice how part of the concrete structure below the giant screen is rearranged in the short, but strong, quake.

4.  **Jump toward freedom.** Surely by now, you have noticed the two floor levels in the north tower that are plainly open and inhabited by aliens. If you had a jetpack you could simply fly over. However, if you like to use your jetpack as much as most people do, chances are that your fuel may not carry you across. The next best alternative is to jump, but clearly the gap seems to be way too wide. Here's a way you can do it: Align your-self with the right column below the giant screen. (See Figure 6.10.) Use the crosshair to help you. Back up as much as you can, and take a run-ning jump toward the column. You will land on the awning below the giant screen. The idea is to reach the point furthest to the north along the broken awning, so you can hop right into the mid-floor office of the south tower.

## Inside the North Tower

1.  **Dislodge the office workers.** Storm the office, and cut a path to the wide stairway along the north side.

2.  **Get the red keycard and flee.** When you come upon the top-level office, hope that you can catch everyone on their break and rain your wrath upon them. Grab the red keycard and all the other visible power-ups and weapons on the shelves.

3.  **Take the RPG launcher, and hit the desk switch.** A panel will open momentarily in the square office. Rush over to get inside. Riddle the troopers and captains assembled there, and grab anything that you can, and of course, we're not talking office supplies.

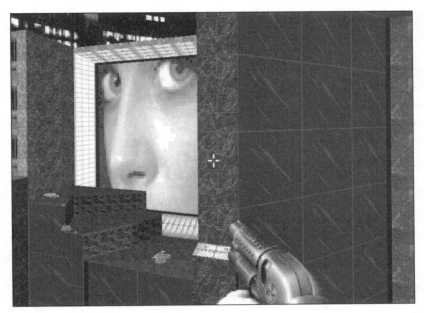

**FIGURE 6.10:** Line your crosshair with the column, and throw caution to the wind as you launch yourself to reach the awning.

4. **Teleport to the landing pad and take off.** Use the red keycard on the latch behind the desk, and step inside the teleporter. Emerge in a small control area overlooking the helicopter you hope to ride out of L.A. Rumble. Walk right over to the exit switch, and pound it one last time.

# ADDED ATTRACTIONS IN L.A. RUMBLE

Expect to fight for every yard in L.A. Rumble, especially in the early going, when you attempt to skirt the boulevard's perimeter and when you finally manage to penetrate the south tower in the East Town Towers complex.

## Skirting the Boulevard

There is a ledge that starts on the west wall and goes around the north tower, ending up against the eastern wall. There are also key sniper spots all along the boulevard because the surrounding buildings are very tall. It's a scary thought, but at any moment, you could be under someone's sights. It makes sense, then, to take out at least some snipers, lest you become too exposed for your own good.

Stepping out of the tunnel you dug in the dark passage, notice the first set of sniper pig cops at the north end, standing on the ledge where you want to reach yourself. Take cover behind the metal air units, hop from the small one to the bigger one, and grab the RPG launcher and its ammo. Set your sights and send one or two rounds in their direction. Drop from the air unit to a small space near the very front of the building, but still on a ledge, and look to the right for the next group of snipers. Again, make handy use of the RPG launcher and your God-given talents. Figure 6.11 shows a detail of this action.

Now you can jump onto the ledge on the south wall and begin your perimeter run. When you reach the place where the ledge stops along the east wall, you will be in plain view of another group of snipers mounted high upon the awning below the giant screen, all the way across the boulevard. This too is a prime opportunity to launch long range shots at the sitting enforcers. Rely heavily on your crosshair, but watch out for the hair trigger. Remember you're carrying the RPG launcher.

FIGURE 6.11: Take the snipers out before they take you.

After taking out a few more snipers, jump over the small gap and continue along the ledge. Pick up everything you can along the way. Begin circling the front side of the north tower.

## Penetrating the South Tower of East Town Towers

If you don't have a jetpack, the only way to reach the north tower is by jumping across, in hop-scotch fashion, from the south tower to the giant screen's awning and then to the middle floor of the north tower. But getting to the top of the southern tower isn't exactly a matter of hopping on an elevator and enduring a bit of muzak. In fact, if you're not on your toes every second, you probably will never get off of the bottom floor.

As you descend down the sloping side street leading to the tower's entrance, make wise use of the RPG launcher and pelt the congregated pig cops from a good distance away. Enter through the open door, and dispose of the single trooper. Before entering the second lab-like chamber, walk up to the panel on the right and push it open to claim more ammo for your devastator. If you need them, also pick up the NVG on the counter top.

Before stepping into the lab, drop a few bombs behind you. As soon as you cross the threshold into the lab, wait an instant to hear the growl of the enforcers and then hit the detonator. Pick up the survivors with impunity. While in the lab, grab the blue keycard if you want to open the front door to this building; otherwise, ignore it. But one thing you don't want to pass up is the hidden atomic health unit. Crouch and push the cabinet at the very left; the adjacent cabinet will open. Crawl in quickly and take the glowing blue atomic health unit. Back off a ways and blow a hole in the lab's north wall.

Run right through the hole, and drop into the empty elevator shaft at the far end of the dark rectangular room to pick up a devastator, should you need one. And who doesn't? Then get on the functioning elevator, and ride it to a very similar chamber a few floors up. Come out firing your devastator. If you are forced to get near the back of the room, an enforcer will sense your presence and come spinning out of the empty

> ## ☠ WARNING
> Stop immediately after collecting the pipe bomb case. You don't want to step any farther east along the ledge. A few instants after you do, you would hear the assault commander's rocket piercing through the air. If you survived the initial hit, then you would see a small dot growing large very quickly as the commander descends upon you from high above. Avoid loss of limb and life by getting off the ledge at this point.

elevator shaft. Don't be afraid to overheat the devastator. It's a rugged weapon, after all. Once things have simmered in the chamber, go around the wall on the east side to come out overlooking the boulevard, and get ready to cross over to the north tower.

## COVERT DETAILS

There are three secrets you should know about in L.A. Rumble, and Table 6.8 points them out.

### TABLE 6.8: THE SECRETS IN L.A. RUMBLE

| AREA IN LEVEL | SECRET ITEMS | HOW TO GET IT |
| --- | --- | --- |
| Secret tunnel at the east end | freezethrower | Blow up the side wall of the dark passage as you emerge from the entry tunnel. Crawl through the rubble inside the tunnel, and collect the freezethrower. |
| Top of the stairs in the north Tower | devastator ammo | Push the landscape painting as you reach the top level office. |
| The southern tower's bottom-floor lab | atomic health unit | Push the cabinet at the far left. Then crawl in the middle cabinet to collect the item. |

# MOVIE SET

Give the aliens a few weeks in Los Angeles, and the next thing you know, they think they can take over tinsel town too. Movie Set is a nice little diversion into a not-so-reputable Hollywood studio. And once again, the aliens seem to relish playing roles normally destined for humans and a few talking pigs and dogs. But for all the enthusiasm normally shown by newcomers to the industry, don't expect high production values or moving artistic statements from the alien directors and their second rate thespians. Their sensibilities really seem more in tune with the B-movie, drive-in splatter genre. And there is probably nothing the aliens would like more than to have you star in their first feature snuff flick.

The Movie Set consists of two stages where low-budget, sci-fi send-ups are currently under production. About half of the entire space in this level is taken up by an open lot for outdoor shootings, literally. Although the exit switch is only a short distance from your entry point, you will have to collect all three keycards before you take your final bow and leave Movie Set behind. You can also choose to branch off into Tier Drop, the first secret level in Shrapnel City.

## MAPS AND ROUTE

In lieu of a script for the Movie Set, check out Figures 6.12 and 6.13 for a preview of coming attractions.

## THE GOODS

Besides the usual studio equipment, props, and cameras, Movie Set has a few items useful to your cause, as shown in Table 6.9.

### TABLE 6.9: THE GOODS IN MOVIE SET

| WEAPONS | AMMO | POWER-UPS |
|---|---|---|
| 1 shotgun | 2 cases | 3 portable medkits |
| 1 ripper chaingun | 2 cases | 8 atomic health units |
| 1 RPG launcher | 3 cases | 1 armor |
| 1 devastator | 5 cases | 1 steroid flask |
| 1 shrinker | 1 shrinker crystal | 2 jetpacks |
| 1 freezethrower | | 2 NVGs |
| 2 laser trip bombs | | 1 holoduke |
| 2 pipe bomb cases | | |

## BLAZING THROUGH MOVIE SET

There is no point in hanging out at a soda fountain waiting to be discovered. Take your destiny in your own hands. Blaze through Movie Set, and rise to major stardom in no time flat.

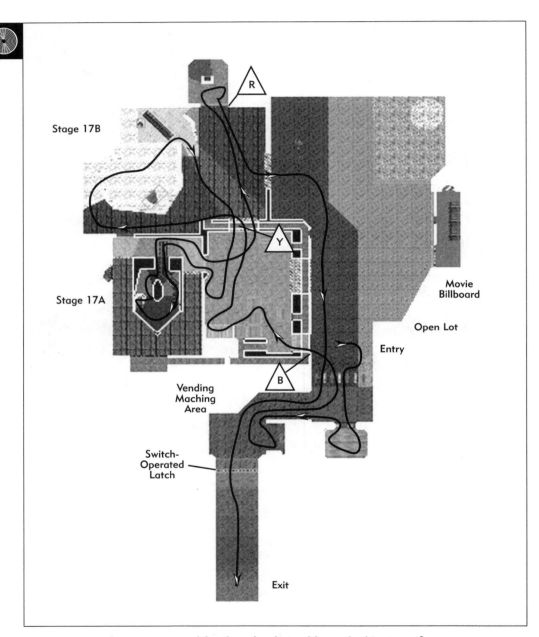

Stage 17B

Stage 17A

Movie
Billboard

Open Lot

Entry

Vending
Maching
Area

Switch-
Operated
Latch

Exit

**FIGURE 6.12:** Are you prepared for the role of your life on the big screen?

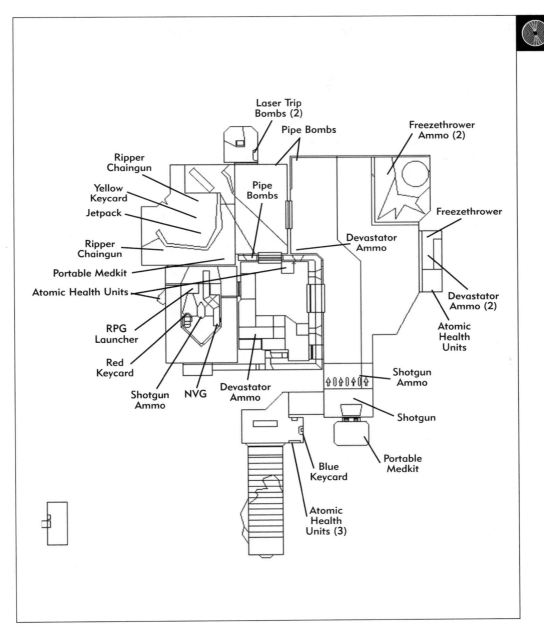

**FIGURE 6.13:** Don't look for a casting couch; just collect as many of these props as you can in Movie Set.

## At the Start

1. **Get the blue keycard.** Without the blue keycard, you can wander all you want in the open lot, but you will never get inside the filming stages.

Naturally, your first move is to find the keycard in question. Look behind you at the entry point—near the south end of the open lot—and pick up the shotgun shells sitting on top of the lane divider. Grab a shotgun and duck from the sights of two pig cops inside a small chamber. Dispose of the pig cops quickly, perhaps with a pipe bomb. Climb over the cash registers, and grab the portable medkit that you pray you don't have to use up too quickly. Climb back out from the small room, and head east toward a dingy vending machine area, where you can snatch the blue keycard by the public phone.

> ☠ **WARNING**
>
> The dark, dingy tiled room is a prime spot to be ambushed by pig cops. It also isn't unusual for an assault commander to show up unexpectedly.

## Inside the Stages

1. **Make the devastator yours.** Use the blue keycard to enter stage 17A. The first chamber is a warehouse of sorts with various wooden crates. You will have to battle a few enforcers before you can attempt to claim the devastator, which is a somewhat tricky proposition. Walk up to the crates lined up along the south wall. Push the middle panel of the crate in the center. Quickly, as soon as you hear the top crate slide open, jump onto the stage light and from there into the open crate.

2. **Score the yellow keycard.** Go north and enter Stage 17B. The production under way on this stage has to do with some gratuitous desecration on the Moon, which is sure to bring a flashback or two of your days in Lunar Apocalypse. Take the studio crew by surprise, and storm out holding the yellow keycard. Now it's time to enter the actual film scene back on stage 17A.

3. **One more card to go.** Open the door to stage 17A, and step inside the back side of the set. Drop a few pipe bombs onto the lower stage before delivering your lines, which are basically, "I'm here to kill you and take the red keycard." Access the capsule prop, and reach inside the pilot's chair to take the red keycard. Your next destination is the small chamber at the extreme north end of Movie Set.

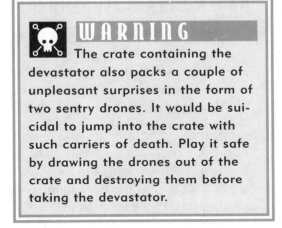

**WARNING**

The crate containing the devastator also packs a couple of unpleasant surprises in the form of two sentry drones. It would be suicidal to jump into the crate with such carriers of death. Play it safe by drawing the drones out of the crate and destroying them before taking the devastator.

4. **Push a crucial switch.** Clear out of stage 17A, and cut through the warehouse area toward the small door at the north end of Studio 17B. Use the red keycard and step inside the small chamber. Do you hear some hair-raising growls in the distance? Stepping into this chamber conjures the dreaded Battlelord. Pound the switch on the right side. Look at the monitor to see the garage-style door lift at the very south end of Movie Set.

**TIP**

While you're visiting stage 17B, consider locating and securing one of this level's two jetpacks, if you don't already have one. This power-up could come in quite handy in the next level.

5. **Dash to freedom.** With all physical barriers removed, make your way back south. If you go out in the open lot, you will have to face a newly materialized Battlelord and his sidekick, the assault commander. However, if you stay inside the stages, you might avoid a painful confrontation. The choice, as always, is yours.

## ADDED ATTRACTIONS IN MOVIE SET

If you ever wanted to shoot a scene at an open lot location, step out to the open lot. But beware of the wrath of two formidable enemies, the dreadful Battlelord and his bloated cohort, none other than the fatuous assault commander.

### Shooting onto the Open Lot

After stepping into the north chamber to push the switch that lifts the exit door (way back at the south end), you are basically clear to leave the set. However, the call of the wild and the growling of the Battlelord in the open lot might be too much to resist. And, of course, there is another potent reason to prolong your stay: You can uncover the secret of the billboard and reap handsome rewards.

Moving very quickly, and staying indoors, outrun the Battlelord to reach the southernmost door on stage 17A. Hoisting a high impact weapon like the RPG launcher or the devastator, step out facing north, and open fire at the encroaching Battlelord. He will soon be joined by the assault commander. Deliver an unhealthy dose of punishment. (See Figure 6.14.) Then sidestep back inside the stage, and close the door behind you. Leave the confused aliens cooling their heels and other extremities outside, and dash back to the north side, inside stage 17B. Open the door and, facing south this time, repeat the same procedure as before. One or two solid RPGs will do the assault commander in. The Battlelord may outlast him, but not for very long.

### The Secret of the Billboard

By now, you might have suspected the billboard hides something. For one thing you may have been hit enough times to know the shots come from somewhere on the east side of the open lot. Before you go investigating what lies behind the billboard, clear the way by firing randomly, but aiming mostly in its center section.

Now there's the matter of getting up there. If you have a jetpack, then you've got no problem; and if you don't, that's no problem either. Just go around the helicopter crash site, and jump along the rubble until you reach a large piece of asphalt you can climb on. From there, it's just another short jump to a narrow walkway below the giant billboard. Walk along to the 3D Realms logo, and step right in. Collect the atomic health

**FIGURE 6.14:** You will soon find out why an open lot "shoot" isn't as glamorous as it is portrayed in the movies.

unit, climb the ramp, and take two cases of devastator ammo and the freezethrower. Then be immediately on guard for another assault commander.

There is not much time to plan your moves. Before you know it, the assault commander will be furiously pounding the billboard with his devastating, albeit, unusually propelled rockets. Your best option is to drop off the platform to reach cover. Then, reach for your newest acquisition, the freezethrower, and, still inside the billboard, step into his line of sight and bombard the assault commander until he freezes solid in mid air. With a flash of flair, flick out the lowly handgun and break the crystallized commander.

## COVERT DETAILS

Do you want to hear about the dirty little secrets of Movie Set? Table 6.10 gives you the inside scoop.

**TABLE 6.10: THE SECRETS IN MOVIE SET**

| AREA IN LEVEL | SECRET ITEMS | HOW TO GET IT |
|---|---|---|
| Stage 17A | jetpack | Jump right through the projection screen showing the blue planet. |
| Warehouse for Stage 17A | devastator | Push the middle panel of the central crate along the south wall. Then jump onto nearby stage lights, and from there jump into the open crate, where the devastator is kept along with a couple of sentry drones. |
| Stage 17B | secret exit | Press the letter on the fin of the rocket to uncover the secret exit right on the side of the rocket. If you step through the door and press the exit switch, you will come out in Tier Drop. |
| Vending machine room | atomic health units (3) | Get inside the small chamber at the south end of the open lot. Push the cash register machine on the right side (there are two machines). Run quickly to reach the secret area behind the vending machine before it raises from the ground to block the space again. |
| Movie billboard on the open lot | atomic health unit devastator ammo (2 cases) freezethrower | Fly into the bottom right or top center portion of the billboard. Without a jetpack, access the billboard from the north side, in the area where the helicopter crashed. Hop along the debris and onto a large piece of cement. From there jump to the narrow walkway below the billboard. Step in through the 3D Realms logo. |

# RABID TRANSIT

This level takes place entirely in the dingy underground. The backdrop is a subway system with two trains and only one route in the shape of a large O. The trains run counterclockwise on a fixed schedule, arriving closely together at the east boarding deck and separated by a few seconds at the west deck. This bit of information is not trivial, when you consider you might have to jump off a moving train or run along the tracks.

Your initial entry point is near the center point of the oval route, in a tunnel close to the east boarding deck. Your ultimate destination is the U-shaped chamber to the south, inside the system's route. The only area outside the periphery of the route is the west boarding deck. This is also the place where the red keycard can be found. The red keycard, as you have correctly guessed, opens the south latch into the U-shaped chamber. However, access to the west boarding deck is only possible with the aid of the blue keycard. Rabid Transit punishes carelessness and rewards fighting skills, dexterity, and sheer guts—all qualities synonymous with the Duke Nukem name.

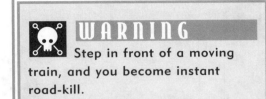

**WARNING** Step in front of a moving train, and you become instant road-kill.

## MAPS AND ROUTE

What better way to get a handle on Rabid Transit than to view the actual route map, as shown in Figure 6.15. Figure 6.16 will help get you oriented to collect everything you'll need.

## THE GOODS

It's dark, dingy, and savage, but Rabid Transit does offer a few good reasons to take a couple of rides on the trains. Table 6.11 shows you the goods.

### TABLE 6.11: THE GOODS IN RABID TRANSIT

| WEAPONS | AMMO | POWER-UPS |
| --- | --- | --- |
| 1 shotgun | 3 cases | 2 portable medkits |
| 2 ripper chainguns | 1 case | 5 atomic health units |
| 1 RPG launcher | 3 cases | 1 armor |
| 2 devastators | 5 cases | 1 steroid flask |
| 1 shrinker | | 1 NVG |
| 1 freezethrower | | 1 holoduke |
| 5 laser trip bombs | | |
| 2 pipe bomb cases | | |
| 1 pipe bomb | | |

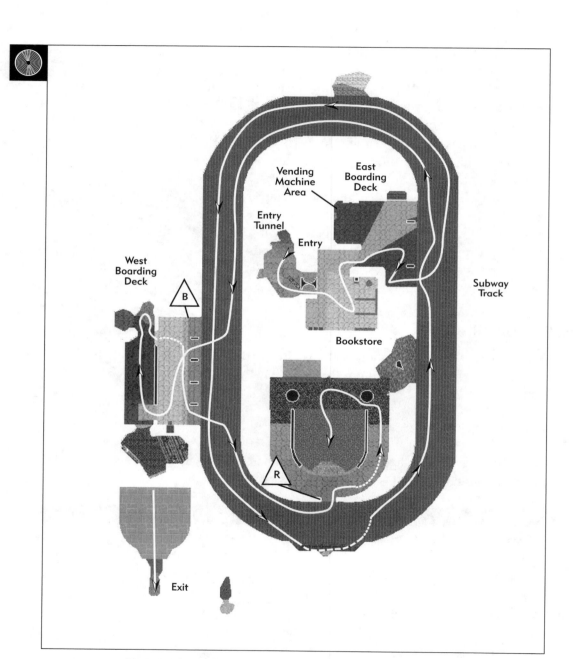

**FIGURE 6.15:** How do I get there from here? Getting around in Rabid Transit is never easy.

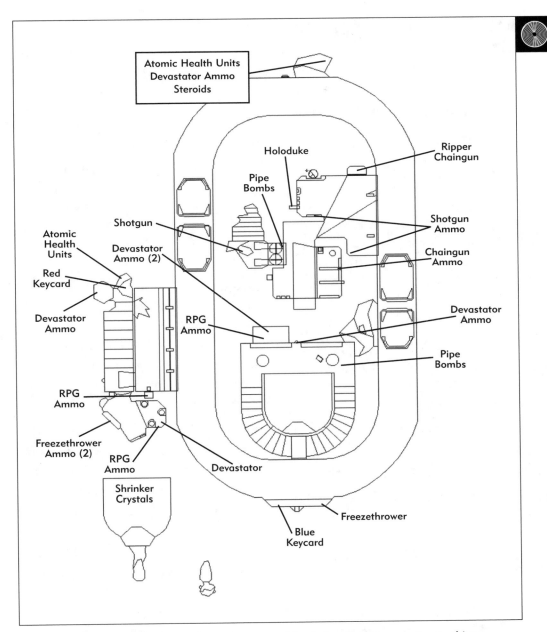

**FIGURE 6.16:** You will discover that going around in circles sometimes gets you things.

# BLAZING THROUGH RABID TRANSIT

You can't get around the fact that you must go around to get anywhere in Rabid Transit. Here is a simple but effective itinerary so you can make all your connections.

## Around the East Boarding Deck

1. **Get some goods right away.** Emerge from the rubble of the tunnel through the revolving doors and into a bookstore. Watch out for the turret at the south end and the encroaching troopers and captains. If you grab the chaingun ammo from on top of the shelf, several pig cops will materialize on the scene.

2. **Take it to the boarding deck.** Mow down a few pig cops as you move into the vending machine area to collect a shotgun. Then look behind the Lunar Apocalypse movie poster, and jump into a small enclosure to grab a ripper chaingun.

3. **Take out the laser trip bombs.** Stand at a good distance and attempt to detonate the laser trip bombs barring access to the trains. A square shotgun blast usually does the trick, but it's hard to fail with a pipe bomb as well.

4. **Wait for your train to come in.** Notice how the second train arrives almost right behind the first one. Get on the last car of the second train. Scoot next to the opposite door. The train makes only one stop. And it is on the west boarding deck.

> ☠ **WARNING**
>
> As far as anyone knows, without a jetpack, it is impossible to get the blue keycard, which rests on an elevated platform at the south end. For that reason, if a jetpack doesn't figure in your arsenal, you should go back to the last level and collect one. If not, your stay in Rabid Transit may well be eternal and not just transitory.

> 💡 **TIP**
>
> Expect to hear a few sentry drones' engines whip up to a frenzy as soon as you reach for the ripper chaingun. Save yourself from serious damage by shutting the compartment as quickly as you can. If you move fast enough, you can expect to hear the drones crash on the wall outside.

## At the First Stop

1. **Don't get off yet!** The first time you come around the west boarding deck, you will notice the entire area is behind metal curtains. It does no good to get off because you still have not scored the blue keycard. Stay in the car and spray bullets at the pig cops patrolling the sealed deck.

## Your First Jump

1. **Get off at the right time.** As the train approaches the south end of its route, get ready to jump off. The right moment is when you see a red-lit platform where a few pig cops guard the blue keycard. Jump off confidently. A small recess below the platform gives you just enough space to avoid being squished by the next passing train.

2. **Get the blue keycard.** Activate your jetpack to reach the platform and wrestle the blue keycard from the pig cops. Look across the way and notice a small yellow latch that leads to the U-shaped chamber, where freedom awaits at the bottom of the wet area. However, don't go for it prematurely; your next move is to penetrate the west side.

3. **Run on the tracks.** It sounds dangerous and it is, but the alternative is to try boarding a moving train, having only a small window of opportunity and no room for a second try. The best time to run is right after a train passes. Run directly back to the west side to put the blue keycard to use.

## On the West Boarding Deck

1. **Bust the pig cops.** As soon as the metal curtains lift, you are at the end of a large rectangular area covered with aliens in blue uniforms. The RPG launcher or devastator is hard to beat in this situation.

2. **Clear the stairway.** Step just inside the stairway, and fire an RPG toward the dark north end, where a bunch of alien eggs are almost ready to hatch. A major explosion will rattle the entire area, causing a tunnel to

form, which connects the stairway and the deck at the north end. Also, suddenly the entire boarding deck will become crowded with octabrains.

3. **Get the red keycard at the top of the stairs.** As you begin your ascent, you will hear the hair-raising growl of the Battlelord, who materializes at the bottom of the stairway.

4. **Get back on the tracks.** As soon as you notice a train go by, jump back on the tracks and then use the red keycard on the latch at the south end.

## In the U-Shaped Chamber

1. **Trash two assault commanders.** Move along the perimeter steps, and try to make each one of your RPG shots count. Avoid hitting the bound female at the bottom of the U-shaped chamber to prevent additional octabrains from materializing.

2. **Dive for pearls.** Although not exactly pearls, there is a shrinker at the bottom of the pool—and a couple of octabrains.

3. **Slide through the final tunnel.** Head directly into the inviting opening at the south end of the pool. Swim upwards into a cavity, where the glowing red switch beckons you to come home in no uncertain terms.

# ADDED ATTRACTIONS IN RABID TRANSIT

By far the most intense moment in Rabid Transit occurs on the west boarding deck. Getting the red keycard at the top of the dark stairway involves engaging some of your toughest enemies. You can't avoid the confrontation, but you can try to control it and pace it in such a way that is advantageous to your cause.

## The Bloody Battle for the Red Keycard

Once you have cleared the dock from the initial wave of pig cops, things will appear to be calm. But don't let your guard down for a second. In this section of Rabid Transit, your enemies

> **TIP**
> You can also reach the red keycard by crawling through the hole you created when you fired the RPG launcher. This way you can avoid the stairs altogether, and prevent the Battlelord from materializing.

materialize only after you take certain actions. Knowing what these actions are allows you to be ready for the ensuing alien attack.

Stepping into the threshold of the stairway, aim north and fire an RPG at the egg hatchery at the north end of the tunnel. A violent explosion rattles the place and causes a multitude of octabrains to materialize in the deck area. Holding your position just inside the stairway, you have an ideal angle to release RPGs at the octabrains outside, as shown in Figure 6.17. Additionally, you can use the dividing wall as a shield from the octabrains' mental energy blasts.

When the octabrains' remains are spread over the deck, get out and approach the north end very cautiously. You want to avoid crossing the stairs because that would only mean that you would be triggering a Battlelord to crash the party. As you get near the north side where the explosion dug a tunnel, be ready to unload a few more RPGs or devastator rounds on the assault commander lurking in the dark. The best time to catch him is when you first hear his sadistic laugh echoing from the tunnel. Fire directly into the gaping dark hole, and prevent the commander from joining you on the boarding deck.

**FIGURE 6.17:** Use your protected position inside the stairway, and do away with the octabrains before making your next move.

## COVERT DETAILS

Rabid Transit houses a good number of secrets, and Table 6.12 lists them all for you.

### TABLE 6.12: THE SECRETS IN RABID TRANSIT

| AREA IN LEVEL | SECRET ITEMS | HOW TO GET IT |
| --- | --- | --- |
| West boarding deck | RPG ammo | Jump on top of the mail drop box, and push against the wall to open a secret compartment. |
| Dark stairway | freezethrower ammo (2) devastator RPG ammo | Push the left side of the wall at the south end. Enter the alien chamber, and collect the freezethrower ammo in plain view. Then activate a control panel at the bottom, right corner of the large screen to uncover an adjoining chamber along the east side. This chamber houses the devastator and RPG ammo. |
| U-shaped chamber | devastator ammo (2 cases) RPG ammo (1 case) | Use your jetpack to lift yourself on top of the bookshelf on the left side. Then hop onto the next bookshelf. This causes the first bookshelf to lower and reveal a small chamber with the goods. |
| Vending machine area | holoduke | Jump on top of the magazine dispenser at the southwest corner. It will lower to show a small chamber where you can crouch and grab the holoduke. |
| Hole at the north end of the tracks | atomic health unit devastator ammo (1 case) steroids | Blow a hole in the north wall, step in, and claim the loot. Of course, you have to negotiate the timing of the trains to avoid being run over when you are in this area. |
| East boarding deck | ripper chaingun | Push the Lunar Apocalypse poster, and jump into the enclosure to grab the weapon. |

# FAHRENHEIT

Who turned up the temperature? This level puts you back above ground, in a part of the city where a TV studio and a fire station dominate the landscape. There is also a small and cozy apartment nearby, a courtyard, and an open warehouse. Like in most major cities, the environment might seem crowded and encroaching. But unlike in most cities, Fahrenheit's environment is run by the aliens you seem to know all too well by now. Sentry drones and assault commanders have a strong presence in this level. But even if you get past them and make it all the way to the exit, you must still face the Battlelord and two of his enforcer minions.

Fahrenheit strikes a pleasing balance of inside action and frisky outdoor encounters. In Fahrenheit, you might start to realize just how effective weapons like the freeze-thrower and the shrinker are in crowded situations. You only need to score the blue and then the red keycards. After that, you are practically home free—except for the small matter of an encounter with the Battlelord. Although the blue keycard is plainly visible at the north end of the waterway, the red keycard is a bit tougher to locate. It is hidden in the fire station's pole, which is inaccessible until you reach and push the appropriate switch. The assault commanders around the fire station complicate matters to a much higher degree. You might not come out smelling like roses, but if you use your weapons judiciously and maintain your health level, you will prevail over Fahrenheit.

## MAPS AND ROUTE

Although you could use the maps to fan yourself, Figures 6.18 and 6.19 can help you cope with the heat you will experience in Fahrenheit.

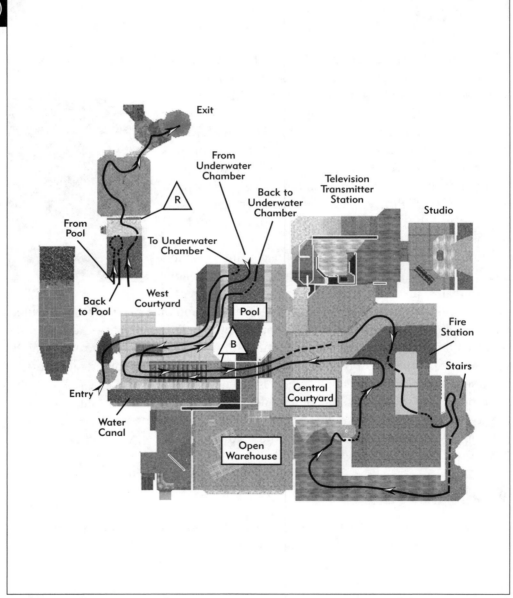

**FIGURE 6.18:** You will see hot action in both close and open quarters in Fahrenheit.

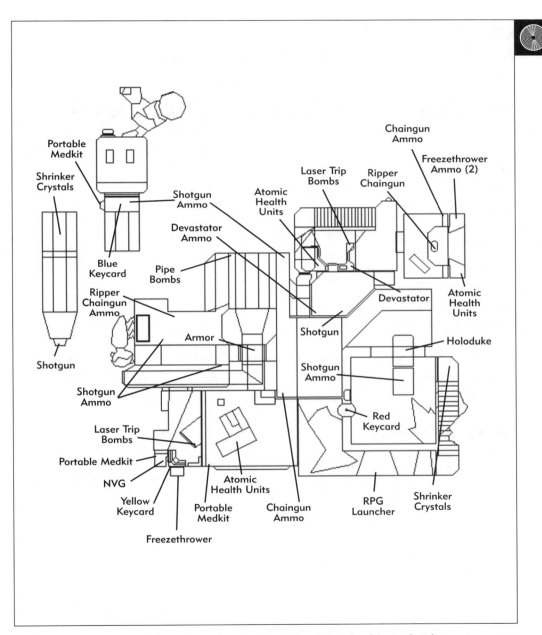

**FIGURE 6.19:** All three keycards are available in Fahrenheit, should you decide to uncover every secret and reap every useful item.

# THE GOODS

Fahrenheit offers almost everything you need to make it through, even if you start the level nearly empty-handed. Table 6.13 shows you the goods.

**TABLE 6.13: THE GOODS IN FAHRENHEIT**

| WEAPONS | AMMO | POWER-UPS |
|---|---|---|
| 2 shotguns | 4 cases | 4 portable medkits |
| 4 ripper chainguns | 1 case | 4 atomic health units |
| 2 RPG launchers | 2 cases | 1 armor |
| 1 devastator | 3 cases | 1 steroid flask |
| 1 shrinker | 3 shrinker crystals | 1 NVG |
| 1 freezethrower | | 1 holoduke |
| 2 laser trip bombs | | |
| 1 pipe bomb case | | |

# BLAZING THROUGH FAHRENHEIT

If you want to explore this level in depth, consider visiting the nearby apartment and the television transmitter station. But to make tracks as quickly as possible, stick to the plan below.

## In the West Courtyard

1. **Kill the pig cops, and loot the area.** Push the metal surface to slide a big Dumpster out of the way and emerge in a small courtyard. Battle a couple of pig cops, and pick up the shotgun shells and chaingun ammo. Head for the north end of the courtyard.

2. **Cook some octabrains in their juices.** Climb on the ledge of the canal, and grab the pipe bomb case. Drop a couple of pipe bombs in succession, and detonate them simultaneously to make short work of the octabrains below. Then dive in and continue north into a larger underwater chamber covered with green growth. Come up for air.

3. **Take the blue keycard, please.** Hop onto a small platform at the north end of the pool, and grab the blue keycard. Notice that the large gate in

front of you requires a yellow keycard. Grab the portable medkit as you dive back into the pool, and head for the west courtyard again. Go down the ramp and use the blue keycard on the gate.

## In the Central Courtyard

1. **Work your way to the fire station.** To better your odds, take out the turret high up in the northwest corner of the courtyard. Then grab the ripper chaingun ammo at the south end. Before rushing toward the fire station, as you ascend the inclined asphalt, look southwest in the direction of a warehouse area. If you haven't already felt its firepower, notice the turret mounted high in the corner. If you have your RPG launcher, take it out and be done with it. Then get ready for a four-alarm fire in the station.

2. **Set the fire station on fire.** Would that you could; but first, you must get what you came here for—the red keycard. Several pig cops will die if necessary to keep you out of this area. Pound them hard and when you get a chance, hop on top of the fire truck to claim a holoduke and a case of shotgun shells.

3. **Blow a hole in the wall.** Either use the RPG launcher or drop a pipe bomb on the east side of the truck to blast an opening into the stairs leading to the top side of the station. Step into the hole and grab the shrinker crystals near the entrance. Then start your ascent into the dark stairway.

4. **Open the pole and slide down.** Reaching the top area of the fire station, notice a switch on the right side, next to the cylindrical enclosure that hides the pole. Push the

> **TIP**
> Expect to hear the very low and ominous laughter of the assault commanders guarding the pole. You should have your RPG launcher ready to fire straight ahead at the first sign of movement. To avoid being reduced to puree, keep a prudent distance by running back into the lower part of the tunnel, if necessary. Normally, the second assault commander stays behind, so you will have to deal with him separately, which is probably a good thing.

switch to uncover the elusive pole. Slide down it and land on top of the red keycard at the bottom. Trace your steps back to the west courtyard. Get back in the water and swim north again.

## In the North End

1.  **Open the last gate and meet some old faces.** Be ready to jump back in the water and get out of harm's way, for as soon as you open the door you are faced with a less-than-hospitable Battlelord and two of his pet enforcers.

2.  **Battle the Battlelord with courage.** An effective technique in this seemingly hopeless situation is to jump in and out of the water like a pogo stick, unloading your arsenal as you break the surface and then rapidly dropping to avoid retaliation. It also helps if you sidestep left and right to keep them guessing.

3.  **Knock out yet another hole.** Enter the medium-sized chamber, previously held by the Battlelord, and grab the RPG launcher behind the compartment. Back off a few steps, and blow another hole into the north wall of the chamber. Climb along the jagged edges of the tunnel. Then descend into the area to the right to find the exit switch.

# ADDED ATTRACTIONS IN FAHRENHEIT

If you haven't had enough fun yet, there are a couple of other places in Fahrenheit that are certainly worth visiting. These places include:

- A nearby cozy apartment
- A television transmitter station with truly questionable programming

## The Cozy Apartment

Tucked away in the southwest corner of Fahrenheit, there is one small but cozy apartment. It overlooks an open warehouse area with a few crates of varying dimensions. The apartment has a TV showroom, complete with multiple screens. In addition, a wet bar and plenty of well drinks make the atmosphere even more alluring. The only way to reach this little oasis in this asphalt desert is to cross the open warehouse area. The sentry drones and enforcers patrolling the area aren't exactly keen on letting just anyone get by, much less you. But you aren't exactly expecting an open invitation either.

So, enter the warehouse carefully, expecting leaping enforcers to pounce on you at any moment. The freezethrower or shrinker will work wonders on the first wave of offenders. But these weapons aren't as effective against sentry drones. Switch to the ripper chaingun or the shotgun to keep the drones from dive bombing into you.

Hop onto the smallest crate and from there into the next larger one. At this point, you should be able to peek inside the windows of a small open space that leads directly into the small apartment. Jump from the middle crate

> **TIP**
>
> A most effective way for disposing of the Battlelord and his pals in this very confined situation is to rely almost exclusively on your freezethrower. If you have enough charges and can maintain a sustained attack where you can unload the equivalent of one charge (twenty-five blasts), then you can shatter his majesty with a simple bullet.

> **NOTE**
>
> If you intend to visit the TV station, you will first have to get the yellow keycard, which, fortunately for you, is inside the cozy apartment.

up onto the narrow ledge right by the windows. Use the wall space between the windows for cover as you assassinate the pig cops inside. Then face eastward and jump onto the larger and longer of the crates to claim an atomic health unit. After that, you're clear to enter the apartment. Hop back onto the ledge, and from there go right through the window and get inside the apartment. These series of movements are graphically depicted in Figure 6.20.

Once inside the apartment, be sure to pick up the devastator and RPG ammo along the north side. Notice the very dark wall next to the RPG ammo. It hides a message for you, but you will need the NVG to read the message; deciphering it is another matter. Head toward the south end, where the entertainment center is found along with a cushy sofa and the aforementioned wet bar. Get up on the couch to reach for the yellow keycard. Also, don't pass up the steroids on top of one of the bookshelves. The

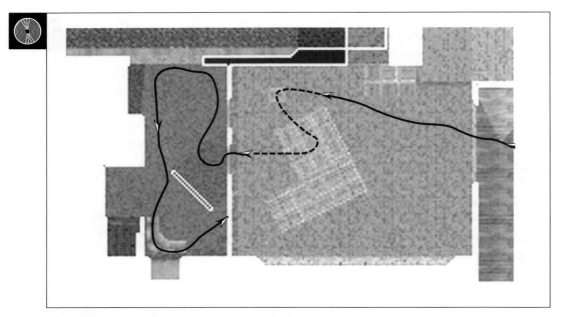

**FIGURE 6.20:** This is how you get to the cozy apartment.

painting behind the couch hides a secret compartment where a freezethrower is kept. Also, if you want to read the secret message on the dark wall, you should grab the NVG on the bookshelf. Having reaped a few goods, you might as well take a load off on the couch, and take in a few moving pictures on the sets.

## The Television Transmitter Station

Don't even think about visiting the transmitter station, unless you have a yellow key-card on you. (If you don't, check out the nearby apartment at the southwest corner of Fahrenheit.) From the central courtyard, head north toward a ramp leading directly to the main door of the station. Use the yellow keycard and smoke the enforcer pages dispatched to guide you on a private tour of the facilities. The ripper chaingun and the shotgun may prove somewhat ineffective in such tight quarters. So without any vacillation, whip out the shrinker and reduce your enemies to the size of bugs. Then step on them.

Proceed up the stairs, resist going into the closed studio doors, and take possession of the security control room. There are only a couple of assault captains in the monitoring room. Be sure not to miss the devastator next to the monitor on the left side.

Take stock of your health. If it needs it, you can give it a boost with the atomic health unit behind a small door near the back of the room. The door actually opens into the back of the monitoring system. Feeling good and mighty powerful, head toward the closed studio doors. Face them squarely and throw them open. Before the doors have finished opening completely, back out to the security control room as you fire a steady stream of devastator charges. If the assault commander hovering near the door manages to expel a rocket, you can sidestep out of the way inside the security room.

Continue sidestepping and unloading charges. The freezethrower is also an excellent weapon from this distance. As soon as the assault commander turns blue, like a grotesque, hovering ice statue, switch to another weapon and break him. Inside the studio you will find a ripper chaingun and some ammo on top of a bookshelf.

## COVERT DETAILS

Fahrenheit is hot for action as well as secrets. Check out Table 6.14 to see for yourself.

### TABLE 6.14: THE SECRETS IN FAHRENHEIT

| AREA IN LEVEL | SECRET ITEMS | HOW TO GET IT |
|---|---|---|
| Security room | atomic health unit | Open the narrow door at the back of the security room inside the television transmitter station. |
| Studio room | freezethrower ammo atomic health unit | Walk right through the curtains behind the stage. |
| Cozy apartment | Portable medkit | Break every bottle and glass on the wet bar shelf, before you can simply walk right through it. |

# HOTEL HELL

If it weren't for the dubious clientele, Hotel Hell might actually be a nice place for serious power lounging. The decor is somewhat Spartan, to be sure, but the hourly rooms are cozy and, above all, functional. The upstairs pool and bar are also a nice amenity. You almost want to order a martini and take in the sun by the poolside deck. Yet, this is Hotel Hell, and its alien management—headed by the Battlelord Sentry and his squadron of enforcers, troopers, pig cops, and RPVs—don't believe in carrying your baggage or taking tips. Forget the leisurely life. In fact, if you don't watch yourself in this level, forget life period. Hotel Hell is also your connection to Freeway, the second secret level in Shrapnel City.

A hotel of ill repute, otherwise known as the Wham Bam, dominates this level. The flickering neon sign outside foreshadows the seediness inside. The hotel is flanked by a wide alley to the north. A large street meets the hotel's main entrance on the east side. To the south, the hotel's side door opens onto a narrow street. On the way to the secret exit, Hotel Hell pays homage to a legendary adventurer and doctor of anthropology, a man inseparable from his bull whip, brim hat, and leather jacket. Might you have heard of him?

## MAPS AND ROUTE

Don't get lost in a second rate hotel. The maps in Figures 6.22 and 6.23 can keep you from straying into an early and final bed.

## THE GOODS

Before checking out of Hotel Hell permanently, make it a point to grab all the loot you can get. As Table 6.15 shows, there is quite a bit of stuff you can lay your hand on.

| TABLE 6.15: THE GOODS IN HOTEL HELL | | |
|---|---|---|
| **WEAPONS** | **AMMO** | **POWER-UPS** |
| 1 shotgun | 5 cases | 3 portable medkits |
| 1 ripper chainguns | 3 cases | 5 atomic health units |
| 1 RPG launcher | 2 cases | 2 armors |
| 1 devastator | 4 cases | 1 steroid flask |
| 1 shrinker | 2 shrinker crystals | 2 NVGs |
| 2 freezethrowers | 1 charge | 2 holodukes |
| 2 laser trip bombs | | |
| 2 pipe bombs | | |
| 3 pipe bomb cases | | |

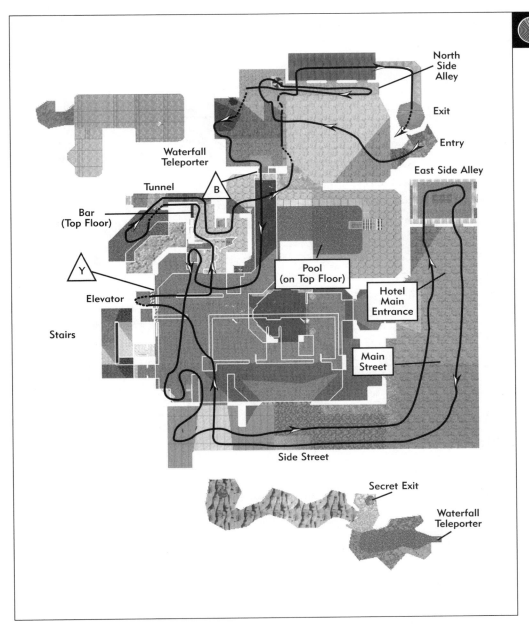

**FIGURE 6.21:** Peril awaits at every turn in Hotel Hell, so take stock of your surroundings and avoid serious trouble.

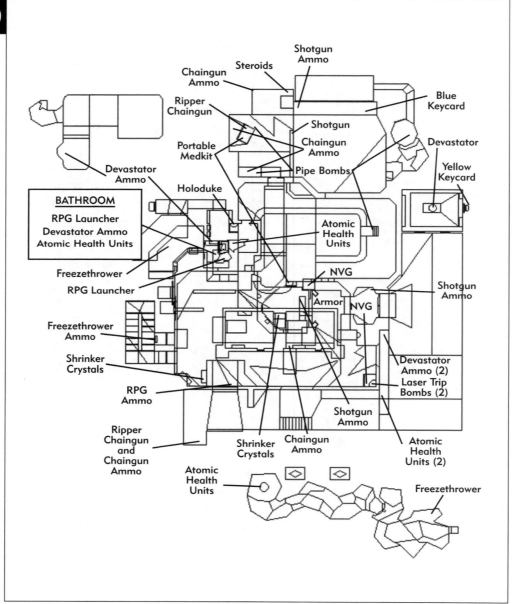

**FIGURE 6.22:** There are two keycards in Hotel Hell, and you will need them both to reach either of the two exits.

# BLAZING THROUGH HOTEL HELL

In this hotel you are charged by the hour, so make every minute count. In fact, if you get done before time expires, consider staying for seconds to reach the secret exit.

## In the North Side Alley

1. **Score a shotgun and down a few bad pig cops.** Hop out of the tunnel you reached at the end of Fahrenheit into a wide alley on the north side of the Wham Bam hotel. Take the shotgun sitting on top of a wooden wall and destroy the pig cops who are sure to sniff you out. Notice there really is no place to go, as the security latch by the door requires you to have a blue keycard.

2. **Grab the blue keycard.** Luckily for you, the blue keycard is in the near vicinity. Hop onto the wooden wall and face north, toward a ventilating unit on top of the short building. Hop again to land near the unit. Finally, a third hop onto the ledge running east and west will place you in plain view of the keycard.

3. **Check into the hotel.** Use caution when you open the door, for there might well be a pig cop on the other side. When you reach the end of the hallway, a blast will open a large hole on the north side of the wall. From this point on, you know you are in for quite a bang inside Wham Bam Hotel.

## Inside the Hotel

1. **Load up on heavy firepower.** Cut a quick right at the end of the hallway, and enter the gaping hole into a dilapidated bathroom. Pick up the RPG launcher from the tiled floor and the devastator ammo on the broken sink.

2. **Skip the soda but take the crystals.** Rush toward the south end of the open foyer, and hop on top of the soda vending machine to take two shrinker crystals.

3. **Face the action outside.** Step out the side door to the south into a narrow side street. You will be instantly met by an assortment of enforcers, pig cops, and an RPV or two. So use every trick in the book, and maybe write a few, to advance into the main street toward the east.

## In front of the Hotel

1. **Stay clear of the entrance.** As you turn north onto the main street, you will be facing an upward slope and several of your favorite enemies, including pig cops, enforcers, and another RPV. As inside the hotel, avoid stirring the Battlelord Sentry by staying away from the entrance. Stand your ground or retreat back to the side street to make the street safer for yourself.

2. **Fight the enforcers from a distance.** Advance northward toward the east office, but stop short of crossing the front entrance of the hotel. By now you will have noticed the enforcers inside the east side office at the end of the street. Pull out the ripper chaingun, turn on the crosshair, and do what you don't get paid to do, but will do gladly.

3. **Rush toward the east side office.** Once the enforcer office party is over, rush past the hotel's front entrance, avoiding detection, and jump right through either window into the office.

## In the East Side Office

1. **Beef up your arsenal and uncover the yellow keycard.** Take the devastator on top of the desk immediately. Then walk toward the compartment on the east wall to claim the yellow keycard.

2. **Keep the devastator handy.** Next thing you know, an assault commander shows up to intercept you. Don't be caught off guard. Be ready to point, aim, and fire in the direction of the sinister laughter that cuts the air like a cold, serrated boning knife.

3. **Head back to the hotel.** If you feel brave enough, go ahead and enter through the front door. Engage the Battlelord Sentry and knock him out

with three to five solid RPG hits. If you want to play it safe, just dash back the way you got to the east side office.

4. **Get to the top floor.** Inside the hotel's lobby, find the elevator and use the yellow keycard to ride up to the hotel's bar and pool area.

## In the Bar and Pool Area

1. **Step up to the bar.** When you open the elevator door, you can be easily overwhelmed by a mob of enforcers. Avoid this sad fate by dropping a few pipe bombs and then closing the door quickly. From the safety of the elevator, detonate the pipe bombs to stop the enforcer menace before it can mount an offensive.

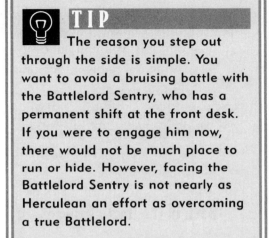

**TIP**
The reason you step out through the side is simple. You want to avoid a bruising battle with the Battlelord Sentry, who has a permanent shift at the front desk. If you were to engage him now, there would not be much place to run or hide. However, facing the Battlelord Sentry is not nearly as Herculean an effort as overcoming a true Battlelord.

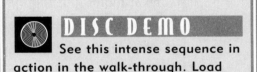

**DISC DEMO**
See this intense sequence in action in the walk-through. Load and play the file E3L8.BLZ from the CD-ROM.

2. **Check out the wine list, but don't overlook the power-ups.** Look around behind the bar counter for a wooden panel at the north end. It is a secret door into a dark and gray hallway where you can take a portable medkit. The hallway leads to the top of a large water tank holding the freezethrower—and a shark. Grab the scuba gear and the case of pipe bombs from the compartment at the end of the hallway.

3. **Dive for the freezethrower.** If you don't already have it, it is really worthwhile to add this weapon to your cache. But even if you have one already, you can always use the extra charges.

4. **Make it to the poolside.** Get out of the tank and walk around behind the bar into the open area where the L-shaped pool is found. Overcome

whatever opposition you find from the roving troopers and captains in this area. Then hop onto the small platform at the north side of the pool, overlooking the initial alleyway where you entered this level. Across the street, you will notice the windows opening on the top floor of the building, revealing a room crowded with aliens of the enforcer ilk.

5. **Fight the enforcers from afar.** The ripper chaingun is a good choice to dispense with the enforcers from where you stand. Turning on the crosshair and the mouse pointing function, you can zero in on individual enforcers. With the enforcers no longer a threat, jump below into the alleyway.

## Back in the North Alley

1. **Reach the top floor of the building to the north.** As in the beginning, hop your way to the ledge of the top floor. Then jump inside the rectangular room.

2. **Go through the duct and down the chute.** Bash the grill on the east side of the room, and hop into the air duct.

3. **Dive to freedom.** Follow the duct as it turns sharply to the south. Then let yourself fall into a semi-circular pit. At the bottom, you will find the exit switch leading to Freeway.

# ADDED ATTRACTIONS IN HOTEL HELL

Because this level is a junction to the secret level Freeway, finding the secret exit is worth exploring in some detail, naturally.

## Exploring for the Secret Exit

Up to the point where you reach the pool, every step for finding the secret exit is exactly the same as when you are only headed for the normal exit. But when you are finally there, you can go either way. Should you choose to go for an extra romp you wouldn't ordinarily see in the course of your playtime, then by all means embark on a search. Who knows what secrets and surprises might await you there.

In the pool area, walk up to the waterfall that feeds the pool on the west side. Step right into the waterfall. You will come out into a natural, rocky terrain at the foot of another, this time natural, waterfall. Head west and explore the north banks along the small water hole to find a freezethrower. Eventually you will come upon a recess in the rocks where a couple of tall palm trees grow. The secret exit to Freeway is well hidden behind the palm trees. Throw a pipe bomb at the foot of the trees to uproot them completely.

Before marching over to the switch, let your sense of exploration heed the call of its primeval instincts. Push against the bloody hand print switch on the broken wall to your left. As the crack widens, step right through the fire into the tunnel just west of the secret exit switch. Follow the sinewy path all the way to the end, where you will find a chamber of sorts with a high ceiling and an atomic health unit sitting on top of a heavy cylindrical stone. But that's not all you will see. You seem to have happened upon perhaps a pagan temple of doom. If the unfortunate college-professor-turned-explorer's body impaled on the wall could speak, he would tell you to be careful.

Realizing the seriousness of the situation, grab the atomic health unit and back out as soon as humanly possible. A good dose of steroids will help you reach the exit before the entire tunnel collapses around and on top of you. Though Duke likes his hair flat on top, this is not the way to achieve it. Having replenished your vitality and health, get back to the secret exit switch and pound it decisively.

## COVERT DETAILS

If truth be told, there are but a few secrets to behold in Hotel Hell, but Table 6.16 comes clean about them.

### TABLE 6.16: THE SECRETS IN HOTEL HELL

| AREA IN LEVEL | SECRET ITEMS | HOW TO GET IT |
|---|---|---|
| Hotel bar (upstairs) | portable medkit<br>scuba gear<br>pipe bomb case | Push the wooden panel on the north wall, behind the bar countertop. It opens into a dark, gray hallway. |
| Hotel bar | holoduke | Push against the wine bottle rack to uncover a small secret area where the holoduke is kept. |
| Remote tunnel, near the secret exit | atomic health unit | Teleport to the area by stepping into the waterfall of the rooftop hotel pool. Follow the tunnel toward the west. The atomic health unit lies on top of a large cylindrical rock. |

# STADIUM

Stadium is the inevitable and much-awaited match of the millennium. A proverbial show-down of colossal proportions, Stadium pits the home-town favorite, Duke Nukem, against the formidable Cycloid Emperor. What's at stake in this final battle is much more than fabulous ratings or the home team's pride. The future of our world rests squarely on your shoulders, Nukem. Please don't let us down. You never have before.

## MAPS AND ROUTE

Considering the straightforward architecture of Stadium and the opposition's caliber, the maps shown in Figures 6.23 and 6.24 might somehow seem superfluous. But think of what's at stake. Every bit of knowledge can become a decisive advantage in Stadium.

## THE GOODS

Power-ups, weapons, and ammo are quite bountiful in Stadium. Of course, judging by the caliber of your opponent, you need everything you can get. Table 6.17 shows you what you can have, should you live long enough to collect. In addition, a *Duff Beer* dirigible floating over Stadium is a veritable weapon and power-up piñata. Fly as high as you can right above the center of Stadium and blow up the blimp to cause a shower of goodies to fall upon the grass of Stadium.

| TABLE 6.17: THE GOODS IN STADIUM | | |
| --- | --- | --- |
| WEAPONS | AMMO | POWER-UPS |
| 1 shotgun | 4 cases | 1 portable medkit |
| 1 ripper chaingun | 1 case | 4 atomic health units |
| 1 RPG launcher | 3 cases | 2 steroid flasks |
| 1 devastator | 2 cases | 3 NVGs |
| 1 shrinker | 2 shrinker crystals | 1 holoduke |
| 1 freezethrower | 1 charge | |

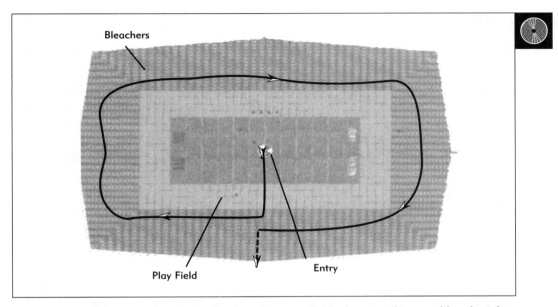

**FIGURE 6.23**: It's game time in Stadium, a wide-open field where anything could and might happen.

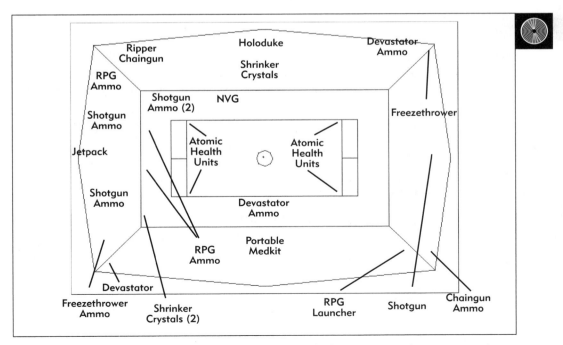

**FIGURE 6.24**: Even if you enter Stadium scarcely armed, there are enough weapons and power-ups to help you overcome the Cycloid Emperor.

## THE MATCH OF THE MILLENNIUM

The kick-off in this level occurs when you emerge from a radioactive manhole cover right at the 50 yard line. The mastodon Cycloid Emperor across the field would like nothing better than to blow you away even before the starting whistle blows. There is absolutely no sense in standing up to the Cycloid Emperor toe-to-toe. It would be a brave but foolish move. Instead, you must use your head, Duke. In a match of fire-power, the Cycloid Emperor has the clear advantage. Your only chance in hell of defeating the Emperor is to remain alive. That means not getting hit. A single hit from the Cycloid Emperor's built-in devastator arms could easily render you into expensive grass fertilizer.

At first glance you might think that there is absolutely no place to hide in Stadium. And you are right. But there are actually a few things you can do to limit the Emperor's target range. For one thing, his massive stature prevents him from climbing onto the bleachers. Secondly, his single eye compliments his single-minded approach to battle. He lives to force you to retire from the game before your time. You can turn this to your advantage. By now you have probably figured out that you need to climb on the bleachers as soon as possible. And if you take to the air, the better off you will be.

If you hop on the bleachers, you want to draw the Cycloid Emperor as close to the bleachers as you can. When he bumps against them, the Emperor's hell-bent nature will keep him trying, in vain, to climb. This renders him practically immobile. If you manage to climb as high as you can in the bleachers, you will also have succeeded in severely limiting the Emperor's fire range. His projectiles might land close, but without much of an angle, you can breathe somewhat tenuously as you plan your next move.

A minor inconvenience in all of this is that a group of troopers at the east end, or dog pound seats, can fire at you from a distance. You can pick them off even with your pistol. As to which side of the stadium to run to, it is up to debate. You should consider which weapons are available and which you would like to get first. Also, keep in mind that the spirited group of cheerleaders in the north end of the fifty yard line, can, and probably will get nailed by the Cycloid Emperor if you rush to the north.

> **TIP**
> If a cheerleader gets nailed, you can count on adding a couple of assault cammanders to the alien line-up. This might not be such a bad thing after all. If you can create a cross fire among them, the short tempered aliens will fight among themselves, giving you a chance to pick up heavier artillery and power-ups.

If you are sitting at the fifty yard line at the top of the bleachers and you don't have about forty to fifty RPG rounds or sixty to seventy charges in the freezethrower, you have no choice but to run around the field collecting what you need. This means getting somewhat exposed. If you are fortunate enough to have a jetpack with you, you can become an elusive target in the air, and drop down in key spots to collect the ammo and firepower necessary. Of course, you should attempt to deflate the hovering blimp at the first opportunity. You will then have just about every weapon and power-up littering the field. Another power-up that can help you even the odds a bit are the steroids. There are two flasks in Stadium—one at the Bad Ass end zone and the other one in your own. Ingest the pills, and you will dash across the terrain like a fearless running back, dodging, cutting, and zigzagging around your opponents. You should try to circle the Cycloid Emperor as you keep him in your sights to pound him with everything you've got (see Figure 6.25).

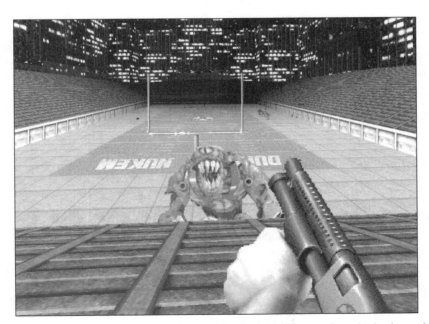

**FIGURE 6.25:** Rain your wrath upon the Cycloid Emperor from high above. It might be your only chance.

There won't be another battle. But if you overcome him, your children and your children's children's children might live to see a better tomorrow. A tomorrow where people can live together and prosper.

# TIER DROP

If you found the secret exit in Movie Set, then you are in for a very special treat in Tier Drop. This secret level is delightful in the four looks and feels it gives you. Four long, wide corridors connected in a simple square design form the perimeter of Tier Drop. Each side of the square has an opening into a very peculiar central courtyard. Depending on which side of the perimeter you approach it from, the courtyard will seem like an entirely different place each time.

Tier Drop asks you to put aside, if only for a while, your common notions about time and space. At each corner of the courtyard, you will find dimensional wells, which appear like ordinary holes in the ground, that will drop you onto another tier in the Tier Drop level. In fact, you might conceive Tier Drop as being four slices of reality stacked on top of one another. Of course, knowing that your concept of what's real and what isn't has just gone out the window isn't exactly reassuring. But take heart, you can solve this level by visiting only two of the tiers.

## MAPS AND ROUTE

To keep you from straining your eyes, Figure 6.26 shows you the two separate tiers among the level's four tiers that are necessary to blaze through the level. Figure 6.27 and 6.28, on the other hand, shows each of the four individual tiers and the locations of all the goodies on each. A line map for this level looks quite interesting, but it isn't very functional for demonstrating the places where these items can be found.

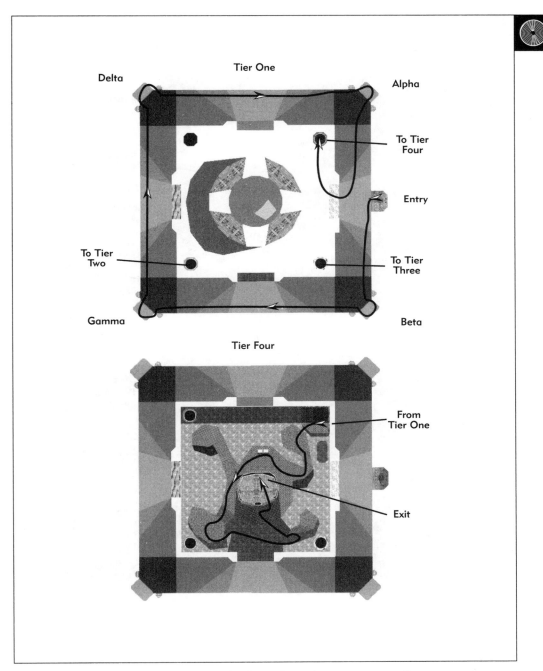

**Tier One**

Delta

Alpha

To Tier
Four

Entry

To Tier
Two

To Tier
Three

Gamma

Beta

**Tier Four**

From
Tier One

Exit

**FIGURE 6.26:** There is much more to Tier Drop than what you necessarily see.

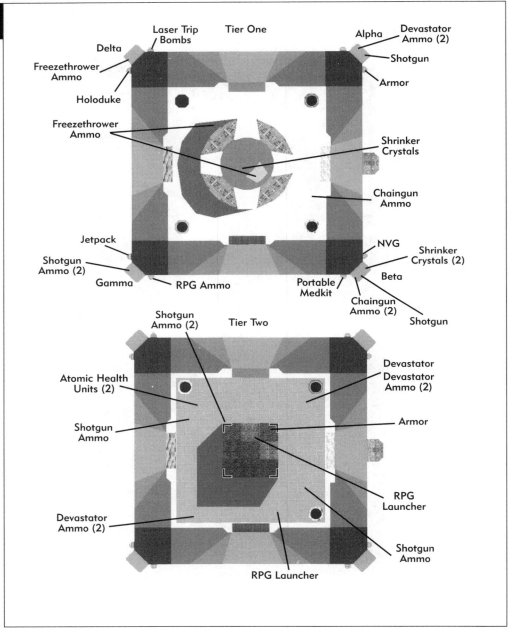

**FIGURE 6.27:** You may not be able to trust your own eyes in Tier Drop . . .

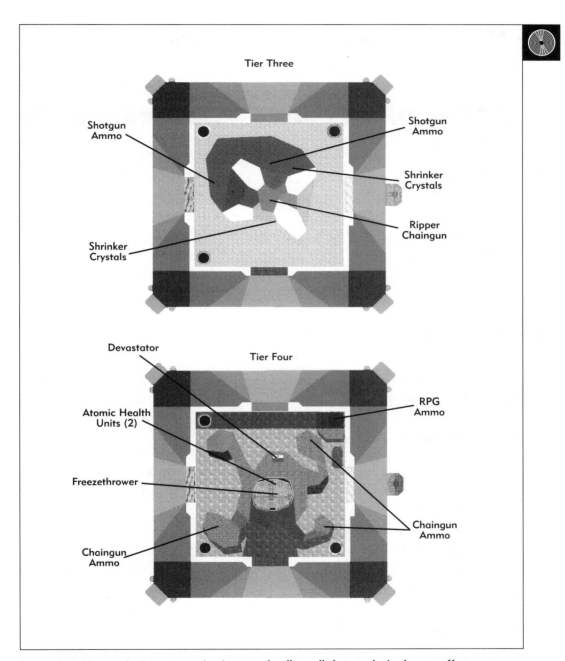

**FIGURE 6.28:** . . . just trust your instincts and collect all that each *tier* has to offer.

## THE GOODS

There is a considerable cache of power-ups, weapons, and ammo, as Table 6.18 clearly points out.

| TABLE 6.18: THE GOODS IN TIER DROP | | |
|---|---|---|
| **WEAPONS** | **AMMO** | **POWER-UPS** |
| 2 shotguns | 9 cases | 1 portable medkit |
| 1 ripper chaingun | 7 cases | 3 atomic health units |
| 1 RPG launcher | 3 cases | 1 steroid flask |
| 1 shrinker | 4 cases | 1 jetpack |
| 1 devastator | 4 cases | 1 NVG |
| 1 freezethrower | | 1 holoduke |
| 3 laser trip bombs | | |
| 2 pipe bomb cases | | |

## BLAZING THROUGH TIER DROP

You can spend a good while exploring every facet of Tier Drop and still not get the entire picture. To get through in a timely and efficient manner, stick with the following outline, but don't be afraid to strike out on your own.

### The Initial Round

1. **Come out and make the rounds.** Get out of the small enclosure and dash around the four corners of Tier Drop: Alpha, Beta, Gamma, and Delta. Pick up everything of value along the way. Pay particular attention to the large and small enclosures in each corner. Your survival and success depends on how much firepower and power-ups you can accumulate early on. Also, if you move fast enough, you can avoid attracting the enemies inside the courtyard.

### The Quick Descent to Tier Four

1. **Drop down to tier four.** After making a full tour around the perimeter, get back to your initial point near the east side entrance to the courtyard.

Make a quick right and drop right into the red glowing well. You will emerge in the northeast corner of tier four.

## On Tier Four

1. **Dispose of the assault commanders.** Use the shotgun to pluck the assault commanders, who normally hover around the south end of this tier.

2. **Climb the central structure for the final struggle.** Climb along the slanted metal of the central structure to reach its top. Move toward the north side where you can take a devastator. Then walk around to the front doors bearing the Battlelord's likeness. Open the doors and do your best to overcome the Battlelord. Then run in and punch the exit switch.

# ADDED ATTRACTIONS IN TIER DROP

The blazing section only introduced you to two of the tiers in Tier Drop. The other tiers have their special features, dangers, and rewards, as you will see in the following short descriptions.

## Tier Two

This tier offers the most polished look of all. It has smooth, cement floors and a perfectly square structure in the center. The central structure, however, is practically carpeted with the web-like matter that seems all too prevalent in and around alien egg nests. The RPG launcher and armor are compelling reasons for venturing into the central structure. The peripheral power-ups and weapons, which include a devastator and two atomic health units, are yet another reason why anyone should spend the time visiting this tier. Tier two, however, is a pig cop stronghold. Take the necessary firepower and precautions, should you decide to drop in for a visit.

## Tier Three

Characterized by a rocky, jagged architecture, this tier is perhaps the most vicious of them all. Tier three is a veritable octabrain spawning ground. If you like using the shrinker, consider entering tier three to grab two crystals. Battling the herds of octabrains inside the courtyard isn't always wise. You will be better off drawing the octabrains to chase you into the periphery, where you can more neatly pluck them off in the air, without being overcome on all sides.

## COVERT DETAILS

The secrets in Tier Drop aren't exactly top secrets, and finding them is not exactly rocket science. Table 6.19 catalogs the secrets, such as they are.

| TABLE 6.19: THE SECRETS IN TIER DROP | | |
|---|---|---|
| **AREA IN LEVEL** | **SECRET ITEMS** | **HOW TO GET IT** |
| Alpha corner | shotgun devastator ammo (2 cases) | Push against the steel panel. |
| Beta corner | shrinker crystals (2) shotgun ripper chaingun ammo (2 cases) | Push against the steel panel. |
| Delta corner | freezethrower charge pipe bomb case | Push against the steel panel. |
| Gamma corner | shotgun shells (3 cases) RPG ammo (2 cases) | Push against the steel panel. |

# FREEWAY

Life at the end of Freeway is about to begin for you. You obviously decided to explore the secret exit in Hotel Hell, and you found it near a manhole cover. Now you're about to emerge out of the drain tunnel into Freeway. This former piece of civilization is built around intersecting roadways. A wide underpass runs east and west. The even wider overpass runs north and south. Surrounding buildings, tunnels, and other chambers offer ample opportunity for exploration. Just don't expect any type of courtesy or road-side manners from the aliens along *this* Freeway.

The path to the exit in Freeway is fairly straightforward, but you must pay a heavy toll to get there. Everyone you meet along this "Freeway" wants not just a piece of the action but a piece of you. With scores of sentry drones, pig cops, RPVs, enforcers, and even a few Battlelord Sentries, you are easily stretched to your limits. How well you fare in Freeway depends largely on how well equipped you are when you enter.

Even if your arsenal is measly at the beginning, there are some good spoils along the roads. Your route in Freeway takes you to the overpass. There, you must climb into an apartment on the east side to grab the blue keycard. Then you will be able to penetrate a compression chamber of sorts, where the red keycard is found. It sounds simple and it would be, were it not for the possibility of becoming a road-side casualty at any moment.

## MAPS AND ROUTE

Don't count on the kindness of strangers to give you directions in Freeway. Rely on Figures 6.29 and 6.30 to get your bearings.

## THE GOODS

The spoils in Freeway are catalogued in Table 6.20.

### TABLE 6.20: THE GOODS IN FREEWAY

| WEAPONS | AMMO | POWER-UPS |
| --- | --- | --- |
| 2 shotguns | 7 cases | 2 portable medkits |
| 1 ripper chaingun | 1 case | 3 atomic health units |
| 2 RPG launchers | 4 cases | 2 steroid flasks |
| 1 devastator | 5 cases | 1 jetpack |
| 2 freezethrowers | 1 charge | 2 NVGs |
| 2 laser trip bombs | | |
| 3 pipe bomb cases | | |

## BLAZING THROUGH FREEWAY

Life on the road has never been easy, and in Freeway it doesn't get much better. The following plan is not exactly a road map to life, but it can help you reach the end of Freeway.

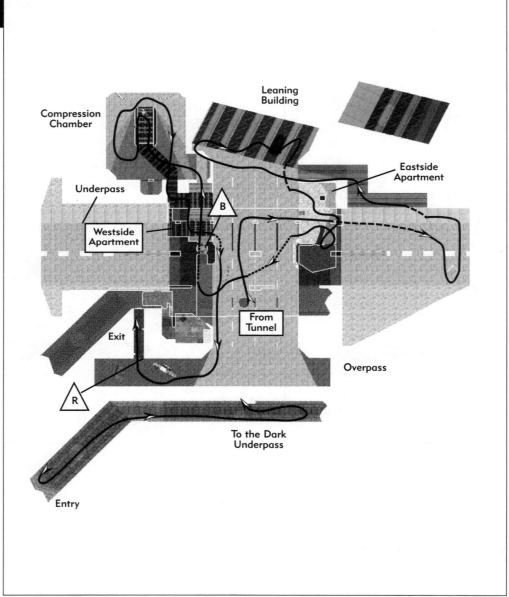

**FIGURE 6.29:** Plan a route and stick to it, if you want to reach your destination in Freeway.

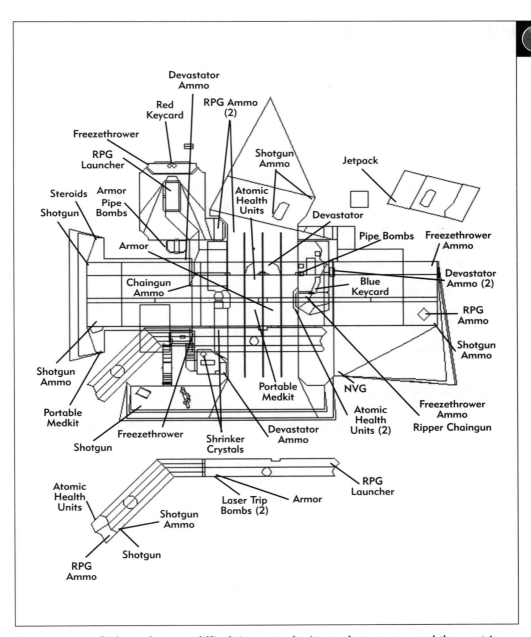

**FIGURE 6.30:** Perhaps the most difficult items to obtain are the two you need the most in Freeway, the blue and red keycards.

## In the Drain Tunnel

1. **Collect some weapons and power-ups, and overcome a few octabrains.** Look behind you to grab a shotgun and some shells. If you have a pipe bomb or an RPG launcher, blow a hole at the end of the tunnel to uncover an atomic health unit and RPG ammo. Then start heading eastward.

2. **Head east and pummel the octabrains.** As you start heading east, three octabrains will try to stop you from reaching the end of the tunnel, where you can collect an RPG launcher. Besides the octabrains, a sentry drone also patrols the east side of the tunnel. If you don't have a heavier weapon, rely on the shotgun and your strafing to open yourself a path past the serrated teeth of the octabrains.

3. **Blow a hole in the tunnel.** Take your RPG launcher and point it toward the crack along the north side of the tunnel. Punch a hole right through the tunnel where you can crawl out and face the action in the dark underpass.

## In the Dark Underpass

1. **Get a devastator and an atomic health unit.** With your shotgun leading the way, come out of the tunnel slowly. Look for the glowing red eyes of the pig cops across the underpass, and fire with impunity. If necessary, fall back into the tunnel to avoid diving sentry drones and a couple of roving RPVs. When the moment is opportune, dash across the way to grab a devastator by the trash can. Kick the trash can to uncover an atomic health unit.

2. **Reach the east side of the underpass.** Use the devastator you just scored to open a path up to the east side of the underpass. Grab the shells behind the wooden crate, and then hop on top of it to take the RPG ammo.

3. **Cut a path through the narrow alleyway to reach the overpass.** Climb along the narrow walkway at the east end of the overpass, and follow it as it turns north.

## On the Overpass

1. **Hold your position for a while.** If you were to rush out onto the overpass, you would be immediately greeted by a group of enforcers and a Battlelord Sentry. Your odds go dramatically down whenever you face the speedy enforcers and the firepower of the Battlelord Sentry in open spaces. Peek out of the alleyway enough to attract the attention of the enforcers, who will come pouncing after you in seconds. Sidestep behind the wall for protection, and then sidestep and fire your single shell shots at the encroaching enforcers.

2. **Deal with the Battlelord Sentry.** Come out of the alleyway to get a good angle at the slower moving the Battlelord Sentry at the south end of the overpass. If you can get off three to five RPGs and avoid the incoming fire, the Battlelord Sentry will not be a factor any longer.

3. **Climb the downed building and get a jetpack.** Dash across the street to take the devastator ammo. Then hop on top of the downed building at the north end. What will seem like a cloud of drones hovering over the building will suddenly focus on you. If necessary, you can run back into the alleyway for protection. Eventually, drop into the gaping hole in the middle of the leaning building. Fight off the single enforcer below, and then grab the jetpack and shells before hovering out of the downed building.

> **WARNING**
>
> The alleyway is mined. Be ready to back out as soon as you turn north and take a couple of steps. The pig cops patrolling the alleyway will die in all likelihood, but you don't have to suffer the same fate.

> **TIP**
>
> Although you can explore another chamber behind the place where you found the blue keycard, you should contemplate whether it's a wise idea. You can blow a hole in the wall behind the blue keycard to reach a chamber that holds one ripper chaingun and a freezethrower charge. However, the second you cross inside the chamber, two Battlelord Sentries will appear out of nowhere on the overpass below.

4. **Hover over to the apartment on the east side.** Take out the enforcers as you drop in from the skies. Explore the room to take the blue keycard along the east side of the apartment. Also, take a moment to explore all the goods to be had in the apartment. There is a case of pipe bombs on top of the soda machine and two cases of devastator ammo behind the bookshelf under the slanted portion of the ceiling.

5. **Hover back to the street level.** Use the blue keycard on the small latch on the west side of the street. Watch out for the pig cop just behind the lifting wall. Then climb aboard the small platform, and ride it to the top.

## On the Top Floor of the West Side

1. **Storm the room with the conveyors.** Stepping off of the platform, do away with the two enforcers, flip the switch that turns off the two conveyor belts in this room, and reach the chamber at the north end—otherwise known as the compression room.

2. **Get the red keycard in the compression room.** Grab the two cases of RPG ammo, and then go inside the dark room that is dominated by a large compression platform capable of flattening any and everything that gets caught inside. Fight the enforcers and reach the north side. Lay down five or six pipe bombs before you use the blue keycard on the latch to open the steel gate. Then, open the latch, step back, and detonate the bombs. If all goes as expected, every enforcer behind the gate is no longer a factor. Take the blue keycard and get back to the main street.

## In the Southern Alleyway

1. **Fight off the pig cops behind car 54.** As you come near the southern alleyway, the police car turned on its side will blow up. Behind it, a squadron of pig cops will come out to shoot and ask questions later. If you have RPG ammo left over, drop a couple of rounds into their tightly packed group.

2. **Open the last door.** Use the red keycard to open the narrow door in the alleyway. Dispose of the pig cop waiting there. Then open a second door, and be ready to confront the last two octabrains standing between you and freedom. If you haven't had a chance to use the shrinker or the freezethrower, this is the perfect opportunity.

3. **Hit the exit switch.** Hop over the dead octabrain bodies, break the glass covering the switch, and then punch it decisively with your clenched fist.

## ADDED ATTRACTIONS IN FREEWAY

The mayhem and destruction in Freeway can escalate even higher if you invite two Battlelord Sentries to the party. And how do you do that? All you have to do is enter the chamber behind the explosive wall in the west side apartment.

### Accommodating Two Battlelord Sentries on the Overpass

If a freezethrower charge and a ripper chaingun are enough reasons to enter the chamber behind the blue keycard, then go ahead and blow a hole in the wall and enter the chamber. Step into the dark chamber, and claim the freezethrower charge and the ripper chaingun. The alien growls you will hear almost immediately will let you know that the guests have arrived. Get out of the dark chamber, and unload a couple of RPGs on the Battlelord Sentries below. It will be hard for them to hit you where you are. However, you can't stay in the apartment forever.

Activate your jetpack and hover toward the south. Come down near the end of the south overpass and jump right through a dark window that leads you into a secret chamber. You can find protection in this chamber and, at the same time, you will also have a clear view of the street outside. However, when you first jump inside, you will have to contend with two enforcers. Take the devastator ammo on the bed, and pummel the Battlelord Sentries outside with a combination of your devastator and RPG launcher. You can then proceed to use the blue keycard en route to the upstairs west side apartment.

# PART

# III

# Duke Nukem's Cognoscenti

This section gives you a chance to get up close and personal with the brilliant minds behind *Duke Nukem 3D*, and it gives you a brief introduction to the game's map editing tools and some cheat codes. Not only are the game's principal developers at 3D Realms talented artists, designers, and programmers, but they, like you, are true connoisseurs of cutting-edge, action-packed games. Chapter 7 provides some interesting insights and behind-the-scenes admissions by the game's producers and the rest of the development team. In Chapter 8, George Broussard, president of 3D Realms Entertainment and the game's executive producer, shares some of the team's sacrifices and tribulations during the entire development phase. Part III concludes with a brief introduction to the game's map and art editing tools available with the full version and a comprehensive list of the game's cheat codes.

# CHAPTER 7

# Duke's Creators Give Us a Piece of Their Mind

To say that Duke's creators are a talented group of individuals would be a gross understatement. Anyone who plays *Duke Nukem 3D* will be dazzled by the 3D virtual environment that Duke's architects have provided in painstaking detail. In *Duke Nukem 3D,* the level design and the technical and artistic elements mesh harmoniously in complete synergistic fashion. Besides its technical sophistication, incredibly rich environment, and totally smooth game play, *Duke Nukem 3D* also boasts a very strong, unique, and rather humorous personality. This did not happen by accident, and it gives the game an additional element of appeal (depending on your temperament, of course).

Despite being a larger-than-life antihero, as well as Duke's brashness and apparent insolence, Duke's motivations are, in the end, most noble. To understand humanity's unlikely savior a little better, it is necessary to get close to the people who engendered him. This chapter includes an interview with Scott Miller and George Broussard, respective presidents of Apogee and 3D Realms Entertainment. In addition, you will also get to hear from the creative individuals who focused their energy and gave their souls to bring Duke from the drawing board into the 3D world of *Duke Nukem 3D*.

# INSIGHTS FROM THE HEAD HONCHOS

*Author's note: I first met Scott Miller and George Broussard in the Summer of 1995. At that time,* Duke Nukem 3D *was in its early developmental stages. In the still impressive, but unrefined version of the Duke Nukem I saw then, Duke had not yet learned to talk. But even back then, when there were only a handful of incomplete levels and many unrealized ideas floating around, it was obvious that Miller, Broussard, and the other talent at 3D Realms knew they had a winner in the making. Their enthusiasm was contagious; their drive was unquestionable. As the months came and went, I was lucky enough to see* Duke Nukem 3D *grow and mature into the Duke we know today.*

*Just a few days away from releasing the full version, Miller and Broussard were kind enough to grant me an online interview that I wish to share with you, the player, who represents the most important variable in the game equation. For after all, no effort was spared to present you with a truly wonderful and advanced 3D game, a game that might well be compared to worthy competitors like* DOOM, Dark Forces, *and* Descent. Duke Nukem 3D *is also a game that stands on its own for its many innovations and for pushing the boundaries of PC entertainment to an entirely new realm.*

**Mendoza:** Tell us about the origins of *Duke Nukem 3D*.

**Miller:** The original *Duke Nukem* game began development in late 1990. Todd Replogle and I were trying to come up with a new project for Todd to tackle, since he had just finished a game titled *Dark Ages,* his third Apogee title. At that time, George was still six months away from joining Apogee. Todd had come up with a list of name ideas, and upon hearing "Duke Nukem," I immediately said, "That's the one!" The idea behind Duke has changed and grown over time, but originally Duke was simply a modern day, post-nuclear war hero who was sick and tired of the continued collapse of society under evil intentions.

His first nemeses was Dr. Proton, who tried to take over Los Angeles with an army of *techbots.* Although defeated in the original *Duke Nukem*, Dr. Proton still escaped and will likely make a return in a future Duke game. From the beginning, Duke was the kind of hero that was never bothered by the incredible odds against him. In the first two games you would always see Duke with his shiny smile and can-do attitude. In *Duke Nukem 3D* we decided that Duke needed more of an edge, dark shades, and a tougher attitude; but beyond that he's still the same character he's always been.

**Broussard:** The original *Duke Nukem* was an immediate hit. Something about the character and his attitude struck a nerve with people, even though the first adventure was just a side-scrolling EGA game. It became sort of an underground cult hit overnight. From that point, we knew we had hit something, so we started developing a sequel about six months later that eventually led to *Duke Nukem II* (another side scroller) in late 1993.

**Mendoza:** How important is the story line in the Duke series? Did you consciously attempt to provide a thread of continuity with previous installments?

**Miller:** Despite popular misconceptions, a story *is* important to us, but in pure action games it's difficult to integrate an in-depth story without slowing down the action too much. *Duke Nukem 3D* picks up just days after *Duke Nukem II* ends, so we do provide some continuity.

**Broussard:** Not to contradict Scott, but "story?" Us? We usually do the story near the end of the game, but with Duke we actually tried to make it all fit together from about halfway through the project. The only real continuity to other games is Duke himself and his unstoppable ego. He is the star of the games and his universe is secondary. We just tried to flesh Duke out more in the 3D version. Adding the voice characterization helped a lot to bring out more of Duke's personality.

**Mendoza:** As you developed your Build engine, was Duke considered as a showcase for the new technology?

**Miller:** Not really. We originally had four games being developed with the Build engine (*Ruins, Blood, Shadow Warrior,* and *Duke*), and we didn't know which would be completed first. Even five months before Duke's shareware release, we were still wondering if we should instead focus on *Shadow Warrior* and get it out first, but *Duke* was slightly further in front so that's where we focused resources.

**Broussard:** Although we didn't know it at the time, Duke did become the showcase for the Build engine. The engine enabled us to be extreme and push all the limits, both in technology and in game design. The team had always done this. Early on, we were doing things with the engine that it wasn't *supposed* to do, like swimming underwater and riding around on subway cars. Todd Replogle, the head programmer, never accepted "no" as an answer and always found a way to implement a weird or extreme idea.

**Mendoza:** What sources of inspiration did you draw upon for ideas about level design or other aesthetic and action components of the game?

**Miller:** Ideas come from everywhere. We are all big movie fans, and many of us read comics, novels, etc. So there's no single source that I can point to. It's more like our collective mind churns out a veritable cornucopia of ideas, many of which wind up in the cutting room, so to speak. Our biggest source for ideas are the people we work with. We try to hire people with creative, twisted minds.

**Broussard:** *Duke Nukem 3D* is about unbridled action, little else. So whenever we design a game, we try to do things that haven't been done before. This leads to stuff like the movie theaters and topless bars that are in *Duke*. We decided after already having over twenty levels done that we wanted a *real* place for Duke to be, so we scrapped the early work and started over, building real cities and other seedy places. So, in essence, the levels themselves inspired a lot of what is in the game. Once we got started, we just went over the top with everything we did.

**Mendoza:** Are there inside jokes in the game we can be privy to?

**Miller:** All the jokes in the game are *outside* jokes because we want the public to see them. For example, in one part of the game id Software's offices are blown up, and Duke says one of his one liners. A lot of people might miss the connection, but we think more than enough will see the subtle—and completely harmless—jab.

**Broussard:** We have lots of cracks in the game. Another crack directed at our friends at id Software occurs in Death Row, when Duke encounters the doomed space marine. We also had some references to a very famous trial in volume one. We had so much fun with these references that we decided to go crazy with them in the full game. There are references to *Star Wars*, Indiana Jones, *The Terminator*, *Star Trek* and many, many others in the game. They are usually in secret places, so it rewards the person for poking around the game and exploring.

**Mendoza:** How would you compare *Duke Nukem 3D* against other significant competitors in the 3D action genre (*DOOM*, *Descent*, *Heretic*, and *Dark Forces* perhaps being the most notable among the competition)?

**Miller:** *Duke Nukem 3D* is innovative in several ways. First, it's the first 3D action game that has a real character with an interesting personality. Second, the level of interaction and realism in *Duke Nukem 3D* far surpasses anything we've seen previously. And third, it's a game strictly designed for adult players without apologies—we set out to make an R-rated game with a gritty, real-world feel and attitude.

**Broussard:** The games you mentioned are stiff competition indeed. But I think Duke holds his own with any other 3D games, due to his personality and environment. Personality has a lot to do with it because Duke is a likable guy, and who doesn't want to become Duke for an hour or so when you play the game? Beyond that, the environment is so interactive that it keeps the game interesting and alive. You can blow up toilets and drink from them, look at yourself in a mirror, turn projectors on or off, blow up nearly everything and lots more. There is just so much to do in a game that it tends to draw you in and keep you coming back for more. As Duke says, "Come get some."

**Mendoza:** Will we see another installment of *Duke Nukem 3D?* Any forecasts as to when?

**Miller:** We will release one or more add-on level packs for *Duke Nukem 3D*, but the next big Duke game will have a new cutting-edge engine. I don't expect another *Duke Nukem* to be released prior to 1998.

**Broussard:** We intend on franchising Duke Nukem everywhere. A 3D sequel will begin in 1996 when we create a more advanced engine for Duke. Each new Duke game should shake up the establishment a little. We will try to have some add-on mission packs for the current game in time for Christmas 1996. In addition to computer products, we've been contacted by everyone from comic book companies to movie studios to merchandise Duke products, so I expect you will see a lot more of Duke in the future. And I know he'll be glad to hear that. You just can't keep a big ego down.

**FIGURE 7.1:** George Broussard accepts a Spotlight Award at the 1996 Computer Game Developer's Conference.

**FIGURE 7.2:** The *Duke Nukem 3D* team. Front row, left to right: Duke Nukem, Doug Wood, Richard Gray, and Chuck Jones. Middle row (kneeling), left to right: Dirk Jones, Mark Dochtermann, and Lee Jackson. Standing, left to right: Greg Malone, Stephen Hornback, Todd Replogle, James Storey, Allen Blum (wearing hat), David Demaret, George Broussard, and Jim Dose.

# MEET *DUKE NUKEM 3D*'S TEAM

Every person who participated in the making of *Duke Nukem 3D* deserves special recognition. It was through their sacrifices and efforts that Duke Nukem acquired his special talents, personality, and, of course, his undeniable good looks. In this section, *Duke Nukem 3D* team members were asked a series of questions about their experiences during the game's development and other matters of philosophy and life experiences that contributed to their particular involvement during different stages of development.

## THE HEAD PROGRAMMER

Todd Replogle, the head programmer, provided some logical insight on the game's development, from initial conception to final product.

**Mendoza:** What were some of the most fun things to program in *Duke Nukem 3D*, and why?

**Replogle:** The fun is in seeing things go BOOM—explosions, flying debris, it's all a wonderful visual experience.

**Mendoza:** How many lines of code are there in *Duke Nukem 3D*, and how long did it take to write the game?

**Replogle:** Approximately 45,000 lines of code over about 2 years.

**Mendoza:** What are your plans now that *Duke Nukem 3D* is released?

**Replogle:** Seek new adventures in life, and start to work on a better Duke game.

**Mendoza:** How did you wind up in the video game business.

**Replogle:** I got really lucky.

## THE MAP DESIGNERS

Allen Blum III and Richard Gray (Levelord), the game's map designers, offered their experiences during the development of *Duke Nukem 3D*.

**Mendoza:** Describe the process for making a map in *Duke Nukem 3D*.

**Blum:** There are many places in the world to destroy, so the first thing to do is pick one. The second thing to do is push the engine till it breaks, and then go to work and make it playable on slow machines.

**Gray:** Well, first you have to think of a cool idea for the main theme of the level. Usually I get my best theme ideas from movies and illustrated books; if it looks cool to me, then I know it will be a cool level. Ideas for cool sector effects stuff (moving contraptions, player tricks, etc.) usually come to me in those twilight times between sleep and waking up. The process of actually making the map is simple, once you have a cool theme. I always start in 2D mode and build the basic layout. Then it's off to 3D mode to do the texturing, sprite placement, etc.

**Mendoza:** What is your least favorite thing to do while making a map?

**FIGURE 7.3:** Richard Gray (a.k.a. Levelord)

**Blum:** I think aligning textures is the worst, it takes so long sometimes. The best thing is knowing that what I'm doing is going to make people's heart rates triple, and they will love it and ask for more.

**Gray:** The hardest thing about developing good maps is building one that is good for single players (critical path, bad guys-to-goodies balance, flow of game play that starts off easy and climaxes with near-death action) as well as multiplayers. This may not be apparent to the common Duke player, but these two objectives often oppose each other. As a simple example, a good single player map will be large and offer lots of places to explore. On the contrary, a good multiplayer map *must* be small so that everyone can find each other quickly.

**Mendoza:** What is your favorite map that you designed?

**Blum:** I think my favorite is volume 1 level 6, the secret map, when you get to blow up the rocket ship. It was pretty confusing to build, but I love to blow things up. My current favorite level is Hollywood Holocaust because everyone in the world knows that map is the best for DukeMatch. I know that whenever I play someone on TEN (Total Entertainment Network), on Local Network, or over Modem, everyone knows this map and is ready for me. Then I kick their butt!

**Gray:** Well, my best is Fahrenheit in volume 3 of the game. My all-time favorite, though, was done by Allen and is one that no one will see until we do a bonus pack. It is the best DukeMatch level. What I like about it is that it had a stronghold where the person in it had supreme weapon/ health capabilities, but the stronghold had

FIGURE 7.4: Chuck Jones takes a breather.

FIGURE 7.5: Dirk Jones hard at work.

a few weaknesses that the other players could use to approach and, hopefully, become the next *king of the castle*. I really like sieges, I guess.

## THE ARTISTS

*Duke Nukem 3D*'s artists, Dirk Jones (no relation to Chuck Jones), Stephen Hornback, and Chuck Jones (no relation to Bugs Bunny's creator) provided the following insights on their roles within the design team.

**Mendoza:** What type of art did you do for *Duke Nukem 3D*?

**C. Jones:** I did the character designing. Most started on paper or in my head. I built and textured the characters. I also animated them: dying, flying, attacking, and shooting. I was also able to do the small cinematics; I'm looking forward to doing more. I'm a one-stop monster shop!

**D. Jones:** As with all the pixel artists, I did art that covered the range from weapons to backgrounds. From the small [elements] (like the 8 × 8 pool balls) to the large (like the 256 × 300 night sky backdrop), the requirements of the artwork covered a large range of sizes. I also did some clean up and retouching of some of the rendered artwork.

**Hornback:** I did a combination of several types of art for *Duke Nukem 3D*. I developed explosions and special effects, individual sprites (like the scuba gear), the backdrops, weapons, doors, walls, ceilings, floors, etc. I really enjoyed all the variety of art that I worked on.

**Mendoza:** What is some of your favorite art that is in the game?

**C. Jones:** I think the cinematics because they were so much fun to make.

**D. Jones:** I have a lot of favorite art in the game, but nothing brought me more pleasure than creating a nice wall or floor tile and seeing the level designers using it to help build their worlds with it. I also got a kick out of seeing level designers using tiles in ways I never intended.

**Hornback:** My favorite art for the game are some of the bosses and the explosive battles that result when trying to defeat them. Them gals ain't bad neither! (I got to work on them too—a lot of people at work were envying me those weeks!)

**Mendoza:** What technical, artistic, and personal qualities did you bring to the team?

**C. Jones:** I brought my artistic ability to Duke and my visualizing power. I have a gift of seeing what's in my head and translating it to the outside world. My personal qualities are I like to laugh, and I like seeing other people laugh too. I've also played games for so long; from D&D to *Ogre* to *Asteroids* to *Street Fighter*.

**D. Jones:** This was the first game I have done art for. I had been doing computer art for a hobby. Though self-taught, I have won some awards for my art work. My art has a crisp draftsman-like look that had to be dirtied up to blend in with the other artist's work. I also have a very logical and pragmatic mind that helped when we were discussing game elements as well as when testing *Duke Nukem 3D*.

**Hornback:** The technical abilities I lend to the game come from the development of past games with Apogee and 3D Realms. It's like there's a never-ending learning curve of new software and new techniques on a daily basis. Then when you apply your work to a new game engine, you have to learn how the advances in that game engine affect how I need to develop the art for the game. Having a good understanding of what the creative director and producer have in mind cannot be overemphasized. I really try hard to get into their heads, so we're all seeing the same picture.

# The Making of Duke Nukem 3D

This chapter gives you a behind the scenes look at the making of *Duke Nukem 3D* from the unique perspective of the game's executive producer and President of 3D Realms, George Broussard. Just how many gallons of blood and sweat were poured into the making of *Duke Nukem 3D* is something we may not be able to quantify. But the results are self evident and don't need belaboring.

## IN THE BEGINNING

The project's concept began near the end of 1993. Scott Miller (my partner at 3D Realms), Todd Replogle (Duke's programmer extraordinaire), Allen Blum, and I all knew that we were going to make a 3D version of Duke Nukem, who had already appeared in two previous side-scrolling games we had made. What we needed was an engine.

Around the end of 1993, we hired Ken Silverman, who wrote the Build engine and all its tools. We knew at once we had found a 3D engine worthy of Duke and began early design on the game before the engine was even done. Todd and Ken worked out early engine problems, and we all pitched in with an endless list of *features* we wanted Ken to add to the engine. At the same time, Allen started making basic maps for Duke and experimenting. We were all just trying to get *into* the tools we had to work with—which were still several months from completion—to see what kind of game we could really make. After a few months of experimenting, the engine started to solidify enough that we could actually start work on a real game, instead of a prototype.

So we started the real design of the game . . . well, kind of. The fact is we were still learning what we could do with the engine near the end of 1994. Todd kept coming into the office with these amazing things he had done—things like the ability to swim under water or ride in shuttle cars. Up to that point, none of that stuff had ever been done in a published game, so we started to design around some of Todd and Allen's wild ideas.

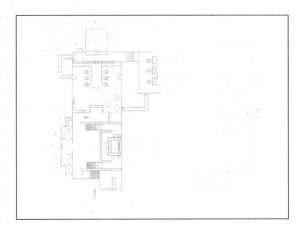

## ASSEMBLING THE DEVELOPMENT TEAM

In early 1994, we had reached the end of the experimenting and we started to build the real core team. We realized that Allen could not do all the maps alone and brought on Richard Gray, who we had met online. We checked out some of his *DOOM* WAD's and saw that he had the skills we were looking for in a level designer. In addition to Stephen Hornback (our sole artist at that point), we hired Dirk Jones and James Storey. Then we moved Chuck Jones (no relation), who had just finished getting his feet wet on *Rise of the Triad*, over to the *Duke Nukem 3D*

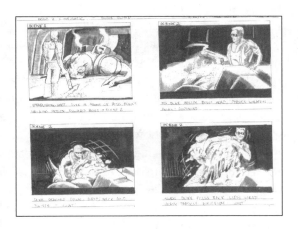

project. We also brought on Greg Malone as a producer to help me guide the project along on a daily basis.

### Working through Delays and Problems

A lot of the game was done by mid 1995, and we wanted to release the game around August. The game could likely have gone out then, but we were not happy with it at all—it would have sucked. It controlled *weirdly*, for instance, and the network code as well as the modem code needed major overhauling and finishing.

From the start we had decided that Duke would be a very detailed single-player game, with very realistic settings and places. We didn't want a *maze* game. Our second goal was to design the maps so that they could accommodate multiplayers over networks and modems. Unfortunately, these two ideas are in direct conflict with each other, and this presented an endless supply of problems.

For instance, how do you make a map that is large enough and interesting enough for single players, yet keep it small and tight for fast action multiplayers? Our early maps were great for single players, but they were way too large for net play (you would never find the other guy) and they also had frame rates that were way too slow. This was something that had eluded us until somebody suggested we see how Duke runs on that old 486 in the corner. To our dismay, the maps ran at less than 8-10 frames per second—way below acceptable frame rates for lower-end machines.

We hacked the maps down in size to achieve better multiplayer capability and also redid lots of architecture to increase the frame rates. Allen and Richard had these *magic numbers* taped to their monitors, so they would always be reminded of the target frame rate.

October 1995 came fast; we had missed our August deadline. Then another month rolled by, and the reality that the game would not be out for Christmas set in. Nobody went home for the holidays, and everyone stayed at the office and worked around the clock for a release.

After Christmas, however, things started to look up. An excitement started to build in the team, as we realized we had finally crossed that *hump* in game play that separates good games from average games. Since about October, we had all been putting in 10 to 12 hours a day, seven days a week, with little time off for other things. The game was always "two weeks away" it seemed. But now, we smelled blood and started to see light at the end of the tunnel.

## FINISHING THE FINAL VERSION

By early January 1996, while there was little to do in the design process, there were some major bugs in the code to hunt down. We had our eyes on early February for a release of the shareware version, so while Todd tracked down the bugs, we played the game over and over. We used the time to improve the game in every area we could. We added more speech to Duke's ever growing personality and used the time to add detail features like tipping the dancers.

After a couple of weeks of testing we were ready to release the shareware version, which we did in early February. The response almost knocked us over. Everyone was playing the game and talking about it, and the game seemed to be an overnight hit, albeit a two-year overnight hit.

This was all great, except that we had spent the last four months focusing on six shareware levels. Now we had to finish the entire game with 22 new levels, and we had to do it by mid-April. We worked around the clock from that point onward. Fortunately, at that point the team was so finely tuned that we had the process down to a science. After the first six levels of volume two were done in a little over a week, we breathed a little easier. The whole process became like an assembly line. We just did the work like tireless cogs in a giant machine.

## The Final Push

Early April rolled around and the game was very close, but we seemed to be stuck in the proverbial *two-week mode* again. Tension was high and Todd had shattered his third keyboard by now. We just wanted to finish the game so we could all collapse and die. Finally we got to *final testing* day, around April 15th. This is the day that if we test

for 12 hours or so and find nothing, we will burn a CD and ship it off for duplication. Between us all, we had played the game at least four million times by now, so we knew it was pretty stable. However, at the end of the day, we found enough little things to warrant another full day of testing.

After another full day of testing, we would find some items and back to *final* testing we would go. This happened three or four times, and each day it seemed like the game would be done. Each day that it wasn't, we would get four hours sleep and start over. About the fifth day of this, we were totally burned out. Finally, we did test the game heavily one more time and found nothing wrong; so about 7 A.M. on April 19 we decided to stop testing. We left the code on Joe Siegler's desk for a CD-ROM to be burned, and we all went home to sleep.

It was an exhausting five- or six-month process to finish the game, but I wouldn't trade it for anything. Finishing *Duke Nukem 3D* was the very definition of teamwork. The *Duke Nukem 3D* team thanks you for buying this book and the game and promises to return in the next *Duke Nukem 3D* game, which will be starting production sometime in 1996.

# Modifying Level Maps and Using Cheat Codes

This chapter provides a brief introduction on using Build to modify or create level maps; its counterpart, Artedit, for modifying the game's art elements; and cheat codes that allow you to play the game with immortality, so you can delve even deeper into the world of *Duke Nukem 3D*—if you dare!

## MODIFYING LEVEL MAPS

The makers of *Duke Nukem 3D* at 3D Realms want you to have fun. That's the primary reason why they breathed life into *Duke Nukem 3D*. Taking fun one step further, they would like you to be the master of your own gaming environment. That is why 3D Realms includes two programs Build and Edit Art. This chapter describes briefly Build and Edit Art and provides some basic information for getting started with these programs.

### WHAT IS BUILD?

Think of Build as a design or modeling tool that lets you create brand new *Duke Nukem 3D* levels, essentially by modifying existing ones. Build is the front-end to 3D Realms' acclaimed Build engine, the powerhouse behind *Duke Nukem 3D*. This same engine will soon be deployed in upcoming games from 3D Realms, including *Shadow Warrior* and *Blood*.

While Build will appeal mostly to those with more than a passing interest in programming and level design, if you have the patience and dedication, use Build to create your own levels and share them with your friends, or upload them for other dedicated Nukem gamers. Build lets you work in both 2D (top-down) and 3D views. The 2D view is ideal for laying out a level, which is composed mainly of walls, ceilings, and floors. Use this view to create sectors and other level divisions. The 3D view is better suited for working with textures and bitmaps. It lets you see your creations and changes immediately in real time. Although modifying levels can become quite complex, rudimentary adjustments, such as raising or lowering a wall, are fairly simple, as are other seemingly complex level design operations.

## What Is Edit Art?

Artedit is a useful program for viewing, importing, and altering the game's bitmap images. Although Artedit can be used as a stand-alone utility, it is typically called from Build whenever you press V to view the existing tiles for any given level.

## USING BUILD

Like all disciplines and fine arts, level-building might take a while to master. But those who feel the call will find that, after some practice, the Build tool is extremely useful and fun. Maybe your creations will not hold a candle to the Eiffel Tower or the Roman Coliseum, but you might yet surprise yourself and gain the admiration of your friends.

The 3D Realms CD-ROM containing the full version of the game has an extensive help file, called BUILDHLP, that covers the fundamentals and some advanced techniques for using Build. It walks you through the first steps in creating a sector and then it builds from that point. Although you will definitely need assistance from the help file to get started with Build, nothing will stop you from discovering the joy of building levels from scratch or modifying existing levels once you are familiar with the tool. Read Build's help file, and follow some of the examples to begin. And, remember, 3D Realms is always looking for good talent.

# DUKE NUKEM 3D CHEAT CODES

Even the most daring players might need a little bit of help from time to time. That is why 3D Realms provides the cheat codes for the game. After all, why allow your frustration level to interfere with your fun. Like all good things, use the cheat codes sparingly. Save them for those moments when you really need them. Just keep in mind that some cheat codes really don't have a tremendously beneficial effect. They simply cause amusing messages to appear or some interesting effects. To use the cheat codes, simply type the appropriate characters as you are playing a level. To turn off a cheat code, simply type the code a second time. Table 9.1 lists the various cheat codes you can use when playing *Duke Nukem 3D*.

## TABLE 9.1: THE *DUKE NUKEM 3D* CHEAT CODES

| CHEAT CODE | EFFECT |
|---|---|
| DNKROZ (or DNCORNHOLIO) | This code puts you in God mode. In God mode, you are in effect completely invulnerable and can face off opponents without fear and danger of losing your life. Your health status will remain at a constant 100 percent the entire time. |
| DNSTUFF | This code gives you every weapon, power-up, and all the ammo you can carry. In addition, you also get all of the keycards. |
| DNITEMS | This code gives you every power-up and keycard, but no weapons or ammo. |
| DNSCOTTY # ## | This code lets you warp to any episode and level. For example, DNSCOTTY 3 03 puts you in Flood Zone, the third level in Shrapnel City. |
| DNHYPER | This code gives you the steroids so you can run around like a madman and kick like a mule. |
| DNVIEW | This code turns on the "chase" view, where you can see yourself from behind, as though you were placing a camera behind you. |
| DNCASHMAN | After typing this code, press the spacebar to throw dollar bills around. This cheat code may not help you overcome your enemies or solve levels, but it infuses you with a false sense of financial security. |
| DNBETA | This code shows the message "Pirates Suck!" This is obviously an inside jest among the 3D Realm developers. |
| DNALLEN | This code shows the message "Buy Major Stryker," a not-so-subliminal message to promote a game in which level designer Allen Blum had a major part. |

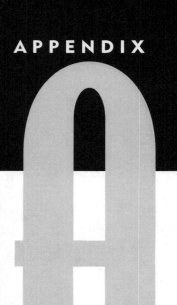

APPENDIX

# Installation and Setup

## INSTALLING *DUKE NUKEM 3D*

Installing *Duke Nukem 3D* on your system is very easy. Whether you are installing the shareware or the full version, all you have to do is run the Install program and then simply follow the on-screen instructions and respond to a few prompts. The Install program anticipates the most common settings and makes default decisions that you can override.

If you have the full version of *Duke Nukem 3D*, insert the CD-ROM into your CD-ROM drive. If you downloaded the shareware version, access the directory where the *Duke Nukem 3D* files are stored. Then, follow these instructions:

1. At the DOS prompt for the appropriate drive and directory, type **install** and press Enter. If you are installing the full version, the program will prompt you to select the game to be installed. If you are installing the shareware version, you will be prompted for a destination directory (folder) where *Duke Nukem 3D* should be installed.

2. If you are installing the full version, select **Duke Nukem 3D** and press Enter. (You can install any of the other shareware games later by following essentially the same steps.) Then type the letter for the drive where the game will be installed and press Enter. The program will suggest DUKE3D as the directory where the game will be stored. Accept this default, or, if you wish, specify another directory or subdirectory.

The install program will begin copying the necessary files to the directory for the game. The process will take approximately eight minutes. When the installation is complete, you will see the confirmation.

3. Press any key to continue with the set-up procedure.

Refer to the next procedure to set up *Duke Nukem 3D* for your system's components.

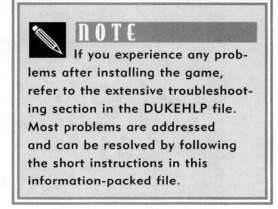

**NOTE** If you experience any problems after installing the game, refer to the extensive troubleshooting section in the DUKEHLP file. Most problems are addressed and can be resolved by following the short instructions in this information-packed file.

## SETTING UP *DUKE NUKEM 3D*

You can run the setup procedure immediately after you install the game or any time later. When you install the full version, the Install program runs the setup procedure automatically. When you are ready to set up *Duke Nukem 3D*, access the directory for the game. Then follow these steps:

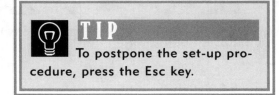

**TIP** To postpone the set-up procedure, press the Esc key.

1. Type **setup** and press Enter. The initial setup Main Menu is displayed (see Figure A.1).

2. Use the arrow keys to select the option you want to adjust and press Enter. Depending on the option you choose, the program will present you with related screens so you can make the appropriate selections.

### Sound Setup

If you choose Sound Setup, you will see another screen where you can choose the various sound settings for your system.

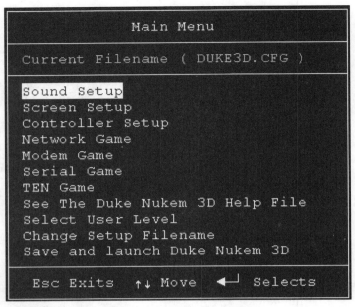

Main Menu

Current Filename ( DUKE3D.CFG )

Sound Setup
Screen Setup
Controller Setup
Network Game
Modem Game
Serial Game
TEN Game
See The Duke Nukem 3D Help File
Select User Level
Change Setup Filename
Save and launch Duke Nukem 3D

Esc Exits  ↑↓ Move  ← Selects

**FIGURE A.1:** The setup Main Menu lets you choose several options to adjust for your system.

To set up your system's sound card so you can hear the game's sound effects, do the following:

1. Select **Choose Sound FX Card** and press Enter. Another screen will show you the available options.

2. After you choose your sound card, you can also adjust its various settings. Figure A.2, for example, shows the adjustments you can make for a Sound Blaster card.

Other options you can adjust for your sound card include:

❖ Number of mixing voices

❖ 8- or 16-bit mixing

❖ Mixing rate

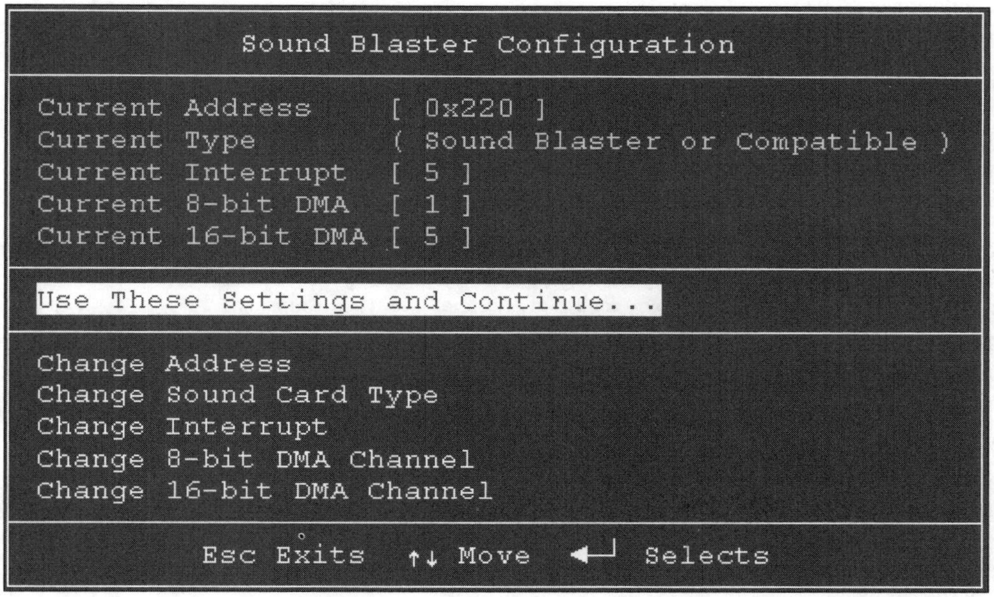

```
          Sound Blaster Configuration

Current Address      [ 0x220 ]
Current Type         ( Sound Blaster or Compatible )
Current Interrupt    [ 5 ]
Current 8-bit DMA    [ 1 ]
Current 16-bit DMA   [ 5 ]

Use These Settings and Continue...

Change Address
Change Sound Card Type
Change Interrupt
Change 8-bit DMA Channel
Change 16-bit DMA Channel

        Esc Exits   ↑↓ Move   ↵ Selects
```

**FIGURE A.2:** The top portion of the screen shows the current settings. Select the option you want to change from the bottom.

## Screen Setup

If you choose Screen Setup from the Main Menu, you can choose between normal or VESA modes. You can get the best screen resolution using VESA modes, but your system must be equipped with a graphics card that supports the VESA standard. In VESA modes, you can specify resolutions of up to $800 \times 600$.

## Controller Type

The Controller Type option lets you choose the device you will use to control the action. The default setup is Keyboard and Mouse. In addition, you can also make other adjustments to your controlling device by selecting other setup options shown on this screen.

## Other Setup Options

The remaining options you can set up during the setup procedure are summarized in Table A.1.

**TABLE A.1: SETUP OPTIONS**

| OPTION | DESCRIPTION |
|---|---|
| Network Game | This option lets you set up and run multiplayer games over networks using the IPX protocol. |
| Modem Game | This option lets you run multiplayer games over your modem. |
| Serial Game | This option lets you run multiplayer games with two computers linked through a null modem adapter. |
| TEN Game | This option lets you dial up the Total Entertainment Network, so you can play multiplayer games over the Internet. |
| See the Duke Nukem 3D Help File | This option lets you display the extensive help file that comes with *Duke Nukem 3D*. |
| Select User Level | This option lets you start a game using a level designed by you or another third party. |
| Change Setup Filename | This option lets you rename the setup file so you can use a second setup file that contains different settings. |
| Save and launch Duke Nukem 3D | Use this option to save any adjustments you have made and to start a new *Duke Nukem 3D* game. |

# Multiplayer Tips and Online Resources

Multiplayer modes include games over an IPX network, modem games, and games over computers that are serially connected. Up to four players can play over a network with the shareware version. The full version allows up to eight players. This appendix does not cover the instructions for launching multiplayer matches. That information is covered extensively in *Duke Nukem 3D*'s DN3DHLP file. Instead, this appendix covers a few tips for making you a fearsome adversary in DukeMatch games or a better teammate in Co-Op play.

## GENERAL MULTIPLAYER TIPS

### CONFIGURATION TIPS

One of the most important aspects of play actually occurs before the game is ever started. Selecting a configuration that is both comfortable and well thought out is paramount to playing well. For the keyboard, assign commonly used functions to keys that are close to one another.

It's important in combat to not take your eyes off the screen when you want to change from one weapon to another or to activate the steroids before making a hasty escape. Doing so means losing sight of your opponent, which could possibly lead to the ultimate loss—the battle itself. By *clumping* functions next to one another, your

fingers can quickly move off your home keys and onto others, then quickly reposition themselves without ever having to look down. Try this technique with your favorite weapons. Your opponent will be amazed at how quickly you can switch between them while remaining in action.

Another useful configuration *trick* is to double assign keys and buttons. When in battle, you may think it is a good idea to get the medkit into action as your health dips below 100 percent. The last thing you want to do, however, is move your fingers off your main control keys to rejuvenate your health. Chances are, your opponent will take advantage of this short pause to end your life before you have a chance to increase it.

A better choice is to double assign keys that are normally used in battle like strafe, jump, or crouch to also include activating the medkit. You can even repeat the assignment of the same function across several keys to make sure you don't miss it when it really counts. For example, while you're dancing around your opponent, you're automatically activating your portable medkit (if it's in your inventory) without having to remember or move your hands around the keyboard. You can use this same technique for other functions, such as opening doors, using NVG, etc.

## CONTROLLER TIPS

Now that you've got the configuration set up, it's time for practice. There are many good keyboard-only players, but the excellent players always use the mouse. With the mouse, you get a greater level of precision and rotational speed that just can't be matched by the keyboard. The down side is the learning curve. Chances are for the first few days of mouse use you'll do more damage to yourself than good. Then, with a little persistence, a breakthrough is achieved.

Use the mouse to run, turn, and fire. If you have a three-button mouse, you can even assign one of the buttons to mouse aiming, which is useful for knocking your aggressors out of their hiding places above and below you. Leave the strafing to your other hand by assigning left and right strafing to the keyboard. To become proficient at this two-handed maneuver, stand at one end of a long street, such as the one in Episode 1, Hollywood Holocaust. Turn on the crosshair, and aim at a fixed point at the opposite end of the street. Now start running forward and, while keeping the crosshair on the *target*, begin strafing to the left and then the right. This left-right motion will later be used to dodge your opponents' RPGs, while sending your own forget-me-nots in return.

Another good exercise is to find a stationary object that is open on all sides. Keep your crosshair glued on the object and begin strafing to the left or right, completely encircling it. With a little practice, these maneuvers will become simple techniques that you'll employ in every battle.

## TIPS FOR BATTLE

With boot camp behind you, it's time to march into battle. To help you FNGs (Freakin' New Guys) live for more than a few seconds, here are some tips that will help you to be more than someone else's chew toy:

- Exercise caution when entering areas that cannot be seen before reaching the entry point. If you make a habit of charging into places full speed ahead, you may run headlong into a web of laser trip bombs or perhaps a nest of pipe bombs. Some players are more direct: They'll just camp out in a certain vantage spot and launch a salvo of RPGs at you when you unexpectedly dash in.

- If you find that you're opponent's play strategy resembles a scene out of *True Grit*, begin wallpapering the walls with laser trip bombs. First choose the ideal spot; blind corners and places that you have to jump up or down to are best. Now start setting traps. Place the laser trip bombs high and low and fairly close to one another. All it takes is for just one to be triggered and the entire lot will blow in a chain reaction. The beauty of laser trip bombs is that they remember who set them. If you set a bomb and are subsequently killed, you will still get credit for a kill if your opponent is unfortunate enough to stumble into

> **TIP**
> If you're unsure that someone is awaiting your arrival just around the corner, use the peek-a-boo trick. Stop short just shy of an entrance or corner and *peek* into the room by using the Insert and Delete keys. Quickly strafing into and out of the area to draw enemy fire is also a safe and effective maneuver.

one. Just remember where you set them. Forgetting could lead to a rather embarrassing loss of a frag.

* Never stop moving. Don't be a sitting duck for chaingun fire; instead, evade damage by strafing, jumping, and flying. Quick erratic movements work best. If you're running low on health, try to pick up health items while you continue battle. Remember to keep your aim fixed on the enemy!

* When using the RPG launcher, it's not always necessary to directly hit your opponent to hurt him. If you can't seem to hit a player, aim at a wall or other object very close to your opponent. The concussion from the explosion will deal a lot of damage.

* Don't stand next to walls or objects when being fired upon by RPGs. Stay in open areas to prevent your aggressor from knocking precious chucks of health off of you from indirect hits. Force your opponent to make a direct hit.

* Use NVG in dark areas. In areas where you can control the lighting, a good technique is to turn the lights off and activate your goggles. Hopefully your opponent will stumble into the area without them, giving you a chance for an easy kill.

* When in trouble, retreat! Don't be afraid to run and fight another time. If you're taking heavy damage, make a fast retreat, and replenish your health as quickly as safety will permit. If someone is hot on your tail, zigzag left and right, jump, repeatedly activate your holoduke, and sharply turn and hide around corners until your opponent runs past you. Then quickly backtrack the same path that led you there, while your opponent tries to figure out where you went. If outside, you can also jet-pack straight up and very high to a point that is out of sight of your opponent. If you have pipe bombs, drop them as you run, and try to time the detonation to coincide with your opponent reaching the same spot. It's very rewarding to kill your opponent, who definitely has the upper hand on you, by cleverly using this tactic.

✢ Shut up and listen. You can easily get a bead on your opponents by listening to what they are doing. You may recognize certain sounds: a particular door opening, an elevator in motion, the bubbling sound of someone swimming, the "Ohhh" heard as someone takes damage jumping out of a high window, or the "Ahhh" made when the portable medkit is used to replenish health. These sounds will tip you off to your opponent's location. If you run there in a hurry, you may be able to catch him unexpectedly, leaving your opponent amazed at your ability to always show up at the same place he does. Turning off ambient sounds, music, and Duke talk may help you to hear better.

✢ Teleporters not only teleport people, they also teleport certain weapons and projectiles. Throw pipe bombs or shoot RPGs through teleporters before entering them. If someone is standing on the other side, you'll clear the way with your little surprise.

✢ Don't stand in front of teleporters! If you know the teleporter trick mentioned previously, chances are so does someone else. If you engage in battle through the teleporters, always stand to the side and fire away.

✢ Each level has its own set of respawning points. These are particular areas in a map where a player will respawn after dying. Once you do your opponent in, run to the closest respawning points. If you're lucky and the opponent is there, his handgun and lack of shields and extra health will be no match against your chaingun, shrinker, shotgun, devastator, or RPG launcher.

✢ If you just fought a grueling battle that left you holding the short end of the stick, but conveniently find yourself respawned near your opponent, don't be afraid to open up on the opponent with the handgun, especially at longer ranges. If you did a lot of damage to him in the previous battle, pumping a number of handgun rounds into his tattered body will quickly do him in.

✢ If you just fought a winning battle that left you barely alive, stay away from the respawning points and seek out health.

✤ Get into your opponents' heads. Part of being a good player is learning how to intimidate your opponents. Anticipate their moves, take shortcuts to head them off, mesmerize them with unbelievable moves and control, and, when you put them to rest, give them a few Remote Ridicules to think about. You can get opponents so rattled and jumpy that they'll end up fraggin' themselves every time they see you coming.

✤ Use the old bait-and-switch technique. You can usually pull this off only once or twice a game, but when it works, it's beautiful. *Pretend* to only be in possession of less damaging weapons by firing off a few rounds then retreating with your opponent in pursuit. Run to an area that will provide temporary protection from return shots, do a 180-degree turn, switch to your money weapon, and wait. As soon as your opponent enters the area, let him have it. The pleasure experienced from knowing that your opponent was just made a sucker is second to none.

✤ When possible, always enter into battle with 200 percent health, 100 percent shields and the portable medkit. With these levels, you will survive even a direct shot with an RPG once. Between two equally skilled players equipped with the same weapon, the results of a battle are often determined by nothing more than who entered into it with the most health and shields. Learn where health is distributed, especially atomic health units, as well as shields and medkits. After your opponents barely escape battle with heavy damage, run to the health caches and try to catch them as they attempt to repair their damage.

✤ When the respawn indicators are on, pay close attention to them. If they're red and spinning slowly, clear the area—it's not worth the wait. If they are green and spinning quickly, payday is near: stick around for the goodies.

✤ Dead men don't tell tales, but they sometimes leave nice shiny weapons behind for the taking. Sometimes when you kill opponents, they give up one of their weapons. If you see something laying next to the corpse of what used to be your enemy, run over, pick it up, and use it to your advantage. And, make sure to thank them for the free RPGs! This is especially helpful when playing with the No Respawn option.

❖ When playing with no respawns, always keep a portable medkit in your inventory. Once a level has been played for a while, it'll be the only source of additional health.

## CO-OP MODE TIPS

Most Co-Op games eventually degrade into DukeMatch games anyway. But in general, just try not to kill the other guy. Also, help your opponents fight battles and never leave them in a room full of monsters. You may want to separate and send one guy after a key, while the others clear a path toward a certain part of the level or a door.

# ONLINE RESOURCES

Thousands of *Duke Nukem 3D* enthusiasts will find extensive support and resources from various online platforms. Besides the official and established channels, there is also a growing brew of home-spun Web home pages where users congregate to exchange useful information.

Here is a short list of the more recognized online resources *for Duke Nukem 3D*:

❖ CompuServe. Issue the command Go REALMS.

❖ America Online. Use the keyword "3D Realms."

❖ 3D Realms official Web site. Point your browser to www.3drealms.com.

❖ Software Creations Web BBS. Point your browser to www.swcbbs.com.

In addition, you can also hook up with other *Duke Nukem 3D* players and issue or accept multiplayer mode challenges over the Internet.

## DUKE NUKEM 3D ONLINE PLAY THROUGH TEN

*Duke Nukem 3D* is also available for multiplayer gaming exclusively on Total Entertainment Network (TEN). Stop playing *Duke Nukem 3D* by yourself. You can play *Duke Nukem 3D* on the Internet with gamers across the country on TEN. At any hour of the day, there could be dozens of other *Duke Nukem 3D* fans on TEN playing brutal DukeMatches. Why miss out? If you want to know more, check out TEN's web page at http://www.ten.net. You can also call TEN at 800-8040-TEN, or e-mail them at questions@ten.net.

    The TEN software comes on the full-version *Duke Nukem 3D* CD-ROM, and you can install and launch it by running **Setup** and selecting **TEN game** from the main menu.

> **NOTE**
>
> To play *Duke Nukem 3D* on TEN, you will need Windows 95, a 60Mhz Pentium processor, 8MB RAM (16MB recommended), a VLB or PCI SVGA card, and at least a 14.4KB modem.